BORDERLINE PATIENTS, THE PSYCHOSOMATIC FOCUS, AND THE THERAPEUTIC PROCESS

Peter L. Giovacchini, M.D.

JASON ARONSON INC.

Northvale, New Jersey
London

Production Editor: Judith D. Cohen

This book was set in Goudy 10 point by Lind Graphics of Upper Saddle River, New Jersey, and printed and bound by Haddon Craftsmen of Scranton, Pennsylvania.

Library of Congress Cataloging-in-Publication Data

Giovacchini, Peter L.
    Borderline patients, the psychosomatic focus, and the therapeutic
process / by Peter L. Giovacchini.
        p. cm.
    Includes bibliographical references and index.
    ISBN 0-87668-295-6 (hard cover)
    1. Borderline personality disorder. 2. Borderline personality
disorder—Psychosomatic aspects. 3. Psychoanalysis. I. Title.
    [DNLM: 1. Borderline Personality Disorder—therapy.
2. Psychoanalytic Therapy WM 190 G512b]
RC569.5.B67G56 1993
616.85' 8520651—dc20
DNLM/DLC
for Library of Congress   92-49191

Manufactured in the United States of America. Jason Aronson Inc. offers books and cassettes. For information and catalog write to Jason Aronson Inc., 230 Livingston Street, Northvale, New Jersey 07647.

Contents

PART II
THE PSYCHOSOMATIC FOCUS

PART III
THE THERAPEUTIC PROCESS

Preface

The study and treatment of emotional disorders seem to reflect specific patterns. There are trends that perhaps are necessitated by clinical needs. The pursuit of a particular form of psychopathology or of a particular therapeutic approach becomes fashionable. These are popular professional movements and also extend themselves to include conceptual orientations.

The post-World War II generation venerated psychoanalysis, an attitude that is quite foreign today as pharmacological treatment dominates and biological explanations, though far from inclusive and consistent, are attempting to replace psychodynamic and structural formulations.

Both biological psychiatrists and psychoanalysts recognize, however, that psychopathology has to be understood in terms that take us far beyond the frame of reference of the psychoneuroses. They also agree that severe emotional disturbances deserve more attention than simply to be classified and cast in a phenomenological mold. Many of these patients are seeking help. Thus, as clinicians and investigators, we have to explore how we can reach and relate to them in a therapeutic perspective rather than simply write them off as untreatable and confine our efforts to maintenance and management.

As far back as 1965, a few psychoanalysts sincerely believed that severely disturbed patients, including schizophrenics, could be treated psychoanalytically with no or very few modifications (Boyer and Giovacchini 1967). There was a tremendous amount of opposition to these ideas and endeavors because the majority of psychoanalysts held Freud's dictum sacred, and Freud (1914a) had emphatically stated that the psychoanalytic procedure was suited only for the transference neuroses and not the narcissistic neuroses, which include depressions and schizophrenia. This, of course, meant that psychoanalysis was also contraindicated for borderline patients and other patients suffering from characterological problems.

Throughout the years, it has been an uphill battle to justify our treatment efforts with this group of patients. I recall how bitterly I was attacked at the 1965 fall meetings of the American Psychoanalytic Association because I even considered analyzing schizophrenic and borderline patients. True, our conceptual understanding of these patients was rudimentary, and even our understanding of what constitutes a psychoanalytic interaction was either rigidly dogmatic or vague. When I somewhat overconfidently, and no doubt overcompensatorily, stated that psychoanalysis was the treatment of choice for borderline patients, my discussant pounced on me with unrelenting fury. Approximately 20 years later, at a meeting of a local psychoanalytic society, a senior conservative analyst made the same remark and everyone nodded in complacent assent without even raising an eyebrow.

This does not mean that there has been a steady, continuous progress aimed at widening the scope and horizons of psychoanalysis as Stone (1954) has written. Quite to the contrary, the development of psychoanalytic understanding and even more so of psychoanalytic technique has been uneven. There are throughout the world many highly sophisticated analysts who pursue the treatment of severely disturbed patients with optimism and enthusiasm. By contrast, there are what appear to be groups of analysts who seem to belong to a prehistoric time when the development of psychoanalysis was in its infancy. They repeat the same dicta about psychopathology and treatability that were the shibboleths of the devout who considered any extension or modification of Freud as heresy. They do not seem to be aware of the voluminous literature and symposia that make their attitudes appear rigidly naive. Not too surprising, many of these "pure" analysts belong to the younger generation rather than to the old guard who, one might believe, would cling to the tradition that dominated their training.

In spite of the voluminous literature just mentioned, there is still considerable confusion about all aspects of the clinical arena of the borderline patient. I recall a conference in which Masterson, Kernberg, Searles, and I participated and in which we could reach no agreement as to what we meant by the diagnosis of borderline psychopathology (see Masterson 1978). Furthermore, although many clinicians agree that a psychoanalytically oriented approach is feasible for some patients who are more severely disturbed than the traditional psychoneurotic, there are very few similarities to the technical procedures various analysts advocate (Adler 1985, Boyer 1978, 1983, Giovacchini 1979a, Kernberg 1975, Masterson 1976, Roth 1987, Searles 1976, 1984, Volkan 1976). There are some similarities, however, between Kernberg and Masterson in that they both advocate confrontation, which in my opinion emphasizes reality at the expense of an intrapsychic focus. The authors contend that boundaries have to be set so that treatment does not degenerate into chaos. Other clinicians, including myself, believe that many patients suffering from characterological problems can comfortably regress and symptomatically display the manifestations of their psychopathology without disruptively acting out. There are, of course, some very difficult patients who are hard to treat in any psychotherapeutic context.

Although I intend to discuss the borderline patient, I will also refer to patients with characterological problems or patients suffering from primitive mental states in order to broaden the rather circumscribed category of borderline psychopathology that I will continually define and describe in various chapters of this book. When dealing with these types of psychopathology, rigid definitions are inappropriate; the topic is constantly evolving. Clinicians have not yet reached a position in which they can deal with absolutes, either conceptually or technically. I believe that many of our difficulties and much of our confusion about our formulations and treatment of patients suffering from severe psychopathology are due to our not recognizing that we cannot demand closure at our present stage of clinical development.

Nevertheless, some clinicians and their students seek out systems of thought and procedures that will dispel ambiguity. Trainees, especially, often flock around a charismatic teacher who feeds them formulas and clever witticisms that are aimed at explaining and resolving difficult clinical situations. What is being transmitted, if carefully scrutinized, usually turns out to be concrete and simplistic. Sometimes it is merely a subtle rephrasing of what has been said before, but presented as if it were novel. This type of teaching leads to certitudes, but it is not really enlightening or productive.

In our scientific era of rapid change, these "schools" impede progress in that they claim to have all the answers and, therefore, discourage exploration or attempts to "experiment" with psychoanalytic techniques with patients who are not very well integrated. Winnicott (1958a, 1960) considered severely ill patients as research patients, and he relied on the treatment approach to make what he called a therapeutic diagnosis. He could learn about such patients by treating them.

Unfortunately, rigidity and dogma are involved in attitudes that go beyond the discouragement of an open attitude, a therapeutic receptivity toward our patients. In some ways, they are involved with a depreciation of patients and of mental illness in general. In so doing they are moving clinicians away from an intrapsychic focus. Psychic determinism, that is, understanding the causes of emotional disturbances as residing within the mind rather than in terms of the environment's contribution, has receded into the background. Many approaches are phenomenological, and treatment often consists of behavioral manipulation.

Biological psychiatry and psychopharmacological treatment ignore intrapsychic factors and emphasize organic and neurochemical explanations of human behavior. These biological concepts and subsequent therapeutic approaches, for the most part, minimize intrapsychic factors; hence the patient's participation in the production of his problems, that is, in determining his destiny, is ignored. Unlike conventional psychotherapy, the patient's role is passive and there is no basic characterological change; the aim of treatment is symptom relief, but even more important is to make the patient's behavior manageable so those attending him will be comfortable.

Thus, both premature closure and concrete and often naive pronouncements about patients have far-reaching deleterious effects, which are frequently observed in inpatient settings. On many psychiatric wards patients are not treated with respect and as individuals in their own right. They are expected to behave properly and not disturb the staff. Often their disruptions are met with punitive retaliation. Furthermore, there is very little, if any, attempt to view patients as people with intrapsychic problems. They are just bothersome persons who have to be controlled. There is very little attempt to understand or to form empathic bonds with them. As psychiatry keeps searching for organic explanations of emotional disorders, there seems to be a corresponding dehumanization of patients suffering from those disorders.

Attitudes bordering on contempt for psychiatric patients are not confined to ancillary staff and some biological psychiatrists; they are also common enough in the thinking of psychoanalysts and psychoanalytically oriented therapists. Although this attitude may be paradoxical inasmuch as psycho-analysis is based on respect of the intrapsychic focus and the unconscious, it nevertheless exists, especially in the context of the treatment interaction.

When discussing situations in which an analyst may be perceived in a pejorative fashion, it is customary not to identify him. Even though the analyst I am about to discuss is well known, especially in the Chicago area, for the sake of discretion I will abide by this custom. I am referring to a senior psychoanalyst who was a brilliant thinker, clinician, and teacher. As expected, he attracted many students of psychoanalysis and candidates of the Chicago Institute for Psychoanalysis. Initially he held seminars in his home, wearing a handsome silk oriental robe and sitting on a massive chair that resembled a throne. His comments on various patients that the members of the group were presenting to him were delivered with scholarly lucidity and wit, often punctuated with Latin phrases that most of us did not understand but that seemed to be in keeping with the atmosphere he had constructed.

Up to this point I felt a certain degree of awe, a feeling obviously shared by my fellow members of this seminar. The majority of them idealized him, and no matter what he said, he could do no wrong. In spite of the spirit of worship that pervaded the room, I was shocked by what followed.

A student briefly presented the case of a depressed man. As I recall, he emphasized how this patient whined and complained, and I suspect he was demonstrating some annoyance toward the patient. Apparently, our teacher was in the habit of using props. With a beatific look of sublime wisdom, he handed the presenter a card of condolence with a black border and suggested that he give it to his patient. We all gasped. Then another student presented the history of a sexually conflicted woman. Again our leader rose to the occasion: he handed the student a wax banana. The group roared with laughter.

This psychoanalyst was advocating ridiculing confrontations. His followers admired him, but they lost sight of the fact that he was violating basic psychoanalytic principles. He was, in fact, being contemptuous of the manifestations of psychopathology, and he was treating the patient as if he were a freak, undeserving of consideration and respect. These seminars occurred many years ago, but the demeaning attitudes toward patients that were expressed there are still prevalent today. For example, the characteristic atmosphere of many psychiatric wards is mechanistic in that the staff does not really relate to the patients. A nurse once told me that her ward was a "holding tank" in which patients were just medicated but not treated as human beings. No one was interested in taking care of persons with problems.

Movements and orientations generate countermovements. What started over 20 years ago has gathered momentum. As we learn more about defective emotional development and become involved in the psychoanalytic treatment of patients suffering from relatively severe psychopathology, clinicians are once again focusing on the fundamental attributes of the psyche. The study of the borderline patient is pursued in a humanistic context and goes beyond mechanistic concepts that ignore psychic determinism and have no regard for the patient as a person.

The study and treatment of primitive mental states emphasize how mental processes influence all aspects of behavior and interactions within the psyche and soma. In the nineteenth century, that is, during the period that gave rise to the psychoanalytic approach, clinicians concentrated their attention on hysterical patients with somatic symptoms, the conversion hysterics. These patients were undoubtedly the outcome of specific cultural configurations that were related to the repression of sexuality. Today, in most technologically sophisticated nations, conversion hysterics are seldom seen (see Chapter 1). Still, there are many patients with somatic symptoms that have a psychogenic element as an etiological variable.

In the 1950s, psychosomatic medicine was very popular, at least in Chicago. Alexander (1961), then known as the father of psychosomatic medicine, had, with his colleagues, constructed various psychodynamic formulations that he believed were characteristic of patients suffering from severe somatic illnesses that were considered to be psychosomatic entities. There is no need to further pursue these formulations or the illnesses they involved, because they have not been confirmed by further studies and have been proven to be clinically useless. In a similar fashion the psychodynamic approach has not been fruitful for our understanding of psychosomatic problems, insofar as it has restricted usefulness in the study and treatment of psychopathology in general.

As clinicians become more involved in the therapeutic interaction with borderline and other seriously disturbed patients, they are impressed as to how structural and developmental defects are the dominant contributors to psychopathology. These particular defects are often characterized by somatic manifestations.

Psychosomatic medicine represents a bridge between medicine and psychiatry. Students who are interested in both the body and the mind are attracted to psychosomatic medicine because it allows them to work within a psychological perspective and still retain their identities as physicians. For clinicians devoted to a psychoanalytic therapeutic approach, this equation of medicine and the study of mental processes is not particularly important, but for many physicians the involvement with borderline patients as it leads to a psychosomatic focus represents a full circle.

The young physician's attraction to psychiatry often begins with the study of patients who have somatic symptoms. Clinical psychiatry in a modern sense at first concentrated on the explorations of conversion hysterics (Ellenberger 1970). Then the clinician becomes more and more in-volved with mental processes per se and, relatively speaking, withdraws attention from somatic processes. Now, with the study of the borderline and other patients demonstrating defects in character structure, clinicians are again focusing on the relationship between psyche and soma. They have moved away, however, from a predominantly simplistic psychodynamic frame of reference to a much more sophisticated and complex perspective that includes intrapsychic conflict as well as problems in emotional develop-ment and vicissitudes of psychic structure.

As has been noted generally by those involved in the biological sciences as well as in the study of mental processes, what investigators learn about malfunctioning helps them construct a model about nonpathological states and processes. The study of primitive mental states has many implications about psychic development and continuity by virtue of its concentration on maldevelopment and discontinuity. From the observation of states of lack of synthesis, clinicians can make important inferences about levels of higher organization and unity.

It is possible to construct a hierarchically arranged continuum beginning with physiological somatic constellations at one end and highly sophisticated mental organizations at the other. Patients suffering from characterological problems paradoxically demonstrate how mental and physical processes intertwine as they make manifest problems in both these areas. Our clinical experiences also emphasize that there is, in the broadest sense, an inherent human or biological drive that impels the organism toward unity and synthesis. This is obvious in the most immature state of existence, that of the embryo, but it seems to reach into infinitely higher areas of mentation.

1

Introduction

Psychoanalysis has reached a crucial turning point. In our ever increasingly mechanistic society, interpersonal relationships do not play as prominent a role as they did several decades ago. An interaction between two persons is not thought of as being as effective as a neuroleptic drug. Concrete psychopharmacological approaches appeal to concretely minded patients.

Values have changed. In the past, people sought their recreation and tranquility in aesthetic, artistic, and intellectual pursuits. Poetry and conversation were valued. Letter writing had reached the status of an art. Recent reports on the sad status of the educational system and the lack of achievement of modern students are reflections of how society in general has moved away from past cultural values.

I do not mean to idealize the past and imply that everything was well for previous generations. I believe that nostalgia is based on selective remembering rather than calling to mind circumstances as they actually were. Still, when we find ourselves in a violent, drug-ridden society, where the murder rate is higher than ever and the streets are dangerous jungles, we must acknowledge that there have been changes and that many of them are for the worse.

Can we state that something similar has happened in the realm of the treatment of the mentally ill? Following World War II, analysis reached its apogee. Recently articles have been written debating whether psychotherapy should be included in psychiatry residency programs. Psychoanalysis in particular has been much maligned, an attitude that seems to have emerged after the discovery of neuroleptic drugs such as Thorazine. Society was ready to accept mechanistic approaches as it was in the midst of a computer revolution in which machines were placed more and more in the foreground.

This is not to say that psychoanalysts have been the hapless victims of a Star Wars culture. Recently there has been an emphasis on the narrow-mindedness and arrogance of some psychoanalytic institutes, and now, with psychoanalysis becoming available to a larger group of professionals, candidates tend not to passively submit to the prejudices and accept the dogmatic dicta of their teachers. They do not bow their heads at Freud's shrine, nor do they tolerate being called heretics if they question some of his pronouncements. Although psychoanalysis has been damaged by cultural shifts, it is apparent that we have to clean our house, which is what so many current authors are advocating. This book represents an effort in that direction. I believe this task can best be done by examining our current clinical status, how we interact with patients, and how we can help them. It is not enough to smugly isolate ourselves and state that what we have to offer is just for an elite, select few. Patients need and want help, and if we denigrate them by implying they are not good enough for our esoteric type of treatment, they will turn elsewhere, as indeed many have done.

This is where the borderline patient enters the picture. These patients are concrete and mechanistic in their thinking, but many clinicians have had the patience and dexterity to be able to treat them in a psychoanalytic context. Psychoanalysis has the opportunity to reestablish itself by demonstrating that therapists are willing to reach out to these misery-pervaded patients and help them achieve a sense of being and inner values. Analysts may again become prominent in the mental health community when it is realized that they have something to offer beyond the promises of psycho-pharmacology, which are aimed at surface improvements and not the integrity of a patient as an autonomous and worthwhile person. Analysis strives for the expansion of the personality and not for cutting off aspects of the self that may even include symptoms.

The psychopharmacological approach is *culturally syntonic*, whereas psychoanalysis has become *culturally dystonic*. Converting the borderline patient into a sensitive, introspective human being rather than remaining a constricted, concretely minded person may help return psychoanalysis to a culturally syntonic position. Thus the treatment of borderline patients has become a psychoanalytic watershed.

In this context, the first question this book addresses is the definition of the borderline patient. There has been no consensus as to the clinical characteristics of this group of patients. Like Meissner (1988), I prefer to think in terms of a borderline spectrum, and I view the concept of borderline from several frames of reference—phenomenological, developmental levels, and structural defects. The borderline patient is viewed as being able to move into a psychotic state, but with the capacity to reintegrate without the obstacles schizophrenics have to face. Furthermore, these patients make a borderline adjustment to the external world; they do not have the ego executive capacities and adaptations to deal with the exigencies of reality.

There are complex and subtle factors in the structural defects analysts encounter. This book deals with a wider group of character disorders that includes the borderline patient. Our focus is on defects in character structure and as we learn more about them, clinicians become aware of structural discontinuities that help explain why so many of these patients have such a concrete orientation. They cannot get in touch with the inner world that contains unconscious forces and motivation.

In treatment many patients display manifestations of structural defects and discontinuity, often organized at prementational levels, that is, levels devoid of psychological content. These areas of the psyche primarily operate at a physiological level and in certain types of psychopathology become what I have called a psychosomatic focus. In some instances severe psychosomatic illnesses can be cured once the patient gains some unity to the psychic apparatus as he gets in touch with the unconscious, and psychic lacunae disappear. Various levels of the personality become joined by connecting bridges. The study of patients in the borderline spectrum can be fruitful for the study of patients suffering from psychosomatic problems.

Standard psychodynamic formulations that have been considered the essence of classical psychoanalysis are not particularly useful for the study of patients in the borderline spectrum and those suffering from psychosomatic problems. As clinicians continue to explore structural deficits and discontinuity, they are impressed as to how much these patients use splitting mechanisms. Not only do many patients with character disorders use splitting and projective defenses, but often their personalities are fragmented because they have never achieved synthesis.

There has been considerable discussion about splitting mechanisms, psychic fragmentation, and projective identification, but these terms have been used loosely. Projective identification, in particular, has been implicated in many transference–countertransference transactions, but as a concept and a process it is still vague and unclear. Every sensory perception has a degree of projective identification. It is also clinically relevant to distinguish between splitting as a defense and a psyche that is fragmented. The latter is not synthesized and lacks unity.

Fragmented personalities have defective self-representations, which involve problems in the formation of a sense of identity. These defects are not usually manifested by discrete symptoms; rather, these patients have problems in adapting to the external world and in establishing satisfactory and intimate interpersonal relationships. Often, they do not feel themselves as whole persons. They believe that parts of themselves are missing and that they cannot get in touch with an inner core or what Winnicott (1960) has called the true self.

The backgrounds of many patients in the borderline spectrum have been extraordinarily traumatic. They have often been the victims of physical and sexual abuse. They may react to intense and frequent traumas by encapsulating them and splitting them off from the main psychic current. Breuer (Breuer and Freud 1895) wrote about hypnoidal states in which ego fragments encapsulate the trauma before it has been processed. Freud preferred formulations that involved clashes between various parts of the psyche: traumatic moments and memories are buried by repressive forces. Breuer preferred, however, to think in terms of various parts of the psyche (hypnoidal states) as isolated and fragmented; that is, as split off from consciousness and general psychic activity. This fragmentation has various symptomatic manifestations.

Although psychoanalysts pushed Breuer to the background in favor of Freud's psychodynamic hypothesis, Breuer's ideas appear to be more relevant for our attempts to understand patients suffering from character disorders. His concepts of hypnoidal states and encapsulated traumas are consistent with many of our formulations that involve splitting and projective mechanisms.

The healing process involves synthesis of a fragmented psyche. Split-off parts have to be regained, often a very difficult task for the patient. Therapists have to be careful to allow their patients to regress to ego states in which they attempt to reintegrate lost parts of the self. Because these cast-off fragments contain traumatic memories and destructive introjects, the process of incorporating them back into the main ego can be extremely painful. Patients may cry and scream and otherwise indicate how much pain they are suffering. Analysts have to understand that they cannot interfere with this sequence of events by comforting their patients or making interpretations aimed at a much higher psychic level, because what they are observing is so primitive that it cannot be articulated in words. The instinctive reaction of therapists is to give comfort and alleviate pain, but to do so in these instances would be at variance with the therapeutic process.

Analysts have to be there for these patients, especially during these difficult, regressed moments. They may make their presence felt by commenting about patients' emotional states, appearance, and the depths of their feelings, having to create a setting in which patients can have these feelings for as long as they need to.

The treatment of borderline patients has caused clinicians to revise their views about the therapeutic process. In many instances, the formation of a holding environment is more important than insight-producing interpretations.

This is another occasion where much has been written about a phenomenon, in this case the holding environment, but it has not been defined or formulated. As I explore the holding environment in various clinical contexts, it becomes apparent that it is the antithesis of the traumatic infantile environment. The therapy produces a setting that not only supports the patient but provides a contrast that furthers understanding of the infantile environment and early traumas.

It has been useful to conceptualize the therapeutic interaction as occurring in the transitional space. The purpose of treatment is to convert grim reality into playful fantasy. Borderline patients are in a constant struggle with the outer world, which is often viewed as ominous and dangerous. The analyst helps the patient internalize these attitudes, and what was once an overwhelming threat becomes a problem that requires solving in the transitional space.

To achieve this the analyst has to create a safe setting. The analytic atmosphere is intrinsically safe because of its constant reliability. There are clinical situations, however, that inadvertently recapitulate the traumatic infantile environment, what I have called the psychoanalytic paradox. The low-keyed analytic atmosphere may phenomenologically resemble the rejecting or indifferent childhood world. It is difficult to deal with the transference when the patient cannot distinguish the past from the present.

Analysts have to be flexible and construct a therapeutic environment that is tailored to the patient's needs. Previously the analytic setting and ritual were sacrosanct, and patients had to fit into the procrustean bed of analytic decorum. If patients cannot conform to the requirements of analytic protocol, they are judged to be nontreatable. Analysis is contraindicated. Fortunately, this attitude is becoming antiquated as clinicians continue to examine all aspects of the therapeutic process.

This book extensively explores the therapeutic process in the context of the transitional space, the psychoanalytic paradox, and the synthesis of a fragmented psyche. It deals with the treatment of patients suffering from characterological defects. I do not focus on the psychoses, which deserve separate attention. I also do not concentrate on countertransference issues because that is also a topic in itself (Giovacchini 1989a,b). Still, the basic therapeutic interaction is closely examined.

What have been considered to be irreducible dicta are challenged. Freud emphasized that the chief therapeutic task is to make the unconscious conscious. Nevertheless, this does not seem to play a prominent role in the treatment of patients with structural defects.

Freud (1914b) then discussed working through as an essential feature of therapeutic resolution, but he did not explain what constitutes working through, nor is there much in the current literature that illuminates the process. Analysts often refer to working through, but we really do not know how it operates. Our explanations, when closely examined, turn out to be tautologies. The usual formulation involves bringing repressed material into the ego domain, where it is dealt with by rational secondary-process psychic operations. Somehow it loses its traumatic potential; it may be decathected, which is another way of saying working through. This, of course, adds nothing to our understanding.

The third part of this book addresses itself to the therapeutic process in general and involves the mechanisms associated with working through. These chapters discuss the inclusion of various psychic structures and developmental levels, such as the transitional space, as participating factors in the curative elements of psychoanalytic treatment. The therapeutic process also has to be viewed from a multidimensional perspective rather than in terms of a linear psychodynamic sequence.

Finally, the interpretative process is examined, since most psychoanalysts agree that it is the chief therapeutic tool of psychoanalytic treatment. In fact, interpretations have long been considered the essence of the therapeutic interaction. Again, dicta have to be questioned, especially in the context of our expanded ideas about psychopathology and more flexible therapeutic attitudes and techniques. The sacrosanct quality of transference interpretations is called into question, especially the exclusivity of their effectiveness in psychoanalytic therapy. The role of nontransference interpretations is also explored, as is the issue of what constitutes an interpretation and its transference and nontransference elements.

In conclusion, psychoanalytic theory and technique are relevant to the treatment of a broad group of patients. The psychoanalytic edifice is strengthened as it is enlarged to include patients whose psychopathology can be viewed as belonging within a borderline spectrum, as well as patients suffering from psychosomatic problems. This is an interesting example of how the broadening of our therapeutic effectiveness contributes to and strengthens our conceptual basis for the understanding of psychopathology within a psychoanalytic context.

PART I

BORDERLINE PATIENTS

2

Changing Clinical Perspectives

The last 40 years, the decades during which I have studied and practiced psychoanalysis, have brought about sweeping changes in all aspects of psychoanalysis. These changes not only include theories and technical concepts, they also affect the structure and politics of the psychoanalytic movement. Many analysts believe that they represent progress, although 40 years ago psychoanalysis was at its apogee, and today many clinicians believe that psychoanalysis is dead or that it will be completely submerged by the tide of biological psychiatry.

From an esoteric cult proclaiming that any deviation from or modification of Freud was heresy, psychoanalysis has become organized into a series of loosely connected or unconnected groups sufficiently diverse so that there are no central doxologies or immutable dicta. In a sense, it has been converted from an oligarchy to a democracy.

Many factors are responsible for the increasing unpopularity of psychoanalysis, which I wish to simply mention but not to explore directly. We can draw some inferences as we take note of the status of psychoanalysis 40 or more years ago.

Then, analysts maintained themselves in a state of haughty isolation, perhaps as a defense against the ridicule they and their work had been subjected to during the early days when Freud had announced his discoveries and ideas to the world. Undoubtedly he was treated unfairly, but there must have been something about his attitudes, in addition to the inherent provocations of his concepts, that contributed to the way he was received. Mid-Victorian prudishness and anti-Semitic orientations did not cultivate a propitious soil for the acceptance of basic psychoanalytic principles, but as Ellenberger (1970) stresses, Freud's milieu was not as oppositional as he claimed, such that he was forced to withdraw in those "splendid years of isolation" (Freud 1915b).

I do not wish to pursue the checkered history of the psychoanalytic movement. As is well known, there has been considerable strife in the ever-splitting psychoanalytic societies as they become overburdened with petty politics. The American Psychoanalytic Association and a few component branches had set themselves up as the *ne plus ultra* of an aristocratically oriented hierarchy. In the last few years this has been radically changed and the American Psychoanalytic Association can no longer function as a monopoly.

I do not wish to pursue the internecine warfare that has plagued practically every psychoanalytic society ever formed. Rather, I want to concentrate only on clinical issues. Politics has caused interest in clinical matters to recede into the background, or clinical issues have become politicized and used as weapons. In both instances our understanding of patients has not really advanced, nor has our therapeutic perspective broadened in that we might have explored the treatment process further and questioned dicta that have been unconditionally accepted ex cathedra.

I believe that psychoanalysis is now in a propitious position to make solid progress aimed at in-depth understanding of psychopathology and the psychic processes involved in the therapeutic interaction. The psychoanalytic movement has, to a large measure, become decentralized. The energy that has been wasted in striving for power and prestige can be more fruitfully applied to exploring the substance of our profession, that is, how to be of service to patients suffering from emotional disorders.

The study of patients suffering from primitive mental states, which includes borderline and other patients with characterological problems, serves as a good vantage point aimed at expanding therapeutic horizons. *Focusing on this group of patients does not represent a subspecialty of psychoanalysis; rather it is the essence and substance of the psychoanalytic enterprise.*

A HISTORICAL OVERVIEW

Returning to a historical perspective, but now only in terms of clinical issues, the interest in borderline patients was not considered to be a proper psychoanalytic pursuit in that it was believed to take the clinician outside the psychoanalytic domain. As mentioned in the preface, Freud (1914a) explicitly stated the indications and contraindications for psychoanalytic treatment. Generally, he divided emotional disorders into two categories, the transference and narcissistic neuroses. The transference neuroses were hysteria and obsessive-compulsive neuroses, the psychoneuroses; and the narcissistic neuroses were the depressions and what he then called the paraphrenias. Later these were referred to as the schizophrenias when Bleuler (1911) introduced the term. The transference neuroses represented the only group considered to be amenable to the psychoanalytic treatment approach because they form transferences. According to Freud, the analysis of the transference is the essence of classical psychoanalytic treatment, and the patients being analyzed are considered to be classical cases. I call attention to the use of the word *classical* because it has aesthetic implications rather than emphasizing objective clinical observations. The classical analyst and the classical patient seem to be shrouded in an esoteric mystique and involved in a mystic ritual that must be kept secret, although the latter is explained to be in the interest of confidentiality.

There is no question that psychoanalysis has to be conducted in a strict confidential fashion. It is indeed a sacred trust, but it is the only aspect of a basically human interaction that is sacred. This does not require that analysts and their patients be viewed as members of an elite cult, as was the situation at the beginning of my training after World War II, and which seemed to be the attitude among analysts for the several preceding decades.

I recall that when I was a resident an analytic patient was admitted to our ward. Apparently this patient had undergone a regressive episode that rendered him helpless while in treatment with a senior analyst, and he was unable to function at an outpatient level. For us residents to be so close to an analytic patient created in us a mild state of awe. We had a different attitude toward him than we did toward ordinary, nonclassical patients. With them we were much more relaxed, and although we maintained respect, we were not reverential. With this patient we trod lightly, so to speak, fearing we might do something that would upset the delicate treatment relationship. Though we knew very little about the analytic relationship, perhaps because of our ignorance we placed it in a separate category outside the mainstream of the interactions taking place on a psychiatric ward. It was something special, and this was reflected in the general attitude psychoanalysts had about psychiatrists who were not trained at a psychoanalytic institute. Psychoanalysts felt superior to other mental health workers; they considered themselves special and their patients, they of the classical transference neuroses, were also special.

The special position of psychoanalysts has relevance to their clinical approach as well as their relationship to colleagues. As stated, their patients were placed on a higher level than patients who were being treated by "inferior" nonanalytic methods. As Freud (1919) stated, they were subjected to the "copper of suggestion" rather than the "pure gold of psychoanalysis." There was generally a disdain for patients suffering from primitive mental states, who in some circles were considered as having weak egos, but the word *weak* had a moral connotation. This was a throwback to Janet's (1929) evaluation of hysterics, who, he believed, were to some extent degenerates and inferior.

From a historical perspective, we have reached a position that is the total antithesis of what I have just described. Once, the prestige of a residency was related to the number of residents who were accepted as candidates by a psychoanalytic institute. In the fifties, Michael Reese Hospital, the University of Chicago Clinics, and the University of Illinois had highly acclaimed residencies because their residents were usually accepted for training by the Chicago Institute for Psychoanalysis. Today, I understand that the University of Chicago Department of Psychiatry focuses predominantly on psychopharmacology, and psychodynamic psychotherapy is hardly ever taught. I know that at the University of Illinois very few residents apply for admission to the Chicago Institute for Psychoanalysis.

Furthermore, psychoanalysts are no longer special. In many circles they are considered obsolete, and in some training centers there has been some debate as to whether psychotherapy, especially psychoanalytically oriented psychotherapy, should be included in the teaching curriculum.

Besides the influence of psychopharmacological discoveries, there are many complex reasons involved in the unpopularity of psychoanalysis. Undoubtedly, psychoanalysts themselves have contributed to the downhill course, and there may have been reactions against the previous mystique and its accompanying arrogance. Returning to the clinical focus, I wish to emphasize some paradoxes that have caused shifts in emphasis on the substance of psychoanalysis, both in its conceptual underpinnings and attitudes about therapeutic orientations and technical maneuvers.

To repeat, Freud stressed that only the transference neuroses were capable of being analyzed, and by implication, other patients who did not belong under this diagnostic rubric were unworthy of the treatment method. Freud did not exactly say this, but this attitude was prominent in clinical seminars at psychoanalytic institutes at a time when patients seeking psychoanalysis were plentiful. It is a rare occurrence when a patient has to be worthy of a technical treatment approach, but psychoanalytic patients had to be suited for the procedure rather than the opposite, which is generally true, that the procedure has to be fitted to patients' needs and their pathology.

As we pursue a historical perspective from a clinical viewpoint we are immediately faced with a paradox. Freud's dicta concerning the indications for psychoanalytic treatment caused us to examine his classical cases, which he used as data to formulate the psychodynamics of the various transference neuroses such as obsessional neuroses and anxiety hysteria. Reichard (1956) has studied the patients discussed in the *Studies on Hysteria* (Breuer and Freud 1895) and concluded that they were much more severely disturbed than one would expect with an ordinary psychoneurosis. Most of these patients could be conceptualized as borderline in that they were bordering on the edge of a psychosis or at times were actually psychotic, as was the case of Anna O. The paradigmatic cases that furnished the data Freud used to conceptualize the psychodynamic factors that distinguished the specific psychoneuroses have also been questioned in terms of their diagnoses (Giovacchini 1972, 1979a). Little Hans (Freud 1909a), for example, proved later in life to have had more problems than could be explained by a simple phobia. Apparently he was sadistic toward women and acted out in a provocative manner that was more consistent with that of a person suffering from characterological problems. Similarly, Dora's (Freud 1904) behavior indicated that her emotional makeup involved more than hysterical mechanisms. Deutsch (1960) interviewed her when she was an elderly woman and discovered that she was a cantankerous, narcissistic, malevolent person who had alienated most of her friends and family. The Wolf Man (Freud 1918) was supposed to illustrate psychic mechanisms characteristic of an infantile neurosis with obsessional features, but in a subsequent analysis (Brunswick 1928) proved to have delusions that were the manifestations of a paranoid psychosis. Regarding the Rat Man (Freud 1909b), we do not have sufficient data to make any statements about his diagnosis because he was killed in World War I.

If these patients were, in fact, examples of borderline psychopathology, then Freud was analyzing patients who, he stated, were not analyzable. He was dealing, to use his terminology, with the narcissistic neuroses rather than the transference neuroses. I again emphasize the paradox that Freud dealt with patients psychoanalytically who, had he known the correct diagnosis, would have been considered to be examples of nontreatable cases. Freud founded the psychoanalytic method with patients whose psychopathology contraindicated an analytic approach. Classical analysis was performed on nonclassical patients.

I do not wish to imply that Freud was not an astute diagnostician. Rather, I believe that he was a product of his time and inclined to observe and conceptualize in terms of the current scientific tradition. Scientific models were mechanistic and based on vectors and shifting energy patterns. The first two laws of thermodynamics, the first postulating the constancy and conservation of energy and the second dealing with entropy—that is, the movement from states of organization to states of disorganization—fit well with Freud's psychodynamic concepts, which are based on accumulation, tension, and energic discharges. Freud was working within the prevailing scientific paradigm and his observational mode was shaped in terms of hydrodynamic concepts and linear causality.

The treatment process, in turn, would be described in the same language as concepts about psychopathology and would be derived from them. The aim of treatment is to make the unconscious conscious. How this brings about or contributes to the cure of a neurosis is still poorly understood. Freud (1914b) simply stated that the gaining of insight as occurs when the unconscious is revealed is accompanied by a process known as working through, and somehow this leads to the resolution of conflict. If we examine these processes it becomes clear that they are also based on hydrodynamic principles.

Presumably the unconscious is a seething cauldron (Freud 1923) seeking to explosively express itself. There are counterforces, however (that is, repressive barriers), that keep it in a bound state. Impulses and needs reside in the unconscious, and as they intensify they seek release and satisfaction. This is a tension–discharge sequence and the process of discharge is supposed to be ameliorative, but this discharge has to be accompanied by insight. Otherwise, discharge can become a therapeutic obstacle, and then clinicians are dealing with acting out, which has to be curbed.

The treatment process was also viewed as a series of energic shifts that had to be controlled by the analyst. That control was exercised on the basis of the authority attributed to, and the respect given to, the analyst. Physicians were commonly held in awe during the mid-Victorian and Victorian eras and, at best, took advantage of the esteem in which they were held by being benignly paternalistic and directive. This enabled Freud to make certain demands of his patients.

The patient had to lie on the couch and was instructed not to withhold expressing any thoughts or feelings, that is, to free-associate. In daily life patients were asked not to make any serious decisions, not to discuss what occurred during the sessions, and in some instances to refrain from having sexual relations or otherwise becoming involved in intimate relationships. Analysis had to be conducted in a state of abstinence in order not to discharge feelings or impulses that had to be contained in the analytic setting.

The analyst, through the pressure of authority, attempts to control specifically the building up of tension and discharge. Free association – the relaxation of control, selection, and suppression – opens up the gateway to the id. The patient's associations, although they are not direct reproductions of the id, represent derivatives of the unconscious. Free association is designed to make the unconscious conscious. Topographically there is a movement from deeper unconscious layers of the personality to surface conscious levels. What has been kept pent up is released, and this is a discharge phenomenon. The analyst does all he can to promote this type of discharge.

Analysts encourage the patient to relax repressive forces. At first, this is related to free associating. Patients invariably put up resistances to free associating, and analysts apply pressure against these resistances, which usually take the form of withholding. Actually, Freud first discussed the concept of resistance when he described the pressure technique. He literally pressed his finger on the reclining patient's forehead and exhorted him to tell whatever came to mind no matter whether he felt it was trivial, embarrassing, or shameful; that it was vital not to withhold anything. In spite of his exhortations, patients nevertheless did not express their thoughts or feelings the first time pressure to the forehead was applied (Breuer and Freud 1895).

The essence of analysis was a struggle against resistance. Perhaps the most important aspect of these early, classical analyses is that they were conducted in the context of struggle. For the most part, therapists and patients were antagonists rather than collaborators interested in learning about the operation of the patient's mind. *They were involved in an adversarial relationship.*

The psychoneuroses were the outcome of clashing inner forces. Freud would side with one part of the intrapsychic conflict. As stated, at first he was on the side of the id and against the ego's repressive strivings. He was, at the same time, against the id, not against the unconscious revealing itself at ego-conscious levels, but against expressing itself in action. To repeat, he was forbidding patients from acting out their unconscious and usually destructive impulses.

Analysts encouraged and discouraged tension–discharge sequences. Although they seemed to have gone beyond Breuer's (Breuer and Freud 1895) abreaction-cathexis procedure and to have achieved considerable sophistica tion since those early days of the "talking cure," classical analysts were, in essence, operating along similar lines. The difference resided in that later analysts did not limit their attempts to achieve psychic discharge of only encapsulated unconscious or split-off memories of traumas.

Viewing the therapeutic interaction in terms of energic shifts makes it difficult to understand what Freud (1913) meant by neutrality because the classical analyst was not impartial about mental processes. Some were good, such as those related to revealing the unconscious, and others were decidedly bad, such as resistance and acting out. The therapeutic interaction was fought on a battlefield (it is interesting that Freud was particularly fond of battlefield and martial metaphors), a situation that obliterates neutrality and emphasizes moral evaluations.

The psychoanalytic viewpoint is supposedly nonjudgmental. But Freud's edicts and confrontations indicate that he had very definite opinions as to what was right and wrong and he sometimes made remarks about patients that went beyond scientific objectivity. For example, Edoardo Weiss (personal communication 1953) once told me that Freud referred to a patient that he had written to him about as being a scoundrel.

These early analysts preached about being nonjudgmental, impartial, and neutral, but in actuality they often stressed and practiced just the opposite. The mid-Victorian patient often accepted the analyst's moral bias and made it his own, but by no means could this have represented the formation of an autonomous true self. The therapeutic relation was not based on an alliance. Rather, it was a grossly uneven dyad in which the therapist, at times, imposed his biases on the patient.

One can well ask what the circumstances were surrounding the patient's so-called acquisition of insights. Freud initially described his therapeutic innovations and techniques in the *Studies on Hysteria*. He made an interpretation to a hysterical woman, who refuted it. Freud emphatically repeated what he had said. Again she refused to believe him, whereupon he became angry and literally shouted at her that she had to accept what he said. Later he asked her a question, and she gave the required answer that would have indicated she accepted his interpretation. He was pleased but apparently not willing to leave well enough alone. Freud asked why she believed what she did, and she replied something to the effect that he insisted that she accept what he said, and she was simply complying.

Kardiner (1977) was less direct and outspoken than Freud's earlier patient. During a session of his analysis with Freud, he was aware of feeling some anger and was preoccupied with death wishes. Freud interpreted that the patient wanted to kill his father, whereupon Kardiner mildly protested that he did not believe this was an accurate appraisal of his feelings. He gently suggested that he really wanted to kill Freud rather than his father. Apparently Freud lost his temper and accused Kardiner of being a bad patient. If he did not like what Freud had to say, he could go back to America. Since Kardiner wanted very much to be in analysis with Freud, he agreed that the Professor must be correct.

These clinical descriptions are considerably at variance with Freud's (1911–1914) recommendations in his technical papers. He wrote that the analyst must forgo therapeutic ambition and that he should follow the clinical material with an open mind and no preconceived notions. He should be surprised at every turn of the material. This would indicate a benign, relaxed attitude rather than a feisty therapist ready to do battle with the recalcitrant patient who is supposedly resisting.

Inasmuch as technical procedures have to be consistent with the underlying theory, Freud conceptualized the treatment relationship in the same manner as he did psychopathology. I am again referring to the psychodynamic viewpoint, which emphasizes clashing intrapsychic forces or vectors. Freud could be viewed as being conflict-seeking, and in the treatment relationship he himself entered and became part of the conflict. The model for the therapeutic interaction is a reflection of forces and counterforces that characterize the various psychoneuroses.

I believe that Freud's formulations were, to some extent, forced on the data, and as mentioned, were consonant with the scientific atmosphere surrounding him. This should not, however, be construed as a criticism and perhaps the word *forced* is somewhat too strong. I believe, however, that all investigators, *more or less*, impose their biases on the field of observation. It was Freud himself (1912) who stressed that there are always preconceived notions that are intruded into our formulations, but he recognized that these formulations represent the surface of conceptual systems and can be easily discounted when better or more efficient hypotheses can be constructed.

As Kuhn (1962) discussed, the history of science is punctuated by paradigms, models that characterize various generations of science. These paradigms color observational methods and determine how hypotheses will be structured. The language of the paradigm is used for the making of, and the conceptual understanding of, new observations. It is the next generation that can change that language as it rallies around a new paradigm.

CURRENT PERSPECTIVES

Probably the data of psychoanalysis as they refer to basic psychopathology have not fundamentally changed. As Reichard (1956) has discussed, the early patients in psychoanalytic treatment can be formulated in terms of models that emphasize structural factors and object relations rather than conflicting intrapsychic forces. Various levels of the psyche may not be smoothly integrated into a cohesive whole, and this can lead to certain behavioral manifestations and symptomatic expressions that have been associated with the borderline personality. Drive theory has become decathected, so to speak, as many clinicians have stopped to think in terms of the psychoeconomic hypothesis.

The current generation of behavioral scientists has rallied around the paradigm of structural psychopathology, which has led clinicians to diagnose their patients more frequently as borderline personalities rather than as psychoneurotics, Freud's transference neuroses. This has occurred because our conceptual orientation has changed.

Our formulations focus on defects in psychic structure and faulty emotional development. Consequently, adaptations to and relationships with the outer world are disturbed as a result of maldevelopment or deficiencies in the ego's executive system. Emotional development is still viewed as an hierarchically arranged series of mental stages, but these stages or mental states are defined in terms of relationships between inner mental states and the outer world, that is, in terms of object relationships (see Chapter 5).

This emphasis is somewhat different from Freud's (1905b) theory of development, which describes a series of psychosexual stages. He also included in his formulations relationships with external objects, but they were not given any special importance in the production of psychopathology. Rather, he concentrates on the sexual impulses, libido, as it is directed toward bodily functions and later at persons. It is the vicissitudes of this libido rather than difficulties in object relationships that are responsible for emotional disorders (see Chapter 3). True, Freud (1924a,b) later wrote about disturbed relationships with reality but he confined them to significant factors in the psychoses. Today our conceptual orientation has changed in that it gives more significance to developmental problems and their effects on object relations than to libido.

Conceptual orientations, of course, do not spontaneously change. Clinical necessity has forced us to view our patients in a different light. Many therapists found it difficult to keep patients in treatment if they followed Freud's dicta about neutrality, confrontation, and the undesirability of countertransference (Freud 1910). Young psychoanalysts tried to emulate their elders, or at least what their elders taught, but they found this to be a difficult and often impossible task. To modify the therapeutic approach meant that the analyst was abandoning analysis.

This was evident among analytic candidates. The clinical seminars at the Chicago Institute for Psychoanalysis were divided into three groups, which dealt respectively with the beginning, middle, and end of treatment. Usually the candidates in the group that was devoted to the beginning of treatment began therapy enthusiastically, with a certain degree of optimism. Frequently, the instructor and students felt the prognosis was favorable, and the patient was often diagnosed as a hysterical personality with good ego integration. Psychodynamic formulations seemed to be appropriate, and for the most part the patient seemed to respond well to the formality of the psychoanalytic procedure.

A year later, at the second-level seminar, the clinical situation had drastically changed. Many of the previous year's hysterics and other psychoneurotics had become transformed in that short period of time into schizophrenics or borderline personalities. Although these control patients had been rigorously screened by both an individual clinician and later by a board of senior psychoanalysts, in treatment they proved to be much more seriously disturbed than had been initially diagnosed.

In part this was due to these patients' sophistication: they covered up their symptoms because they would not be accepted for a low-fee analysis if they revealed the severity of their emotional problems. This was true of my first control patient. He was a black adolescent, an overt homosexual who, on occasion, had auditory hallucinations. He kept both his homosexuality and hallucinations hidden, and did not discuss them even with me until he had been at least 6 years in treatment. The Institute no longer mattered, because I had graduated and the patient knew I was committed to his therapy. Furthermore, he had become sufficiently successful that he paid an almost standard fee.

The third-level seminar discussed patients who were in the termination phase of analysis. Practically none of the patients who had begun analysis 2 to 3 years earlier were presented, because they were no longer in treatment or were nowhere near ready to be considered for termination. The treatment of those patients who were presented seemed anticlimactic. The formulations we made struck me as drab in that they consisted of a series of poorly strung-together cliches. They usually took the following form: The candidate analyst spent a good deal of time analyzing defenses. When they were worked through, he would come to grips with the Oedipus complex and this would in turn be worked through. This seemed to be the standard formula for the treatment process and applied to practically all patients.

The only differences were related to the nature of defenses, which were acknowledged to be pregenital. As a rule, we were discussing oral defenses, which were manifested by passivity and dependence. In an orderly analysis the patient would indicate feeling dependent on the analyst and wishing to be taken care of. The therapist would interpret the patient's receptivity and dependence, sometimes in a critical tone, the implication being that the patient should grow up and not be a baby.

Nevertheless, senior analysts stressed that these feelings had to kept in the transference context, that is, directed toward the analyst. Patients were supposed to curb their passive-dependent impulses in the outer world since this would constitute acting out, and acting out was a potent source of resistance. Suppressing acting out, as far as I could determine, was the essence of working through. I recall with some amusement being asked how I defined psychoanalysis. I replied that this was simple; the analyst discovered the symptoms and then forbade them.

Forbidding the expression of symptoms or symptomatic behavior also applied to the Oedipus complex.

One of my patients, a young woman in her middle twenties, after having gone through a protracted period in treatment when we concentrated on her dependent wishes, began a series of affairs with Italian men. I interpreted how she was defending herself against erotic feelings toward me by displacing and thus dissipating them in the outside world. I repeatedly confronted her with how she was avoiding facing the sexual transference, and this represented resistance to treatment. My supervisor supported my interpretations, but the patient's behavior did not change. Both my supervisor and I felt that interpretations should curb acting out, but they did not have a prohibitive effect. After several months during which the patient continued her promiscuous behavior, we agreed that I would have to be more forceful. Thus I explained to my patient that there was no point to continuing the treatment if she kept on draining her feelings in her various affairs. If she wished to remain in analysis, she would have to stop being sexually involved with these men who were surrogates for me. She acquiesced to my demand, but she was by no means pleased with my edict.

The patient continued in treatment for 4 more years, a total of 8. She became aware of a mild erotic transference. She later divorced her gentile husband, the patient being Jewish. She then became engaged to a Jewish doctor, whom she married at the end of her treatment. In a final dream, she was getting married and I was giving the bride away. The patient was asymptomatic and apparently pleased with the outcome of analysis.

It would seem that this was a successful treatment and that my intervention was crucial in breaking up an impasse, but there are many lingering doubts about this patient. She never forgave me for my "interfering with her life," which she saw as an attack on her autonomy. She attributed the progress she made as occurring in spite of my prohibition rather than because of it.

My supervising analyst believed that everything had gone well, but at a postgraduate clinical seminar the group was somewhat skeptical. They felt that the course of analysis was too pat. What I had reported was the course an analysis should take as we then believed. The resolution of pregenital oral defenses took us to the oedipal position, and then she was liberated from an incestuous attachment. Her first marriage represented an acting out of a defense against her sexual attachment to her Jewish father, her husband being gentile. At the end of the analysis she was presumably able to marry a Jewish physician, a choice her family very much approved. Her husband, however, was sufficiently different from her father so that the relationship was fairly free of incestuous elements. It was interesting that the group was suspicious of an analysis that proceeded as it should have. It was too simple and straightforward, to an extent that made us believe our formulations were naive and simple-minded.

Several participants stated that perhaps she had not worked out the erotic transference, that it was still in force at an unconscious level. She could not, because of oedipal conflict, express her sexual attachment toward me; instead, she bolstered my self-esteem and ego ideal by giving me the present of a successful analysis.

These formulations are still cast in the mold of drive theory and psychodynamic constellations. Structural factors are totally ignored. Furthermore, none of these formulations take my intervention into account.

Looking back at this patient from a current perspective—that is, a perspective that does not promote an adversarial treatment relationship—I believe we might gain further understanding if we pay attention to what she said. We supposedly always pay attention to what patients say, but do we believe them or do we believe only what we want to believe, or what confirms our preconceived formulations? The patient emphatically stated that she resented my prohibition, and experienced it as an intrusion on her autonomy. If that is the way she experienced it, then it is significant and has explanatory value. My supervisor and I tended to underplay her feelings, which are of course part of her psychic reality. As analysts we were not paying much attention to psychic reality, certainly a nonanalytic attitude, if not a travesty of the psychoanalytic approach.

Thus I am advocating that we not only listen to our patients but that we believe them. This may sound trite, but what I have heard at clinical seminars, panels, and presentations of clinical papers indicates that we analysts tend to respect our own beliefs more than the patient's. Furthermore, this is an orientation that is consonant with the classical psychoanalytic relationship because in such analyses the prevailing opinion is that the patient tries to hide the truth rather than reveal it. Again it is the old struggle between the analyst and the patient's resistance.

If my supervisor and I had taken what the patient said at face value and admitted the possibility that my intervention was, in fact, intrusive and an attack on her autonomy, then we might have looked at the course of her treatment from a vastly different perspective. During the final phases of the therapy she felt submerged by me because I threatened her individuality and identity sense. This was also a father transference since she had disclosed similar feelings toward her father, but I had reinforced this transference by making her stop having affairs. Actually, her promiscuous behavior was more than just a displacement and defense against an erotic transference. She was also feeling threatened and fearful of fusing with me, and her outside involvements represented an attempt to escape from what she perceived as a smothering experience. True, it was her transference projections that had created such an atmosphere, but I participated in that I behaved as would have been characteristic of her father. If I had literally accepted what she said when she protested, I would have learned a good deal.

It is also possible that part of her wanted to provoke me into a confrontation so that she could bring the infantile ambience into the consultation room, but these possibilities were obviously not explored. If they had been, the last dream she had might be viewed differently. My giving her away as a bride could have been a wish-fulfillment in which she was separating from me. She also might have forced the termination of treatment because of her need to liberate herself from me. Here is another instance of a literal approach that can be applied to a dream as well as to her associations. The manifest content of this dream can be directly translated as a wish-fulfillment.

Clinicians might protest that patients do indeed hide and distort the truth because of inner conflicts, and therefore we cannot believe everything they say. Distortions, however, represent manifestations of a conflict and perhaps psychopathological mental states. We can still learn from them. They are part of the patient's psychic reality, and in most analyses this is all that matters. I do not wish to be engaged in a discussion of historic truth versus psychic truth. I am simply emphasizing that whatever the patient brings us is worthy of our attention and deserves equal time. This de-emphasizes the importance of resistance.

It is also noteworthy that the reexamination of my patient did not make oedipal feelings a central core; rather, I focused on structural elements, primarily the self-representation. The oedipal aspects of a neurosis and structural problems, however, are not mutually exclusive. I also call into question the value of confrontation, a parameter that some clinicians, even contemporary clinicians such as Kernberg (1987) and Masterson (1976), might feel is required to set limits so that the analytic process does not disintegrate into chaos. To the extent that such confrontations become technical ingredients, analysts are carrying on a heritage that belonged to the early days of classical psychoanalysis.

This does not mean that analysts should always avoid taking actions that are intended to set limits. Many patients are so disorganized or have so very little control of their impulses that they cannot be treated unless the therapeutic setting is able to contain them. Still, once we become involved in this kind of management, our capacity to analyze the transference may be diminished because we are, in fact, assuming the role that goes beyond an exploration of mental processes and is, perhaps, similar to that of some punitive person of the past. Patients who require this type of restraint may be very difficult to treat from a psychoanalytic perspective or in an outpatient setting.

Many of the patients clinicians see today seem to have a concrete orientation and are not particularly psychologically minded. They are impulse-ridden and action oriented, and these qualities do not make them good prospects for psychoanalytic exploration. Insofar as this group of patients are in the majority, are psychoanalysts faced with a crisis characterized by a lack of, or very few, psychoanalytic patients? If this is true, psychoanalysts are faced with an identity problem. If they are to survive as psychoanalysts, they have to practice psychoanalysis. They have to find patients who can be analyzed or they have to modify their treatment approach to suit their patients' needs and still be able to remain within a psychoanalytic context.

What has happened to the patient population? In the course of a year, the patients mentioned in the clinical seminars changed from hysterics to borderlines. Nevertheless, they had been accepted for analysis by highly skilled diagnosticians. A year later, they were still the same patients they were a year before. Treatment could not have produced such drastic, negative characterological changes. Perhaps the initial interviewers sensed that there was something positive in these patients' mental status that indicated they were capable of being analyzed. Possibly the interviewers felt, most likely unconsciously, that they had to justify this feeling by viewing these patients as psychoneurotics. I do not believe they were distorting the data; they were simply emphasizing the positives and maybe narrowing their vision to exclude the more serious and primitive aspects of psychopathology. This could lead to an accepting and receptive attitude that might be propitious for the construction of an analytic relationship.

As I have emphasized, Freud's classic cases, in terms of the severity of their psychopathology, were probably not particularly different from the patients we see today. Nevertheless, he and his followers were able to enhance their psychoanalytic identities by treating patients psychoanalytically. This could mean that psychopathology is basically the same; only the manifestations of emotional disorders have changed. Cultural factors may also be very much involved.

Actually, we can investigate the cultural variable by observing how the patient population has changed in countries that have moved in the direction of accepting the mores and values of Western capitalistic civilization. For example, several years ago I was in Morocco. Psychiatrists told me that the majority of their patients had been conversion hysterics. They had somatic symptoms that were created by intrapsychic conflict associated with the repression of sexual impulses, much in the same fashion as the patients demonstrated by Charcot in his Tuesday lectures, which Freud attended as a young man. What was most remarkable was that since Morocco had become independent from the French, the types of psychopathology gradually changed and conversion hysterics were becoming increasingly scarce. Correspondingly, there was an increase in borderline and schizophrenic patients. Again, conversion hysterics, borderline and schizophrenic patients are the same people, but the structure and values of that society have drastically changed since they started governing themselves and the French had left. The family, which had been a tight, cohesive group, had become much more loosely organized. Formerly there was an extended family, and children remained with their parents when they reached adulthood and married. Currently the importance of the family has receded, and children have the same goals and desires as children in our country. They strive for independence and material acquisitions. Even their music changed in that rock and roll is extremely popular. The Moroccan culture seems to be moving in our direction, and inasmuch as this has occurred, their patient population is becoming more like ours.

In Russia something similar has happened, and it was predicted at least 20 years ago. The director of a state hospital in Moscow was asked whether delinquency and drugs were problems. She replied that alcoholism was their most severe problem. She said, "No, drugs and delinquency are not a problem, not yet." Her prediction has come true.

The salient point is that these are the same patients. If they could be treated psychoanalytically when they were seen as hysterics or as having other types of psychoneuroses, why can they not be treated now as borderline patients and perhaps even some as schizophrenics? Many clinicians believe that these patients can be treated, a belief that may help analysts overcome their professional identity crisis. By trying to bring the analytic method to the borderline group of patients, clinicians are functioning as psychoanalysts and retaining their psychoanalytic identity.

As stated earlier, a conceptual system that stresses structural defects as they are involved in psychopathology represents a new paradigm, which, in a sense, is forced on us because of the manifest changes in the patient population. Within this context we can maintain our psychoanalytic identities, but to complete the cycle there have to be corresponding modifications in our attitudes about treatment, which will, in turn, affect our technical responses.

As stated in the Preface, there is still considerable confusion as to what is meant by borderline or borderline personality organization. I will discuss this question further in the next chapter. I bring this up again because I believe that this confusion is due in part to our attempts to establish a new paradigm. When a new paradigm is established, the previous paradigm does not completely disappear. Many clinicians still cling to the psychodynamic-psychoneurotic analysis of the resistance sequence, which represents the conceptual, diagnostic, and treatment aspects of the old paradigm that has been labeled classic. The attempts to operate in both frames of reference simultaneously can cause confusion; or, at least, clinicians may develop a viewpoint that is so individualistic or idiosyncratic that it cannot be shared or accepted by colleagues.

Can drive theory and the structural approach be reconciled? May there not be clinical situations that are best understood in terms of drive theory, and other instances (the majority of instances), in which the structural and object relations approach is preferable? This would be similar to the relationship between Newton's physics and Einstein's relativity theory. The former can be applied to certain macroscopic phenomena leading to a sufficient degree of accuracy, whereas the latter is confined to the explanation of much more subtle interactions. Within the domain of psychoanalysis, the further question can be asked as to whether the classic and structural paradigms can be simultaneously applied to the same clinical data. The mind is so multifaceted that it might require two theoretical models to understand it. This would indicate that drive theory and the structural approach can be reconciled and that they are not mutually contradictory.

As we further examine the two paradigms, it becomes apparent that attitudes about therapy present us with the greatest difficulties. Clinicians may disagree about formulations, but it has frequently been stated that most of us treat patients in more or less the same fashion, no matter what our theoretical persuasion might be. I do not believe this is true; I feel our conceptual foundations determine how we act toward patients. This must be the situation among professionals, otherwise anyone without any training can set himself up as a therapist, as is often the case, unfortunately. Consequently, we can narrow our question as to whether classical therapeutic approaches can be compatible with the approaches required for borderline patients.

I do not believe the adversarial relationship that characterizes classical analysis can be reconciled with a therapeutic approach designed to be suitable for the patient's needs. I admit that there may be some patients who can adapt to the relatively silent, neutral analyst, who do not require much of a holding environment and who are capable of obeying the rule of abstinence. Such patients, however, are rarely seen, thus requiring clinicians to modify their therapeutic approach so that it remains in synchrony with the new conceptual system. The treatment of the borderline patient has ushered in a new era of psychoanalysis and has contributed to its preservation.

3

The Borderline

Concept

Over 40 years ago, psychoanalysts began to realize that neither Kraepelin's (1883) division of patients into two categories, the neuroses and psychoses, nor Freud's (1914a) classification of the transference and narcissistic neuroses were as inclusive as they were believed to be. Clinicians realized that there was an in-between group. As the years passed, this group seemed to increase in size, or, to be more precise, was becoming more recognizable. Knight (1953) observed that these patients were neither neurotic nor psychotic, but at times hovered around the edge of a psychosis. They could become psychotic, but they frequently reintegrated sufficiently to cope with reality and minimally function. He labeled this group borderline, meaning that it belonged somewhere between the neuroses and the psychoses, and could on occasion move into the realm of the psychoses, but never, without therapy, could they become neurotics.

I will not review the voluminous literature on the history of the concept of the borderline patient. It has already been ably done by Adler (1981), Kernberg (1984), Masterson (1976, 1978), Meissner (1988), and many others. Suffice it to mention that most investigators of the early period of the study of borderline patients remained, as Knight did, on a phenomenological level. In approximately the last 20 years this has changed as we explore psychodynamic, developmental, and structural factors.

Kernberg (1984), for example, discussed borderline patients' pregenital organization, the underlying rage and orality and the use of splitting mechanisms. Masterson (1978), Rinsley (1982), and others focus on the fixation on the stage of separation-individuation as an etiological factor in the production of psychopathology. There are many other formulations dealing with regression to primitive pregenital phases and the use of primitive defenses such as denial and projective identification (Grotstein 1981, Ogden 1982). Modell (1963) emphasizes psychopathology involving the transitional space as characteristic of the borderline personality.

As discussed in Chapter 2, many psychoanalysts have been treating borderline patients without knowing it. The situation has changed considerably in that most practitioners know that the patients they are treating are not classical transference neuroses. They acknowledge they are treating borderline patients and, in some instances, psychotic patients or patients with a psychotic core. Still, clinicians are not dealing with a homogeneous group. The patients that have been diagnosed as borderline may vary considerably in their symptomatology and character structure. This is because there is not as yet a theoretical consensus to encompass a wide variety of clinical phenomena.

Abend and colleagues (1983) have formulated borderline psychopathology in the context of drive theory and psychodynamic conflicts. Others have more or less de-emphasized drive theory and are concerned about structural factors, psychic development, and adaptation to the external world, which includes object relations. Many of these investigators, however, cling to Freud's phases of emotional development, that is, his psychosexual stages. Some have adopted Mahler's (1968) sequence of psychic maturation which emphasizes a progression from an autistic to a symbiotic phase, followed by separation-individuation and then by explorations of the outer world, characterized by practicing and rapprochement periods and, finally, object constancy. Melanie Klein (1952), ignored for many years in the

United States, has gradually gained some popularity. Her ideas about the paranoid-schizoid and depressive positions have been useful in understanding what has been considered to be borderline psychopathology. She also formulated the defense of projective identification, a concept that has helped explain many clinical phenomena and treatment interactions (See Chapter 5).

Freud's (1905b) stages of psychosexual development did not stress the development of the ego's executive techniques, which determine adaptations to the outer world. His theories are more concerned with the development of libido rather than of the ego, as was discussed in Chapter 2.

Other theories of development, with the exception those of Mahler and Klein, only deal with specific stages rather than the total spectrum from infancy to adulthood. Erikson (1959) has covered the course of development up until old age, but he and others do not include the maturation and integration of all parts of the psyche, or at least those that are involved in psychopathology.

SYMPTOMS, AFFECTS, AND PSYCHIC STRUCTURE

The borderline group of patients have difficulties in relating to people. They are often afraid of intimacy and making commitments. They also have problems in functioning in general, and responding to the exigencies of the milieu. As a rule, they do not have discrete symptoms such as phobias and obsessions and if they do, they are ego-syntonic rather than ego-dystonic. They may be somewhat depressed, but this tends to be a pervasive mood that reflects their views of the world. These patients may also be anxious, but again this is an all-encompassing feeling, usually not related to specific situations, feelings, or persons. Affective responses are manifestations of character configurations rather than responses to internal dangers that call into action various defensive patterns. Thus these patients display character traits rather than ego-dystonic symptoms when they reveal the essential features of their psychopathology.

Their affective states are part of a general ego state. They are also responses to internal difficulties, as is generally characteristic of affective responses. In contrast to the psychoneuroses in which anxiety is a response to aberrant, usually sexual, drives, painful affective reactions in the borderline patient are frequently manifestations of defective character structures. The simplest example is that of patients who are overwhelmed by anxiety because they find themselves in situations in which they cannot cope or they need to feel anxious in order to survive. I believe this is a typical borderline constellation. For example:

A woman in her late thirties complained of being in a state of constant anxiety. She could not attribute it to any particular precipitating traumas, nor could she predict situations that might calm her. She felt, for the most part, incapable of being soothed. She claimed, however, that not being anxious was also perceived as traumatic.

At first I thought in the context of psychodynamic factors and tried to understand her anxiety in terms of Freud's (1926) signal theory of anxiety. Therefore, I looked for events that she might have perceived as traumatic in that they may have cathected internal representations of infantile traumas or stimulated conflictful impulses that she had to repress. The patient witnessed my attempts to uncover such traumatic impingements with amused and benevolent tolerance (Giovacchini 1956, 1984). She tried to tell me that I was on the wrong track, that I was trying to find something that did not exist. I felt that she was being oppositional, that she was defending herself against painful feelings she did not want to reveal. In other words, I was convinced that she was resisting.

The patient kept telling me that I was imposing onto her formulations that were true of other patients. Her tone was not harsh or perturbed; instead, she was indulgent. To prove her point, she demonstrated that it was, at least to some extent, under her conscious control. She stated, "Now I will feel anxious," and she showed me goosebumps on her forearms and rivulets of perspiration on her brow. She then "decided" not to feel anxious, and these vegetative signs of anxiety disappeared.

This dramatic display caused me to reflect upon and question my therapeutic stance. In my mind, and sometimes actually, I challenged her accusations that I was attributing a degree of psychic organization and sophisticated intrapsychic conflicts that she felt were beyond her level of development. I was, in a sense, not listening to her in that I did not give credence to what she was saying. I wanted to believe what I had been taught rather than what she was trying to teach me. However, after her demonstration, I heard her.

She used her anxiety as a characterological defense. Later in therapy, she viewed it as a vehicle that reassured her that she was alive, like a person pinching herself to prove that she is awake. She gradually revealed that her anxiety was, on the surface, generating a sense of aliveness and protecting herself from a more basic, fundamental, and devastating anxiety. The latter might best not be classified as anxiety if anxiety is defined as an affect with a certain degree of coherence and organization. We were dealing with a state of fundamental terror, an existential catastrophe. The patient referred to these deeper feelings as the manifestations of a basic apathetic terror, a description Federn (1952) wrote about; but my patient had never heard of Federn.

She repeatedly indicated that she had no firm sense of identity, that for the most part she felt that she did not exist. As expected, this was accompanied by an almost total lack of self-esteem and a devastating sense of inner emptiness. She was overwhelmed by feelings of self-loathing. Anxiety, although painful, served as an organizer of psychic structure and generated sufficient feelings to protect her from existential annihilation. It defended her against the devastating effects of a structural defect, a crumbling, loosely held together self-representation.

She had other defenses that served the same purpose, but they were also operating in an anxious context. She clung to her friends and had to schedule her social life to such a degree that she was practically never alone. Or if she was alone, she knew where she could reach at least two of her friends by telephone. She filled up all her weekends almost a year in advance and she had New Year's Eve parties planned for the next 5 years.

She needed to maintain a tie with reality so that she would not be submerged in a morass of anonymity. If she could keep herself outwardly directed and hold onto her grip on the outside world, she could pull herself out of the quicksand that threatened to swallow up her sense of personal being.

This patient illustrated how an all-pervasive affect achieves a degree of psychic equilibrium that is threatened by a structural defect that involves the self-representation. Anxiety, as is usually the case, was not, however, entirely adaptive; it was also the manifestation of a partial psychic breakdown. I believe that in character disorders and borderline patients, integrative and disintegrative processes can be embedded in the same tissue and operate simultaneously. In this patient, this means that the same anxiety can have a defensive, adaptive function as well as being the affective manifestation of a regressive, psychically disorganizing process. The former is a character defense, whereas the latter is an example of psychic disintegration (see Chapter 5).

As stated, the patient clung to her friends in order to remain in the external world and also to be rescued by them. This was a prominent transference feature emphasized by her clinging to me for succor and salvation. She constantly stressed how helpless she felt and how much she needed her friends for support and as her guide to life, which meant how to function in a civilized society. She had to be taught how to perform what, for others, were pedestrian tasks. For example, there were certain destinations that were too difficult to find while driving. Someone would have to either drive with her and give her directions or be her chauffeur. When thus regressed, she could not organize a shopping list and go to the store and purchase what she needed. Again she required a friend to accompany her. Her inability to accomplish these tasks contributed to her anxiety. It also intensified her self-loathing and low self-esteem, which generated depressive feelings.

Affects, in this instance, represent a response to a structural defect, or to be more precise, an ego defect. She did not have the adaptive techniques to cope with the exigencies of everyday existence. This was a lack rather than an inhibition or repression, which, as I will discuss later, is characteristic of borderline psychopathology. She was exhibiting a defect in the ego-executive system as well as a disorder of the self-representation. In this instance, however, the affects generated were not restorative or adaptive; they were simply the manifestations of anxiety and depression that are characteristically found in patients who feel helpless and vulnerable as they face a world they cannot comprehend or master. They feel themselves to be victims in an unfamiliar and, to them, hostile milieu. Of course, this orientation affects all facets of the personality, but the core defect is primarily found in the self-representation and the ego-executive system. True, structural defects involve the total personality, but there are certain psychic areas that are central in the construction of psychopathology.

The borderline group of patients, though they may not often regress to fixed psychotic states, nevertheless have problems in maintaining psychic stability and integration. They are loosely organized and lack emotional coherence and cohesion and, as stated, this is reflected in various psychic systems. This results in a decreased tolerance for both internal and external stimuli. Many patients indicate that they find it difficult to process experiences that others would find routine, and they use unique methods in order to achieve equilibrium.

The subjective and behavioral manifestations of such coping strategies constitute the borderline patient's symptoms, although this concept of symptom formation is considerably modified from our usual formulations about compromise formations, which define the various psychoneuroses. The reconciliation of the id and ego in a compromise formation is the essential feature in the construction of symptoms, and this is especially clear in the reaction formations of the obsessive-compulsive neuroses (Freud 1909b). To repeat, in the psychoneuroses, symptoms are the subjective and behavioral manifestations of defenses designed to maintain repression of a dangerous impulse; in the obsessive-compulsive neurosis this refers to sadistic, destructive feelings that have become erotically tinged. Patients suffering from character disorders do not have the same discrete problems of clashing internal forces. They are preoccupied with the all-pervasive problem of holding themselves together.

Affects can be used in many different ways as organizers and vehicles to achieve psychic equilibrium or, at least, to protect patients from uncontrollable regression, a total disruption of their internal household. Beside filling voids, as was illustrated by the patient just discussed, they can serve as an impetus to the formation of psychic structure. They may be binding forces that lead to cohesion and relief from internal chaos. Something similar happened to the patient just discussed, but the clinical phenomena I will describe occur much more in an interpersonal context.

I believe many affects have this binding potential. Let us begin by discussing anger. A young man in his middle twenties indicated even during his first session that he was displeased with me as a person and challenged the efficacy of the psychoanalytic method. Nevertheless, he decided to enter treatment, but for the first year he constantly attacked me. I was insensitive, nonempathic, incompetent, and totally uninterested in helping him. I tried to view his material in terms of projection, a transference in which he was assigning me the role of an inadequate parent. I was surprised, however, as to how quickly such a transference developed, which would have pointed to its psychotic nature, Still, I had the feeling that his reality testing was intact, and at most, I thought of him as borderline in a phenomenological sense. I was more surprised at my reaction in that I felt relatively comfortable with his litany of complaints and tirades despite the fact that he rebuffed my interpretations that related to the transference meanings of his material. Furthermore, the patient showed no inclination to terminate treatment in spite of his apparent dissatisfaction.

The patient had initially complained that he was generally irritable and did not get along with people. He was a loner and felt alienated from his peers. He had had a girlfriend but shortly before he sought treatment she had left him. In fact, her departure was one of his reasons for seeking treatment. I realized that he was behaving toward me as he had done with his few friends and associates. He was displaying various character traits in the consultation room.

There was one notable difference. He felt irritable in the external world, but this was felt as an internal agitation rather than as anger. He might have felt some chronic, mild annoyance, but it did not have the definitive feeling of anger. With me he was unmistakably angry, an affect that was obvious both physically and emotionally. He was pugnacious toward me, something he had never previously experienced. In the external world he usually withdrew rather than being assertive. Although therapy was useless, his relationships had markedly improved. He had become more active socially and had made several new friends.

I believed that he had succeeded in confining most of his disruptive behavior to the consultation room, and therefore in his daily life he could act in a much saner fashion. The anger seemed to be created de novo. After about a year of treatment, I made some remarks indicating that his behavior had improved because he had been able to move with greater ease in the outer world and form comfortable friendships, since he was restricting to our relationship what had been passive provocations. With me he was angrily assertive, whereas with his friends he was being productively assertive. Previously he had simply paid little attention to my attempts to view his reactions as projections of parental imagoes; now he was furious. He accused me of protecting myself and wanting to take credit for a successful therapy when it was anything but that. He felt he had improved despite, rather than because of, the treatment. For the first time, he mentioned the possibility of not continuing and said he had to seriously think about whether he wanted to remain in treatment with me. He left that session on these sour notes.

His reaction was so intense that I expected him to cancel his next session and never return. Borderline patients can be volatile and unpredictable. He had certainly demonstrated his volatility in almost every session, but his unpredictability was striking.

To my immense surprise, he returned to the next session in an expansive, friendly mood. He stated that I was looking well and this pleased him. He also complimented me about my professional decorum. He went on to explain that when he left after the last session, he had felt considerably relieved. He had begun to feel a calmness and equanimity that he had never experienced before and gradually it had led to his having good feelings about me.

When he returned to his apartment from my office he was still in a rage state. He could not tolerate how completely I had misunderstood him. How could anyone be so obtuse? Then he made a conscious effort to enumerate all the qualities that made me a bad therapist. At that moment he had what at first seemed to be a mental block. Absolutely nothing came to mind. Instead he could only think of good things: my not fighting back, my patience and willingness to listen to him in a nonjudgmental and noncritical fashion.

He recalled his life before therapy, when he had hardly ever felt anger. As he stated, he could not enjoy the luxury of anger, because he would be severely punished if he expressed any hostile or rebellious feelings. Strong feelings were simply not tolerated and he was expected to behave properly, which meant not to do anything disturbing or disruptive, or anything that would make him stand out as a distinct person. His family, in turn, displayed mitigated feelings or, as far as he could recollect, no feelings at all, at least toward him.

Then he felt vulnerable and, as I have mentioned, he was generally irritable. He also had moments in which he experienced mounting internal agitation, which made him feel extremely anxious, but his feelings never reached the intensity of a panic state. Rather, he felt loosely organized and disjointed. These were often manifested as identity confusion, when he believed he was falling apart. At times he would momentarily feel he did not exist and could not even remember his name. Later in treatment he demonstrated this loss of identity, which, on the surface, resembled Erikson's (1959) "identity diffusion syndrome." During these episodes his capacity to feel and to have feelings was minimal.

He reported that being able to generate mild annoyance gave him a rudimentary sense of security, but his family would withdraw from him, more so than usual, if he showed a spark of feeling.

It became apparent that the anger he had directed at me represented more than the outcome of frustrated reactions to his caregivers. He felt safe in my office and, in a sense, reveled, as he later disclosed, in having a place in which he could generate affects. He needed a comfortable setting that would neither interfere with his need to have feelings nor reject him for feeling angry. Being angry gave him a sense of comfort, and though his feelings were intense, the angry experience had a calming effect. Anger seemed to structuralize what had previously been described as disorganized, disruptive, and chaotic internal agitation. He was grateful to me for not taking a defensive adversarial position and for allowing him to get in touch with a feeling that eventually led to a heightened level of self-esteem and a strengthening of his sense of identity.

This patient also demonstrated the connection between the capacity to generate an affect and the consolidation and cohesion of the self-representation. Affects are responses to either inner or outer stimuli. They can be pleasurable or unpleasurable, being the manifestations of an ego state. To be able to construct an affect requires a certain degree of ego integration, as has been repeatedly observed in developmental studies (Emde et al. 1976, Spitz 1965, Stern 1985). The development of psychic structure is linked to the development of affect. Both are disturbed in patients with character defects.

The faulty psychic structures of borderline patients are related to deficits incurred during early developmental phases when there are difficulties in internalizing experiences that are potentially adaptive and structure-promoting. These early object relations are crucial. The interaction of sensori-motor systems with the external world leads to the formation of functional introjects (Giovacchini 1967) that consolidate psychic structure and expand the capacities of the ego's executive system, which, in turn, helps strengthen the coherence of the self-representation.

The child first relates to external objects on the basis of their function. At first, the mother is perceived in terms of her ability to nurture and to satisfy her child's needs for sustenance and soothing. The baby initially internalizes this nurturing function and forms an endopsychic registration of a gratifying interaction. I have referred to this primary internalization as a nurturing matrix that consolidates a functional introject.

Winnicott (1955, 1958a) referred to children who have constructed a nurturing matrix as experiencing deprivation when their needs are not met, that is, when they are frustrated. Other children who have never internalized a gratifying nurturing experience do not know gratification, and suffer from what he calls *privation*.

When dealing with clinical situations and psychopathology, nothing is absolute. This is especially true when we are investigating standard patterns and developmental sequences. As a rule, borderline patients demonstrate uneven development rather than a total developmental arrest or a complete absence of a nurturing matrix. The latter would be an extreme situation; probably the infant could not survive unless there has been some gratification of internal needs. Some patients suffering from primitive mental states might have a minimally functional, poorly constructed nurturing matrix or functional introjects, but they must have at least some. They must be able to have experienced at least minimal gratification and frustration.

To have needs met leads to a sense of aliveness, which is the essence of the human condition. Patients suffering from character disorders often question whether they are truly alive. As described, this is frequently expressed in terms of an existential crisis, as was the situation with the patient who had the capacity to spontaneously feel anxious. Anxiety, however, was an affect created to protect against feeling dead. This is another instance in which borderline patients, instead of presenting discrete symptoms, suffer from a lack of energy and vitality, a vitality that is characteristic of a person who is involved in living and relating to the world. These patients, on the contrary, have learned to withdraw from painful and confusing situations and to live in a narrow shell, as one patient stated; or to find themselves in a tight, constricted, colorless milieu, which they have created. They are often obsessed by their lack of accomplishment, a preoccupation that frequently pervades the therapeutic interaction.

There may be rare instances where there has been practically no development of a nurturing matrix; these are as close as possible to examples of Winnicott's formulations of privation. As an extreme instance, I recall with horror an 8-year-old girl who presumably had spent all of her life chained in a closet. She was about 2 feel tall and looked more like a monkey than a human being. She crouched and walked in an apelike manner. She had no capacity to speak; rather, she grunted like an animal and showed no emotions or affects that could be recognized at an interpersonal level. The only feeling observers could identify was anxiety, which occurred when she seemed to be confronting a situation that was too complex for her limited mentality, her initial reaction being confusion. This happened when someone tried to talk to her.

She ate when food was given to her, but there was nothing positive about being fed. She grabbed the food in a greedy manner and devoured it. She did this with a pear that was handed to her. She literally pushed it into her mouth and in no way acknowledged the person who gave it to her. She seemed devoid of feelings, as one might expect in some subhuman creatures. It was difficult to think of her mind in the usual terms of ego integration, introjects, self-representation, or affective attunement. At most she seemed to be operating at a reflex level, with little mentation but with some perceptual awareness. It would have been ludicrous to ascribe to her her internalized regulatory psychic structures designed to obtain gratification and to relate to external objects beyond their caretaking potential.

Spitz (1945, 1946) wrote about a group of children who resided in an unidentified orphanage. Their physical needs apparently were taken care of, but there was no other contact with them. The children were in cribs that were placed in cubicles, the walls being high enough so that the child could not see beyond them. Periodically attendants would feed them, but they made no effort to go beyond simply giving them food. They did not talk to the children or otherwise try to relate to them. According to Spitz, these children did not develop in a sequence in which "organizers" consolidated the acquisition of various functions and modes of relating. They sank into a state of apathy, and none of them survived beyond early infancy. Many of them died during a measles epidemic, apparently not having been able to develop an adequate immune system.

These are extreme examples of global developmental arrests, that is, states of fixation sufficiently severe that they are not compatible with living. The orphans died because of a lack of psychic development, which is the outcome of being totally ignored, emotionally speaking.

For life to continue there has to be an accompanying psychic development to physical maturation. An embryo has to grow to a certain degree of maturity before it can survive, and then it has to be placed in a caretaking environment in which it can continue to differentiate. The fetus becomes a baby, which requires a reciprocal interaction with a nurturing person until it reaches sufficient autonomy so he or she can independently exist, but no one achieves complete independence. A certain amount of dependence is healthy and characteristic of adult intimate relationships.

Borderline patients suffer from developmental arrests, but these are only partial, and thus these patients survive and can, to some extent, have feelings, produce affects, and relate to the external world. These accomplishments are marginal, however, because of a defective psychic structure, and a relative lack of, or weakly cathected, functional introjects. Furthermore, as discussed, affects such as anxiety and anger are used in a unique fashion, that is, as adaptations to protect against devastating states of inner emptiness.

The lack of a stable nurturing matrix makes it difficult for the psyche to construct pleasurable affects that are the outcome of having experienced gratification. There is a reciprocal interaction between the mother and infant, a positive feedback sequence of satisfactory nurturing experiences leading to the endopsychic registration of these experiences, that is, the nurturing matrix and the production of pleasurable affects. The latter enhance self-esteem and impel the ego to seek further levels of gratification, which, in turn, are internalized and add to the stability and scope of the nurturing matrix.

When this positive feedback sequence is not established, serious disturbances occur in the course of emotional development that characterize specific types of psychopathology, including the borderline state. Affects are no longer structure promoting because they are not the outcome of gratification and are thus not pleasurable. Instead, they have acquired defensive functions to make up for the lack of psychic structure and functional introjects. These are developmental defects that affect the cohesion of the self-representation and the competence of the ego's executive system, as has been discussed. Thus affects play a central role in emotional development and have a stabilizing effect when maldevelopment occurs.

Classical psychoanalytic formulations make the Oedipus complex the central core of the psychoneuroses. Sexual impulses that characterize the oedipal phase are involved in the production of psychopathology as well as in emotional development. When encountering patients with character defects, clinicians often wonder what happened to Oedipus. Has he been replaced by Narcissus? Therapists hear a good deal about narcissistic injuries when treating borderline patients, but, especially with younger patients, there is also considerable sexual material.

Unlike the cases Freud and his followers described, the patients I have seen do not seem to be particularly conflicted about their sexual feelings and impulses. They may often feel, and are, rejected when they make advances, but they do not appear to have any internal conflicts about their sexual impulses or to construct any repressive or inhibiting defenses against them. Some patients are particularly free about gratifying sexual needs, to the extent that they are promiscuous and sexually acting out. Thus erotic feelings are frequently expressed by borderline patients, but they are not associated with oedipal levels of development or conflicts about incestuous wishes.

In clinical seminars this type of sexual material has been diagnosed as pregenital sexuality, meaning that earlier preoedipal stages of development and their subjective and behavioral manifestations have been erotized (Giovacchini 1990). Erotic feelings, like other affects such as anxiety and anger, also have adaptive and defensive functions besides being involved in an oedipal triangle and consequently being repressed during the latency period as Freud (1905b) postulated.

A supervisee reported a case of a young man in his middle twenties who would periodically feel extremely agitated. These disruptive states were usually the outcome of having internalized his mother's agitation. The mother was quite adept at maintaining her sanity while driving all those around her insane. The patient, her oldest son, was most often targeted for her inner chaos and tension. She was able to disturb him by behaving in an unpredictable fashion and thereby succeeded in remaining calm. Once, she quietly picked up a shotgun, walked into the backyard, and killed the family cat, which she allegedly adored.

The patient would initially feel confused and was overwhelmed by a mounting tension that caused him to feel restless and tremble uncontrollably. He would pace back and forth incessantly and then go to bars and drink heavily. This was followed by a spree of sexual activity, both heterosexual and homosexual, as well as frequent bouts of masturbation. He had relations with as many as three or four persons a night.

He told his therapist that his immersion in sex had a palliative effect, more so than drinking. Prior to this flurry of sexual acting out, he was overwhelmed with waves of terror that made him feel as if he were losing his mind. He envisioned his body as being hollowed and he was reduced to nothing but an empty shell. All that was left was the exterior of his body, but it had practically no substance. He had the fantasy that his mother had infused a toxin into him that spread throughout his body and mind and, like an acid, dissolved all of his organs.

Sexual activity, according to the patient, filled up the hollow space. It gave him a sense of definition. He had felt that he had lost his identity in the morass of confusion and agitation that was engulfing his mind and body. By setting up a frenetic tempo of erotic pursuits, he was generating feelings that he could sustain. He had to engage in repetitive acts in order to be able to hold on to his feelings, because at the beginning of these escapades, his affects were evanescent and he knew he could not hold on to them. By the brunt of his excesses he was establishing an anchor within himself, which led to organization and a capacity to retain, if not the memory of his experiences, at least the affective tone attached to them. This internalization, as he described it, acted as an organizer, which gave him a sense of being and a minimal amount of tranquility.

For this young man, what was on the surface promiscuous acting out had an adaptive function, which was brought into an analytic focus. True, his behavior had its self-destructive edges but he was somehow able to avoid being hurt. In other instances the outcome can be tragic.

I am referring to one of the most destructive and self-destructive therapeutic interactions—that is, when the therapist has sexual relations with the patient.

I once interviewed a bright young psychoanalyst who had had sexual intercourse with his patient. He was remorseful, but he knew that he could never again practice psychoanalysis. He had irrevocably transgressed his professional ego ideal, and he believed that no matter how much more analysis he had, it would not make up for the damage he had inflicted. The patient, on the other hand, did not blame him and did not understand why he had disqualified himself as her therapist.

Whether this psychoanalyst could be rehabilitated is a moot question. He did not, for whatever reasons, choose to mend his career as a psychoanalyst. What is interesting for our purpose is that in many respects he was similar to the patient just reported. His patient, whom I also saw, was an extremely provocative woman in her middle thirties. During our interview she was extremely anxious and constantly paced back and forth. She created an atmosphere of tension and confusion not only through her motor behavior but also by her speech. She spoke in a staccato-rapid manner. She enunciated clearly enough, but although she seemed to be clear and logical, upon reflection it was difficult to make sense of what she had said. It seemed as if she were conversing in a meaningful fashion, but later it was impossible to discover this meaning. I noted that I was beginning to feel frustrated, and I gathered that I was absorbing her state of inner agitation.

Her analyst reported feeling the same agitation I had, but for him it was totally disruptive. As he became increasingly disturbed, he felt upset by two feelings. He had a desperate urge to hit her, and he later deduced that by killing her, he would be destroying the source of his agitation, which was becoming unbearably painful. At the same time, he felt paradoxically attracted to her. He was overwhelmed with sexual desire that he could not contain. He made what he described as violent love to her, which she enjoyed immensely. He did not know what was happening to him, since he was being driven by forces he believed he could not control. All he knew was that afterwards he felt calm, a state that was becoming increasingly foreign to him. His lust converted unbearable pain to pleasure, which led to relaxation of tension. Nevertheless, he paid a terrible price for his transgression. Not only did he feel that his career was ruined, but he also had to bear the retaliation of his superego as he faced the betrayal of his professional ego ideal.

Both these patients demonstrate how affects can be adaptive and destructive. They attempt to achieve psychic cohesion and, in a paradoxical fashion, a form of soothing, an organization of the internal world. This realignment of the internal world, however, creates problems with the external world. Borderline patients' adaptations are designed to maintain an inner calm, a homeostasis, but their psychic state leads to behavior that is unacceptable and inappropriate to their outer reality. Psychic reality is not in synchrony with external reality, an asynchrony that is characteristic of many patients suffering from ego defects.

EMOTIONAL PROGRESSION AND DEVELOPMENTAL VICISSITUDES

To effectively relate to reality and at the same time maintain emotional balance requires a mental state that has achieved a level of development such that it can master the exigencies of the external world. This means that there has been a movement from self-preoccupation to involvement and relationships with emotionally significant persons and, later, to others who may not be as significant.

As discussed, symptoms and affects in borderline patients have to be viewed from another perspective than that which is characteristic of the psychodynamic concept. The sequence of emotional growth or the vicissitudes of psychic development also have to be examined if we wish to achieve a more specific understanding of the various types of patients suffering from character disorders. I am implying that the borderline spectrum is broad and includes a variety of conditions that have many common denominators but also significant differences. The unique qualities that distinguish different types of emotional disturbances are related to specific traumas that have derailed the ordinary course of psychic development. If there is an innate developmental drive impelling the mind to achieve higher levels of psychic structure and maturation as it differentiates from earlier, more primitively organized mental states, then psychopathology can be understood as the outcome of traumas that disturb the unfolding of such a drive. Thus there are fixations and arrests that contribute to a general maldevelopment that creates difficulties in the patient's general adaptation, both internally and externally.

Before discussing maldevelopment, the clinician has to understand, conceptually speaking, how ordinary development occurs. Both Freud (1905b, 1909a,b, 1916) and Melanie Klein (1952) have constructed systems that outline a sequence from early infancy to stages of relative maturity. As discussed in the Preface, their contributions, important as they are, still lack an emphasis on a positive feedback sequence as being the essence of progression and maturation, or a negative feedback sequence as leading to maldevelopment, structural defects, and psychopathology. As mentioned, Winnicott (1963a), Spitz (1959, 1965), and Mahler (1968) have also made important contributions to our views of the early months of life, but I will only refer to them in passing because many of their ideas will be included in what I consider to be useful current concepts of psychic growth. I will briefly review Freud's and Klein's position because they were the bedrocks of classical psychoanalytic thinking throughout the world: Freud in the United States, and Freud and Klein throughout the rest of the world. I wish to emphasize how their concepts have to be modified in order to be brought in line with our clinical needs.

Freud (1905b) conceptualized an autoerotic phase at the beginning of development. Although Freud did not stress object relations, he still differentiated levels of psychic development as to how they related to external objects. The autoerotic phase is a preobject stage in which instinctual needs are gratified internally, that is, by the self; the infant does not have the sensory capacity to recognize something or someone as being external. At this phase there are no boundaries separating the internal and external world. Infants are not sufficiently differentiated that they can make a distinction between inner and outer processes. The most primitive autoerotic activity is thumb sucking.

The next stage is referred to as primary narcissism, which is discussed principally in terms of energic shifts. This phase is when structuralization begins. Stimuli from the external world initially make their impact on the periphery of a psyche that is relatively amorphous. The mother protects her baby by providing a stimulus barrier. Through her protective soothing and nurture, she modulates the strength of incoming stimuli so that they are not disruptive. This protective shield, the *reizschutz*, as Freud (1920) called it, is an intrinsic aspect of the mothering function, an outcome of primary maternal preoccupation, as Winnicott (1956) described.

These impingements, because they have been modulated, help structuralize the outer periphery of the psyche. Freud compared this process to the blastula stage in embryology, in which development proceeds from an undifferentiated mass. In the previous autoerotic phase, the instincts, if they are viewed as vectors, are moving in random directions. He called them *component instincts*. By contrast, in the phase of primary narcissism, the instincts are directed to the structuralizing peripheral portion of the psyche that is receiving external stimuli, that part of the psyche that is the core of the ego. Instincts are internal stimuli that lead to further structuralization of what will ultimately be the ego, which in turn becomes a modulator or regulator as it faces and controls its three masters, the outer world, the id, and the superego, as Freud (1923) discussed. It is easy to understand how the lack of a protective shield or the absence of stimuli could both have disastrous effects on the early and fateful phases of ego development.

The next phase, the stage of secondary narcissism, is the beginning phase of object relationships. Freud (1914a) stated that the first object relations are narcissistic. During primary narcissism, instinctual impulses are directed toward the ego. In secondary narcissism, however, the external object is incorporated into the ego, and the energy of the instinct, that is, libido, flows toward it. This is ego-libido, but it becomes attached to an internalized object.

Mahler (1968) postulated a similar line of development when she hypothesized that the beginning of individuation occurs after a "hatching" from a symbiotic union. The incorporation of the external object (the mother) into the ego is the outcome of a symbiotic union and is similar to Freud's concept of secondary narcissism. I find certain inconsistencies and flaws in these formulations, which I will soon discuss.

Disturbances during the stage of secondary narcissism are characterized by fears of commitment and intimacy, fears that are characteristic of borderline patients. The incorporation of and fusion with the external object is, as Mahler would emphasize, a traumatic event. The mother may be destructive and devouring. The infant withdraws from the threatening external world and does not progress to the stage of separation-individuation. Later this fixation is manifested by lack of self-esteem, social inadequacy, fear of intimate relationships, and many self-destructive defensive character traits.

Freud outlines a sequence of development based on what he called psychosexual phases. These involve object relations, but as discussed, the infant relates to the external object in terms of inner needs. The first psychosexual phase is basically oral. The nurturing caregiver is the active provider and the infant is the passive receptor. Presumably, this phase, in which the child recognizes the person ministering to his needs, begins around the age of 2 to 3 months.

The next phase, the anal phase, is not at the same conceptual level as the oral phase, as Fairbairn (1954) stressed. Preoccupation with feces and bowel control are not biological necessities or the outcome of instinctual needs. For the infant, there is pleasure derived from playing with and smearing feces, but this preoccupation does not require an interaction with the external world.

The anal phase, nevertheless, is involved with object relations. The child is struggling to maintain control. Anality is a stage when the child has to relinquish power. He has to restrain certain activities, as occurs with toilet training. External objects are no longer just the source of gratification. Now they impose restrictions and are also the source of frustration. This is a stage of acculturation that does not fit smoothly into a sequence progressing from biological orientations to mentational levels dealing with whole persons.

The phallic phase is biologically oriented in that the sexual organ as a source of pleasure is involved. It would indicate a movement from oral to sexual gratification. It does not, however, refer to sexual pleasure; rather, the penis becomes a power symbol and expresses ambition, competitiveness, and attempts at mastery.

When clinicians refer to anal and phallic stages they are referring to modes of relating to persons and the world. They lead to character traits. We speak of anality and anal issues, which are described as orderliness, parsimony, and cleanliness: character traits that are found in the obsessive-compulsive personality (Freud 1908, 1909b). The phallic phase leads to certain characterological orientations that have exhibitionistic and competitive elements. The bowel and the penis determine how certain behavioral traits and adaptations will develop, but activities regarding these organs are regulated and controlled by external objects. The relationship to the mother becomes the prototype for all emotionally meaningful relationships.

Phallic and anal phases are different from the oral phase as they relate to external objects. The penis and the bowel do not directly connect to the parents, whereas the mouth does. When studying character structure or defects in structure, our concepts about development have to follow a consistent sequence.

The final phase in Freud's schema is the genital phase, which ushers in the Oedipus complex. Here, as in the oral phase, a bodily part, the penis, tries to relate to the external object, the mother. Fairbairn (1954) retained the oral and genital phases in his theory of development because of their similarities regarding libido and the wished-for object. They can be viewed as a continuum. The anal phase, as stated, does not fit into such a continuum.

The oedipal aspects of the genital phase involve a triadic, rather than a dyadic, relationship. The child fears the retaliatory, castrating father because of his incestuous desires toward the mother. The relationship to the father is not based on attempts for need satisfaction; rather, it establishes limit setting and prohibitions. This leads to the acquisition of further psychic structure, the superego, which, Freud believed, begins to form around 3 years of age.

What I have described is well known as the foundation of classical psychoanalytic developmental theory. For our purpose it is important to understand that this model does not really follow a hierarchically arranged continuum. Such a continuum is useful for the exploration of development and psychopathology of patients suffering from problems and defects in psychic structure. Furthermore, the phallic phase and castration anxiety refer to a male-oriented model, and it is difficult to apply Freud's ideas to female psychic development. Freud (1931) wrote about the oedipal elements of female development, but his formulations seem contrived and designed to defend his concepts about the sequence of development of the masculine psyche.

Melanie Klein (1952) also wrote about the sequence of psychic development; I will briefly discuss her ideas because they are pertinent to our understanding of the psychic processes characteristic of patients suffering from severe psychopathology. Actually her theories apply more to the study of primitive mental states than to the course of ordinary emotional development. She attributes qualities to the mind that are characteristic of deep psychopathology rather than describing how the mind goes through various maturational sequences.

In her system, the very beginning of psychic life is already object directed and under the sway of the death instinct. The child experiences greed in that he wishes to devour the mother and the father's penis that may be inside of her. He also is consumed with envy because he feels vulnerable to the powerful mother. These feelings are fueled with the energy of the death instinct rather than libido, which represents the energy of sexual instincts.

The psyche internalizes external objects and classifies and splits them into good and bad objects. Around the age of 2 months, the bad objects are projected into the external world, whereas the good objects are retained in the inner world. This is the paranoid-schizoid position, which is accompanied by persecutory anxiety (Klein 1946).

At this stage the child relates to external objects on the basis of projective identification, which involves introjective-projective mechanisms. Children then project parts of themselves onto external objects, parts which acquire synthesis and organization by being received in a better organized psyche. Then they are introjected back into their psyches, having acquired a further degree of structure.

Around the age of 6 months, bad and good internal objects fuse with each other. The mind has acquired the capacity to view the same object in terms of both good and bad. This is the beginning of the capacity to feel ambivalent and, according to Klein, the ability to relate to whole objects. This is the depressive position (Klein 1935).

It seems unlikely that infants are able to relate to whole objects by the age of 6 months. Even if they can put good and bad feelings into the same object, that does not make that person a whole object from the infant's viewpoint. It can still be a part object and be related to according to its function. When internalized it may be treated ambivalently as a part-object functional introject. The anxiety that follows conflicts at this developmental position is called *depressive anxiety*.

It is obvious that Klein is attributing many qualities to the early psyche that could exist only in a better structured, more mature psychic apparatus. Paranoid and depressive mechanisms belong to the realm of psychopathology and are not processes usually associated with ordinary, relatively nonpathological emotional maturation.

Some authors have tried to modify and perhaps modulate her concepts so that they can be incorporated into a system that describes the unfolding of a developmental drive. Winnicott (1963), for example, when referring to Klein's concept of making reparation for having destroyed the internal object, viewed this process as concern for the mother's welfare, a feeling that does not necessarily have psychopathological implications. He viewed the capacity for concern as a developmental achievement.

The value of Klein's formulations is primarily clinical in that she describes mechanisms and defensive adaptations that are characteristic of severe psychopathology. In adults, clinicians often discover psychic constellations similar to the paranoid-schizoid and depressive positions characterized by projective and splitting defenses.

The psychopathological configurations of borderline patients require a developmental timetable that emphasizes the transformations of psychic structure as well as adaptations to the external world, which includes object relations. It should consist of a hierarchically arranged spectrum beginning with early primary-process orientations. Both Freud and Klein recognized that in the course of emotional development, early phases are never abandoned or lost; they are incorporated in later stages and may once again emerge, as happens in regression, creativity, or intimacy. The distinctions between pathological and nonpathological processes are not clear-cut. This should be taken into account when discussing psychic structuralization.

There must be a time in neonatal development when mentation begins. Research involving direct observation of babies places the moment further and further back in the postnatal period (Emde et al. 1976, Klaus and Kennel 1982, Stern 1985). If beginning mentation can be approximately located, there must be a period that can be referred to as the *prementational phase* of development. This phase may be of very short duration, but it can lead to severe types of psychopathology later in life if the milieu is assaultive during such a phase, which must occur immediately after birth.

The prementational phase is basically physiological rather than psychological. It is prepsychological and precedes the mentational elaboration of feelings and experiences. Presumably the infant feels only a state of calm or an inner agitation that is the manifestation of disturbed homeostasis. This seems to be a painful state, but it is not associated with discrete affects. It appears as a general disturbance and tension, often brought about by hunger or other types of discomfort. The mother nurtures and soothes the neonate in order to reestablish an internal balance.

If these babies are not effectively soothed or if their needs are ignored, later in life they are not able to soothe themselves or form relationships in which they can be soothed. They suffer from prementational agitation that cannot be understood in terms of intrapsychic conflict. It can be viewed as the manifestation of a structural defect that affects self-soothing regulating mechanisms and creates problems in internalizing potentially helpful experiences from the outer world.

The next stage is characterized by an amorphous ego organization. The psyche begins to differentiate and to have a dim awareness of needs and stimuli, but it cannot as yet differentiate between inner and outer perceptions. Nor are inner needs precisely located at their somatic source. Obviously these are speculative assertions, but this phase also has its clinical counterparts.

I have seen patients who cannot distinguish various bodily needs and functions. For example, a middle-aged woman remarked that she could not distinguish, at least qualitatively, between hunger and the urge to defecate and urinate. They all felt the same, but the feelings located in the upper area of her abdomen were identified as hunger. The boundaries between her inner psychic world and external reality were considerably blurred.

As the psyche continues to structuralize, the ego begins to distinguish external from internal objects. Freud (1915b) postulated that an external percept can be distinguished by action, such as withdrawal or shutting it out. An internal percept, by contrast, is persistent and its impetus cannot be halted by simply withdrawing our attention from it. It has to be dealt with, usually in terms of gratifying an internal need.

The process that leads to the formation of object relationships involves the construction of the transitional space as first described by Winnicott (1953). He described an area between the ego and the outer world in which the child feels he is the source of his own nurture. Inasmuch as the mother is in tune with her child's needs, she ministers to them at the time they are felt. Presumably the child has the illusion that all he has to do is to feel—for example, hungry—and then gratification spontaneously occurs. At this stage he does not recognize external objects because he can omnipotently take care of himself. Winnicott referred to this state of mind as primary psychic creativity.

As I have already mentioned, I believe the outcome of differentiation and structuralization is the formation of a nurturing matrix. It is the product of a satisfying mother–infant interaction, but inasmuch as the child's needs and the mother's responses are so much in synchrony with each other, the infant does not, as yet, recognize an external source of nurture and soothing. This is an illusory state, but as Winnicott states, the child at first has the illusion of total self-sufficiency, and later he enjoys the illusion as he plays with it in the transitional space. The capacity to recognize illusion represents the beginning of object relations.

The infant forms sensory percepts very early in the neonatal period. What probably does not occur until the transitional phase is the recognition that these percepts have something to do with need satisfaction and internal regulation. Object relations involve more than the transitory registration of a person. The caregiver has to be acknowledged in terms of her functions, and this occurs as the transitional space consolidates.

Many of these formulations are somewhat adultomorphic. The child, at the age of 4 to 6 months, does not have illusions or feel omnipotent in the adult sense. At the most, infants feel a diffuse harmony, which to the outside world resembles security. Again, we can think of homeostatic balance.

The child's internal world extends far beyond visible ego boundaries. The borders of the transitional space penetrate into what the adult views as external reality. The area of overlapping—that is, the space that protrudes into the outer world—is the transitional space, an area of make-believe and illusion as well as of play and creativity.

When external objects are brought into the transitional space, they are known as *transitional objects.* The nurturing matrix is projected into the transitional object, which then becomes a nurturing and soothing modality. Projection, from the infant's vista, is not exactly the mechanism involved, because to project means that something internal is made external. Babies at this stage do not recognize a surrounding milieu. Everything belongs to them, so rather than a part of the self being projected, it is transferred to another part of the self. *Displacement* is a more apt term.

This stage is characterized by a series of displacements as different objects acquire increasing significance. As the child grows older, there is a tendency to view even inanimate objects in terms of the self. Around 1 year of age, when walking and vocalization begin, children often use the third person to describe their actions, and they often anthropomorphize familiar objects such as toys and furniture.

Gradually the transitional space recedes and ego boundaries are established. As this occurs, objects are extruded from the transitional area and enter the external world. At this juncture the child has achieved the capacity to partially distinguish between the internal and external world and is able to relate to objects as separate from the self.

When this happens is still unclear. Some investigators believe somewhere between 4 and 6 months, and others, such as Spitz (1959), conjectured that it occurs around 9 months, the time that the child develops stranger anxiety. Undoubtedly the ability to recognize external objects develops gradually and begins very early during the course of perceptual discrimination. Certainly around 2 months, the time of the smiling response, there is an expression of affect precipitated by external stimuli. Whether this represents a connection to an external object or just a pleasurable response to excitement in a secure setting is still an open question. Nevertheless, at some level the infant is able to incorporate experiences with caregivers at a very early age, perhaps beginning with bonding. This does not mean, however, that the neonate is aware of internalizing processes and is able to discriminate outside from inside.

When object relations are established, ego boundaries are consolidated. The transitional space, however, is not obliterated. It recedes, but during moments of intimacy, immersion in fantasy, or creativity, the transitional space once again expands. It persists throughout life, enabling states of fusion by internalizing loved ones as the self makes contact with deep feelings.

The subsequent developmental progression of the psyche leads to the increased differentiation of the self and the stabilization of internal self- and object representations. The executive system also expands as it acquires further adaptive techniques by internalizing helpful and constructive experiences as well as making self-esteeming identifications.

This developmental sequence differs from those postulated by Freud and Mahler. Both assert that object relations follow the development of the stage of secondary narcissism, whereas this schema does not include secondary narcissism as a developmental stage. Freud wrote about a sequence from autoerotism to primary narcissism followed by secondary narcissism and then the psychosexual stages, which can be viewed as part-object relations. Mahler wrote about a symbiotic phase from which the infant "hatches" as it undergoes separation-individuation and begins to acknowledge and relate to external objects.

Hatching from the symbiotic phase refers to the emerging from a state of fusion, a self-object state first described by Freud (1911, 1914a) when he introduced the concept of secondary narcissism. This concept is clinically useful, but how can it be a precursor stage to the formation of object relations? To fuse with an external object means that there must have been some degree of object relating before being able to form object relations. But how does the infant acquire a sufficient degree of recognition of an external object in order to fuse with it? The introduction of the transitional space helps explain a process in which the internal world is differentiated from the external milieu.

Fusion, or symbiotic, states occur after object relations are, to some extent, established. These states are not developmental stages from which the infant begins to distinguish inner and outer reality. Rather, they are the manifestations of a psyche that has already made connections with the external world and is able to distinguish between self- and object representations. They do not necessarily lead to psychic structure; they are the achievements of a differentiated psyche. Later in life, however, to be able to fuse with another person represents the deepest form of commitment and intimacy attainable.

4

The Borderline
State and
Character Disorders

The reason a consistent development sequence emphasizing psychic structure and object relations is important is that it allows the clinician to distinguish between different types of character disorders. Freud separated the various psychoneuroses on the basis of their points of fixation (a developmental level), the internal conflict, and the defenses used to deal with that conflict. In a similar but not identical fashion, the character disorders can be classified according to the developmental levels they have achieved; they are described in terms of psychic structure and integration and their capacity or lack of capacity to sustain object relations. Rather than dealing with defenses as processes set in motion to maintain repression, in the character disorders I focus on adaptive mechanisms characteristic of a particular developmental level and how successful they are in dealing with the external world, as well as their efficacy in establishing internal harmony. When the capacity to form object relations is achieved, adaptive techniques are directed toward the outer world and are responses to the demands and exigencies of reality.

I am using the term *character disorders* to classify all patients whose main psychopathology can be expressed in terms of defects in psychic structure. As discussed, the psychoneuroses were conceptualized primarily as the outcome of intrapsychic conflict, and very little emphasis, if any, was given to psychic structure. The character disorders encompass a large group of patients who may fall on different levels of the developmental spectrum. Inasmuch as they do so, they vary somewhat in their symptomatic or, better stated, characterological, manifestations. If we lump them all together in the borderline category, then it should be expected that clinicians would be confused as to what exactly defines the borderline syndrome. As discussed, Kernberg, Masterson, Searles, and I were not discussing the same group of patients when we conducted a symposium on the borderline personality (Masterson 1978).

There has been some consistency about the phenomenological aspects of the borderline personality. The very earliest writers who used the concept of borderline (Knight 1953) viewed these patients as hovering somewhere on the edge of a psychosis. They are neither psychotic nor neurotic in the traditional sense. They can become psychotic, but as a rule, this is a transient state. Still, this is just a phenomenological definition, and there can be many variations of character structure and psychopathology that have this borderline quality. All of the character disorders can regress into a psychotic state, but there are significant differences among them that allow us to classify them according to various categories, and these can be placed on different positions of the developmental spectrum.

Freud (1916) made extensive use of the concepts of regression and fixation when mapping out the scope and extent of psychopathology. He also recognized that there is no such state as a complete fixation. The patient traverses all levels of the developmental course, but the more advanced positions are not as strongly cathected; that is, they are not as well differentiated or consolidated. When regression occurs, the resultant ego state is not identical to that stage during infancy. There are still many aspects of later stages operating even during the regressed state. For example, most patients can walk, talk, and be continent, functions that may have not yet been acquired during infancy. Furthermore, there seldom is a clear-cut fixation pinpointed on a particular phase. There is usually considerable overlapping, so the clinical entities that will be described are, in some measure, hypothetical. They are approximations of what clinicians encounter in their practices.

SCHIZOID STATES AND THE PREMENTATIONAL PHASE

Before emotional development is elaborated into psychological or mentational processes, let us first consider a prementational phase. Although this is an extremely early period, some patients' disturbances can be traced that far back. I refer to these patients as *schizoid* personalities because their main adaptation to the external world is schizoid withdrawal. They have developed far beyond the prementational phase, but the core of their difficulties operates on a prepsychological level. This may be difficult to understand, since the question can be raised as to how one can determine whether certain problems or behavioral abnormalities are devoid of mental content.

In the previous chapter I discussed a patient who could willfully generate anxiety and in whom, no matter how hard I tried, I could not discover an underlying conflict or danger, except for the danger of feeling annihilated if there were no anxiety. Anxiety filled up an ego defect, a sense of emptiness and a feeling of nonexistence.

Schizoid patients either deaden their feelings or experience a lack of feeling that causes them to feel dead. They also cannot handle external stimuli, which often overwhelm them and frequently cause severe disruption and agitation.

A 16-year-old adolescent was sent to a residential treatment center because he could not be maintained at an outpatient level. He was failing in school because he would not do any work. He was of superior intelligence and should have been able to do his work, but he simply refused to do it. He was not actively rebelling. His attitude was generally passive. He would take his homework home, put it in his desk, and then forget about it. He showed no anxiety or remorse about the prospect of failure.

Other than attend school, he did nothing the rest of the day. He spent most of his time lying in bed in the fetal position, but he was awake. As far as his parents could tell, there was nothing particularly different in his present behavior. The problem began when school had become more demanding and required the completion of assignments. In the past, he could survive by what he learned in the classroom.

He was always quiet, never spontaneously talked to anyone, and had no friends. He had participated in some games, such as baseball, but he functioned as an automaton. When addressed, he was able to respond and hold a reasonably rational conversation. Again, his role was passive and the other person would have to choose the topic and take the initiative. He was not autistic and showed no evidence of a thought disorder.

The parents did not believe there was anything wrong with him except for his school failure. They were eager to put him in a residential treatment setting where his schoolwork would be supervised. They thought of him as having only an academic problem. He was not a problem for them. Actually, the patient made no demands and did not behave in a disruptive fashion. He was quiet and unobtrusive.

The mother, a woman in her early forties, had been sickly all of her life with numerous somatic complaints. She was excitable and emotionally volatile. She took offense easily and then would cry and sob. These were responses to the slightest provocations. She was depicted as fragile, vulnerable, and hyperactive. She was very anxious when the patient (an only child) was born and was afraid she would cause damage as she tried to take care of him.

She was so excitable, especially when trying to bottle-feed her baby, that she created havoc in the household. Several maids quit because they could not stand the turmoil. The child, during the first 6 months of life, acted as if he were always in pain, perhaps from colic, and constantly cried. The mother was unable to soothe him as she was unable to calm herself. After 6 months, he suddenly became quiet and was no longer any trouble.

At the treatment center, as might be expected, he isolated himself. He withdrew from group activities, and the workers for the first few months did not attempt to push him; they had intended to let him set his own pace. However, after several months, they realized that he would not do anything if left completely alone. Consequently, they did not allow him to retreat to his bed for hours at a time. They insisted that he at least sit with other patients in the recreation room and look at television. They also tried to engage him in conversations with themselves as well as with his peers. He gradually became somewhat more outgoing, participated in occupational and art therapy, and seemed to enjoy watching movies on cable television.

One night there was no worker supervising the recreational room, so a patient turned on an R-rated movie that was highly provocative sexually. Everyone was riveted to the television set, the patient later reported, but he became increasingly tense. His body ached all over, and he felt as if he were going to explode. He felt overwhelmed with cramps, particularly in his abdomen and chest, and he believed that he was "coming apart at the hinges." Finally he started running and screaming. He also became physically violent and started hitting other patients until he was subdued and put in restraints.

He found it difficult to articulate exactly what he felt. This was partly due to being generally disturbed and unable to perceive what was going on within him, as well as his inability to communicate. He was visibly anxious although he could not describe the subjective experience of anxiety. He was hypersensitive to light and sound, and ordinary noises caused startle reactions. He acted as if he had been subjected to an acute trauma. Because his behavior resembled that of posttraumatic stress disorder and he had some of the symptoms of an acute panic disorder he was put on alprazolam and imipramine, and he became calmer although he was still somewhat hyperagitated.

His therapist wondered whether the patient had revived traumatic memories of the primal scene, because his disruption occurred after watching a sexually explicit movie. Other patients mentioned that as soon as some sexual activity or nudity occurred in the movie, the patient cringed and put his hands over his eyes as he tightly closed them. Apparently he was trying to shut out the stimuli coming from the television.

For several months he acted as if he were a hyperactive child and played tricks and pranks on his peers, which caused him to become involved in many fights. His life was punctuated by violence. The therapist was trying to understand his intense reactions on the basis of sexual conflicts that were precipitously released from repression by the sexually oriented movie. The patient continued to talk about inner distress and painful excitement but brought up no sexual material during his therapy sessions. When the therapist ventured an interpretation about his fear of sexual feelings, he did not understand what she was saying.

The therapist stopped making interpretations about forbidden or dangerous sexual feelings because she began to believe that she was talking over his head, that he was not able to integrate and understand material of such complexity. She began to understand his aberrant behavior and disruptive feelings as a failure of internal self-regulation. As he started to give up his schizoid defenses, and rather than withdrawing, moving gingerly into the surrounding world, he was making himself receptive and vulnerable to external stimuli.

This patient could not fully comprehend his environment. Because of the lack of adaptive techniques, inner stimuli were painful and perceived as chaotic. His mother had created a chaotic infantile environment, stimulating prementational agitation rather than protecting him from disruptive stimuli. In the residential treatment center it was a sexual stimulus he could not integrate. He could not internalize it, as evidenced by his attempts to shut it out by shielding his eyes and closing them. This is markedly different from a conflict about forbidden incestuous impulses.

Furthermore, any excitement, if sustained, would eventually become painful.

One evening, several long-term patients who had formed a jazz band had a jam session, which the patient attended. At first he sat there as if riveted and fascinated with the music, but as he continued listening he became extremely disturbed. He did not go berserk as he did when looking at the sexually oriented movie, but he could not sit still. He abruptly left the room and went to his bedroom, where he fell on the floor and rolled over and over, writhing in pain.

In spite of the primitive nature of his psychopathology, he did relatively well in treatment. His therapist – a gentle, protective, maternal figure – in the course of time was able to soothe him. She acted as a buffer for potentially disruptive stimuli. The sound of her voice had a calming effect, and at times, he would telephone her late at night just to hear her recorded voice as she spoke the announcement message on the answering machine. There were many subtle interactions and transference projections that led to the reenactment of infantile relationships, which helped produce a supporting matrix that enabled the treatment setting to modulate potentially disruptive stimuli.

Another patient, a junior high school student, illustrates similar psychic constellations. In this case, there is the added advantage that there is more detailed information about the maternal relationship because I was treating her mother, a middle-aged alcoholic woman. I have already presented this case (Giovacchini 1979a,b) in order to discuss a particular type of trauma during the prementational phase that leads to a state I called *primal confusion*. Now, I wish to emphasize further how my patient's daughter's aberrant behavior was a peculiar mixture of schizoid withdrawal and self-destructive acting out. In some ways she was similar to her mother, but these similarities were the outcome of psychic processes considerably more primitive than identification.

I saw the mother in the morning because she would start drinking at lunch and continue until she passed out in the evening. She never admitted to me that she drank excessively; I obtained this information from the referring internist. Over the years, as I learned more about her proclivities to be oblivious of what was going on around her, I began to believe that she was sincere when she stated that she seldom drank, only a genteel glass of sherry on occasion. She demonstrated an uncanny capacity to use denial, but I am not certain this was denial in the traditional sense of a defensive adaptation. Rather, I believe she had an extremely constricted perceptual system, a narrow view of both internal and external events.

She was an example of a person who had a poorly established nurturing matrix, and as a consequence, her needs were indistinct and undifferentiated. She too could not distinguish hunger from execretory urges. Alcohol both soothed and nurtured her, a voracious activity because of the anesthetic insatiability of her loosely organized nurturing matrix. Its lack of cohesiveness led to an incoherent, frenetic lifestyle.

She could create havoc when drunk—as her husband was sadistically and intrusively eager to confide—but for the most part she was quiet, subdued, and pleasant although she did not seem to have strong affects. Her emotions were similar to her needs, low-keyed and diffuse.

There was a naive quality to her demeanor, and most of the world slipped by her. She did not recognize that her children had problems, that her husband was sadistically humiliating her, and that her brother was schizophrenic. A colleague who had hospitalized him reported that he was in a catatonic state of waxy flexibility; but my patient, who was with him before he was taken to the hospital, believed there was nothing truly wrong with him. He was simply suffering from a sore throat and the hospital was going to prescribe antibiotics.

In my office, I noticed a similar obliviousness. She never noticed a missing painting or a new piece of furniture such as the chair she sat on. She did not even comment when I walked with a cane because I had fractured a foot. I thought at first that perhaps she felt it would be indecorous to comment about different chairs or my infirmity. Months later, however, I asked her how she liked the new chair and in a bewildered tone she said, "What new chair?" I replied that it had been delivered at the time I broke my foot and walked with a cane. Again the same bewilderment and the question, "When did you break your foot?"

Her responses are indicative of the narrow scope of her perceptual system rather than the denial of a percept that is experienced as traumatic. Her world was limited in breadth and was accompanied by fragile narcissistic supplies. Anything beyond her vulnerable narcissistic boundaries simply did not exist, and I believe this included her drinking.

I am stating that to some extent, when she commented about her sparse, genteel drinking—when obviously she was intoxicated daily—she was not lying or shutting out reality by disavowing it. In her own fragmented fashion, she probably was not aware of drinking excessively. Drinking was no longer under conscious volition and control. It had become automated, as is the situation with visceral functions. No one is particularly aware of the air that surrounds us and of breathing. To her, drinking was like breathing. Both were done all the time, breathing to survive psychically and drinking to maintain a fragile emotional equilibrium, a self-destructive attempt to soothe herself.

We would not expect this patient as a mother to form empathic bonds with her children. I have discussed certain aspects of her character as a background to understanding the infantile interactions involved in traumas during the prementational period, which lead to states of inner agitation that cannot be understood in mentational terms. As stressed with the previous patient, this internal disruption is the outcome of the lack of self-regulatory mechanisms and bizarre soothing patterns that are associated with social isolation and schizoid withdrawal.

During a session, for no particular reason that I could discern, she showed me how she had nursed her daughter. She would suddenly grab her from the crib, swing her in a wide arc and, throwing her in her left arm, roughly shove a bottle in her mouth. As might be expected, the baby would cry. Then the patient would start humming and bouncing her up and down, apparently to soothe her, but as she reenacted this little scenario, she was anything but soothing. Her humming had the eerie and disturbing sounds of keening, and her movements would have been more in context with a roller-coaster than a lullaby. Instead of soothing her daughter, her attempts drove the poor infant into a frenzy. She cried louder, which only led to the mother intensifying her efforts. I imagine this mother–daughter interaction reached a crescendo that would have been unbearable to an onlooker and proved devastating to the child.

As an adolescent, her daughter was on drugs and also drank to the degree that she was frequently drunk. She had been expelled from several schools, events that finally forced her to seek psychotherapy.

She was so "spaced out" that she was unable to function as a student or in any other capacity. She was visibly tense and agitated and would often grimace as if she were experiencing pain. She also had numerous allergies and was considered as having stress reactions to her environment. For this and other reasons she spent a good deal of time locked in her room, and although intelligent and attractive, she had practically no friends. This was primarily due to her withdrawal rather than to being actively rejected. She would go out rarely to loud, crowded, smoky discotheques, where she seemed, oddly enough, to gain some calm and peace.

She was different from the previous patient in that she could stand intense external stimuli, but the discotheque was about the only setting she could adjust to. Beautiful scenery, melodic music, romantic movies only served to intensify her agitation, which drove her to drink further and increased her reliance on drugs. Violence, discordant music, and noise, on the other hand, contributed to a transient sense of inner peace.

I recommended a relatively young psychiatrist to her mother, hoping that she might relate easier to a younger person closer to her age than to a therapist who would be more of a contemporary of her parents. This was not a wise judgment. She sat in his office with her legs crossed and blew cigarette smoke at him. She seemed to be quite composed but was reluctant to talk. She volunteered practically nothing, and her therapist felt he had to drag material out of her as she continued to withdraw. Finally, in order to protect the patient and himself, he stopped seeing her and referred her to a colleague when the same set of events again occurred.

Later I learned of an interesting fantasy she had after seeing the second therapist, which she felt to be the core of her existence. I have also discussed this fantasy elsewhere, but it is particularly germane here in order to illustrate how patients suffering from prementational agitation use certain schizoid defenses that become involved in the treatment setting, in these instances in order to disrupt it. At the same time, these patients put their agitation into other persons and thereby achieve some degree of soothing.

In her fantasy the patient was able to feel calm if not contented. She saw herself driving up to her high school's faculty parking lot, which was not available to students. It is winter and the lot is covered with ice. She sits in the car with locked doors, knowing it is forbidden for her to park there. She is quite content as she nonchalantly and calmly smokes cigarettes. Two policemen approach her and attempt to give her a ticket and force her to leave. The patient ignores them, and they cannot get at her because the doors are locked. They angrily pound on the window and demand that she open the door. This amuses her and she blows smoke toward them. They become increasingly angry and pound harder on the windshield. As they become further disturbed, her composure correspondingly increases.

This fantasy is not too different from what happened in each of the two psychiatrists' offices. She succeeded in frustrating two therapists as she frustrated two policemen in her fantasy. She could isolate herself from a disruptive world, imposing her rules, and maintaining control over her environment by partially withdrawing from it, but still relating to it in a destructive fashion. She did not belong to the cold, unfeeling (depicted by ice), violent world outside her car, and she could find comfort in the car's smoke-filled cramped interior. As she created the fantasy, she also created, as mentioned, an external world by putting her internal agitation into it. Her psychiatrists had also absorbed it, and they had an urge to seek relief by erotizing it or organizing it around the affect of anger.

The mother's demonstration reenacting her attempts to care for her daughter proved that being fed was a disruptive and painful process. Soothing was equated with agitation and being upset. She seemed to be operating on the basis of the oxymoron disruptive soothing, which led to what I have described as *primal confusion* (Giovacchini 1979a,b). As an adolescent she sought such disruption in order to feel some sense of calm. She was unable to integrate a truly soothing experience, as most of us know it, in her psyche, because she lacked a matrix that would make such internalization possible.

Again, I can compare this situation with one of Winnicott's (1963b) concepts, mentioned in Chapter 2. To repeat, he distinguished between privation and deprivation. In the former, children could not feel gratified because there were no gratifying experiences in their backgrounds that would help them recognize and accept a potentially satisfying experience. To be able to relate to various external situations, there has to be some endopsychic representations of similar past experiences, which were internalized at the appropriate developmental phase. Deprivation, by contrast, means that there has been some internalization of good nurturance, a nurturing matrix, so that the child recognizes its absence, which causes frustration. The baby who has experienced privation does not know what gratification is, so she cannot recognize its absence. She has not achieved the capacity to be frustrated. Her reaction is usually apathy and schizoid withdrawal.

With the adolescent patient under discussion, there has been no internalization of a calming, soothing experience, so there is no *soothing matrix* that makes it possible to take in calming interactions. To seek internal relief she had to find a jarring experience similar to the one provided by her mother, although as an infant she was only agitated further.

The patient derived some benefits from her relationship with her mother, whom she viewed more as inadequate rather than as destructive and malicious. Her mother was inept but she tried to nurture her children. As the patient grew up she became increasingly aware of the mother's weakness and vulnerability and her inability to cope with the exigencies of a mature adult's world. The daughter had similar difficulties in coping with the usual demands made of an adolescent, although she was, in spite of her debauching, physically fit and had above-average intelligence.

The point is that she could be soothed in a paradoxical fashion, as evidenced by her fantasy and her calmness in discordant, noisy environments. She must have had some soothing matrix, but it was pathologically distorted and not solidly constructed. The mother, in a childish fashion, had affectionate feelings toward her daughter, and the daughter, in turn, was fond of her mother. These were not deep feelings, but there must have been some bond, weak as it might be, between them. This bond led to the establishment of some capacity to be soothed, and therefore she was not exactly subjected to privation, where there is a greater absence of the capacity to be gratified and to take in potentially helpful experiences.

Unfortunately, the positive elements involved in the mother–child relationship developed later in childhood rather than in early infancy. There are optimal moments for the internalization of structuralizing experiences. Langer (1948) develops this thesis, concentrating on the development of speech. She writes about a chattering phase occurring around the age of 11 or 12 months. The child finds pleasure in vocalizing and interacts vocally and vigorously with the environment, primarily the mother. If she does not reciprocate and share the child's excitement, there will be difficulties in the development of language. Langer refers to the so-called feral children, presumably raised by wolves, who had no experiences with human beings early in life but were brought back to a family group in later childhood. They were able to learn considerably, but they could never learn to talk. Similarly, whatever positive, soothing elements that were developed between mother and daughter did not occur at an optimum moment, but they still had some effect.

The internalized disruptive experiences of early feedings became associated with soothing and led to the adolescent patient's paradoxical reactions to noisy and disruptive environments. Her resorting to drugs and alcohol was also an attempt to gain inner calm, but it created chaos rather than tranquility. As discussed, she created a similar chaos in her relationships with her two therapists.

The daughter asked her mother whether she might be able to see me. Because I was treating her mother, I was ambivalent about giving her an appointment. My patient was eager for me to see her daughter, and I finally consented to do so because the mother was not in analysis, and I concluded that not seeing her daughter would cause more complications than seeing her. The mother viewed my relationship with her daughter as part of a supportive network that included the two of them and brought them closer together.

The first time I saw her, she was sleeping peacefully in my waiting room. She felt very comfortable talking to me, telling me that she planned on dropping out of school and getting a job as a bank teller in a small country town. She was now in her twenties and had access to a fairly sizable trust fund. We left each other on an agreeable note, and she asked me if I could see me in several months, to which I agreed. For the next several years I saw her every 4 to 6 months, during which time she married and had a child. All of her tumultuous and frenetic behavior apparently had disappeared. She seemed to have developed the capacity to soothe herself in a nonpathological manner.

How can this have happened without intensive therapy designed to achieve characterological changes? She indicated by sleeping in my waiting room that she was ready to be soothed in the context of our relationship. She had attributed certain qualities to me that were able to calm her inner agitation, and these may have been related to my treating her mother. I had learned from her that although her mother kept drinking, she was no longer subject to crying spells and screaming at the servants and reviling herself for her ineptness. The beneficial effects of therapy consisted in that the mother would quietly fall asleep after a day of heavy drinking. She was, however, quite dependent on our relationship, and the daughter sensed that it was the basic reason that kept her from being institutionalized. The therapy had provided a holding environment that helped maintain some degree of psychic integration. The daughter saw me as supplying something that her mother had been unable to give her, at least to the extent that she had needed as a young infant. I had been able to transform a disruptive mother into a nonthreatening one. She had never been experienced as assaultive, but in her frail fashion, she was able to upset people.

Because of her mother the daughter was able to find someone who could soothe her nonpathologically. Inasmuch as I could, to some degree, contain the mother's feelings she unconsciously felt that I was an all-encompassing mother and she could use me in the same fashion as her actual mother. I did not disrupt her, and she did not have to withdraw from me as she did from the two young psychiatrists. I suspect that this was in part due to my age, inasmuch as she did not feel sexually threatened by me.

I do not mean to give the impression that she underwent a miraculous cure. Quite the contrary, she is far from well. She is still a highly dependent person and still capable of becoming agitated. However, she does not use drugs or alcohol to calm herself. She has married a man who seems to need to have a relationship with someone he can take care of. He is very protective.

Many patients whose internal agitation stems from the prementational period are able to obtain considerable relief without the acquisition of penetrating insight. By supplying something that was missing in early life, such as a protective, understanding environment, some patients are able to establish psychic equilibrium. This has been frequently observed clinically, but the interplay of specific caregiving experiences and the fragility of the infant's psyche have to be precisely understood. The assumption of a role, however, is experienced as intrusive rather than helpful.

BORDERLINE STATES AND AN AMORPHOUS
EGO ORGANIZATION

The term *borderline* appears again, but this time it is in a different context, which goes beyond a phenomenological frame of reference. All the patients that I have included under the rubric of character disorders are borderline in that they can regress or disintegrate into a psychotic state.

The patients I will discuss are also borderline in the sense that they make a borderline adjustment to the outer world. I repeat that I am viewing patients with characterological problems from various frames of reference, as Freud did with the psychoneuroses. I have emphasized the structure of the psyche in terms of the dominant developmental phase and will now also stress how well the ego adapts to reality. The schizoid patient almost totally retreats from the milieu, whereas the patient I have designated as being essentially borderline moves toward the world, but in a clumsy, inept fashion. These patients do not have sufficient adaptive techniques to cope with the complexities of reality. One patient aptly commented that he had an arithmetic mentality in a world of calculus complexity. The ego executive systems of these patients are constricted and attuned to an infantile environment that is markedly different from the contemporary milieu. I emphasize that these patients really are lacking in techniques and knowledge rather than repressing some functions and techniques because of intrapsychic conflict.

Borderline patients often keenly feel their basic inadequacies, but they also attempt to construct overcompensatory defenses. On a superficial level they have narcissistic qualities, but these patients have to be distinguished from those with narcissistic personality disorders, which will soon be discussed. They may be arrogant and, to some extent, offensive, but their attempts at self-aggrandizement are so inept that they appear pathetic. Furthermore, their narcissistic orientation is fragile and can be easily undermined. They are then quick to reveal how weak and helpless they are, and seek help by clinging to persons to whom they attribute omniscience. They then hope to absorb these persons' wisdom in order to feel a modicum of competence.

They differ from narcissistic personality disorders in that they are much more polarized. They lack basic structures rather than suffering from fluctuating low levels of self-esteem. They also have low self-esteem, but it is based on an actual deficit rather than on low narcissistic supplies. Their inadequacies are paraded side by side with boasts and claims about their superiority.

I repeat, there are no clear-cut diagnostic distinctions when dealing with emotional disorders. Borderline patients who stabilize their overcompensatory defenses become patients with narcissistic personality disorders. The borderline patient overlaps with all of the character disorders, and I believe that is why clinicians continue to use the word *borderline* to cover a wide spectrum of patients with emotional disorders who have some defects in the ego's executive system.

The identity sense, as has been discussed, is also involved in the production of psychopathology. How a person relates to the outer world, that is, the range of a person's adaptive mechanisms, is a significant aspect of the self-representation. If there are deficiencies or defects in the repertoire of the ego executive system, they will be reflected in the identity sense and may range from an almost total lack of a sense of being, an existential quandary, to inappropriate, poorly functioning false selves (Winnicott 1960). The borderline patient is often engaged in a battle to maintain some sense of identity while struggling to meet the demands of the surrounding milieu and to extract some gratification from the external world.

I recall one patient who presented innumerable paradoxes.

A 20-year old college student, he could present himself as a scholar whose function in life was to enlighten mankind but among his presenting symptoms, to use his own words, was that he was "neither fish nor fowl." He claimed to know how to do many things, from cooking gourmet meals to being an expert mechanic. Yet he had two sports cars and a motorcycle, and most of the time he was unable to use them. He would have to take the train to my office.

When I first saw him, he displayed the mixed picture of arrogance, helpless vulnerability, and ineptness. He was even inept in his movements in that he was markedly uncoordinated and physically clumsy. I feared for the safety of a lamp as he stumbled into the room and nearly knocked it over.

His clothes were bizarre. Although we were in the middle of a Chicago winter, he was wearing Bermuda shorts. He literally did not know that this was inappropriate, and later in the session I asked him if he did not think shorts were improper attire in view of the weather; in those days they would not have been acceptable in the downtown section of the city even in the summer. He defended this choice of wardrobe by stating that because he wore a heavy long overcoat his legs were warm, and that most buildings were heated and often overheated, so he was quite comfortable with his exposed legs. Nevertheless, in spite of his seeming assurance, he asked me whether I thought he could wear a sweater to the prom rather than a jacket and tie. I was quite certain that these were sincere questions; he was not mocking or trying to manipulate me.

For approximately one year, he constantly demonstrated the vulnerable and helpless sides of himself. When he drove to his sessions, he frequently got lost. Often his car or motorcycle broke down. He complained that he could not get a date, which he attributed to his naivete. He stressed that he had no social skills and very little knowledge of what was acceptable or unacceptable.

As far as he could recall, he was always clumsy. He had hated courses in manual training because he could never complete a project. He suffered from the helpless feeling of not even knowing where to begin when he was told, for example, to make a small cabinet.

He had similar problems with his courses in college. Although he had been in college for 3 years, he had only managed to get low Cs in the basic courses. He never completed any of his other courses. Fortunately for him, this university did not have many time requirements and some students remained in residence for many years. His intentions were to bypass the bachelor's degree and to go directly to the master's, but he had made no progress in that direction. He would let papers, books, and mail accumulate on his desk. To get started on his thesis, he had to clear his desk. This might take as long as a week. When he finally finished, he was so exhausted that he had to rest a while, but in the meantime his desk was once again cluttered. It was an endless cycle, and he never had started working on the thesis.

He sought treatment because he was basically dissatisfied with himself, although at times he denied it and rationalized his numerous failures. He had no sense of who he was and the purpose of his life. He wanted to do something significant in the field of mental health, but he was far from convinced that he was particularly interested. He would also fantasize being a powerful business tycoon or a painter who could sell his paintings for millions of dollars. He was extremely confused and, at times, bitter about his inability to do things that his classmates found to be pedestrian. Then he would lament how inept and inadequate he felt.

His attempts at denial of his lack of identity and accomplishments were interesting and sometimes contributed to his being viewed as peculiar and bizarre. I have already mentioned his clothing. His apartment was set up in a highly unique fashion. He slept in the kitchen, ate in the bedroom, and used his living room for his desk and storage of items that would ordinarily be put in closets or basements. In the very few closets he had, he put in his hi-fi equipment and numerous audiocassette recorders. He also ate lobster on Thanksgiving rather than the traditional turkey. At baseball games, he would bring cartons of sushi and vodka instead of hot dogs and beer.

He had to stand out from the crowd. Otherwise, he would be swallowed in an abyss of anonymity, a state of abject terror. To protect himself he had to be different. He even changed his name in order not to be just one of many members of a large family. Still, he desperately craved love and affection, but his antics only pushed people away from him. He was pathetically lonely.

Several years before I saw him, he had a bout of regression that was diagnosed as an acute schizophrenic episode. It occurred during the first week of his freshman year, when he stopped eating and bathing and isolated himself in his dormitory room. He also had moments of confusion in which he could not even remember his name, and his fellow students felt that he was listening to voices. He was hospitalized and given Thorazine. After 2 weeks he had fully recovered; he was no longer confused and having auditory hallucinations. It was not clear whether this was a true schizophrenia or an identity diffusion syndrome as described by Erikson (1959).

Clearly, this young man had identity problems and defects in the ego's executive system. He did not know how to perform tasks that most people would think of as routine. To bolster his self-esteem and to establish some cohesion to his self-representation, he had developed some grandiose and unrealistic concepts about his capacities. His narcissistic defenses, however, were weak and poorly constructed and most of the time he felt insecure and anxious. His adjustment to reality was, at best, borderline.

CHARACTER NEUROSES, NARCISSISTIC DEFENSES, AND EXTERNALIZATION

Unlike the two groups just discussed, these patients have achieved the capacity to relate to external objects and have a repertoire of adaptive techniques that enable them to adjust moderately well to the surrounding milieu. When the equilibrium between the ego and the outer world is disturbed, there is a corresponding psychic disruption, which can manifest itself in two possible ways. The patient suffering from a character neurosis may experience anxiety and feelings of inadequacy or may have erected fairly structured narcissistic defenses.

These qualities appear similar to those exhibited by those patients whom I have considered to be predominantly borderline. Besides having a more structured and adaptive ego executive system, as mentioned, they have better constructed defenses. The borderline patient's narcissism remains in the context of low self-esteem, helplessness, and vulnerability, whereas character neurotics are stable and their narcissism is more or less constant, not betraying their underlying inadequacy and insecurity. These patients exhibit the familiar narcissistic personality disorders. If, on the other hand, they reveal their basic character structure, their feelings of inadequacy are not as pervasive as in the case of the patient just described, and as a rule these patients can function quite well. They move into the world rather than withdraw from it and they are able to adapt to segments of their environment.

There is a discrepancy, however, between the infantile environment and the current setting. These patients have learned to adapt and to construct defenses in the early milieu. Insofar as that environment corresponds to that of the adult world, the psyche will be in balance with the current reality and be able to meet its demands and satisfy inner needs. The greater the differences between the two, the harder it will be to adjust to the contemporary world, and a character neurosis may develop. Most well-equilibrated persons can find segments of reality that are similar to the world of infancy. They have learned the basic techniques to deal with segments of reality early in life.

Again I emphasize that there are no clear-cut distinctions between various categories of patients suffering from emotional problems, and this is especially true of character disorders. Some highly narcissistic patients, for example, feel hollow and empty and have very little cohesion and structure to the self-representation. Some of these patients are known as "as-if" characters (Deutsch 1942). The borderline group I have just discussed often blends into that of the narcissistic personality disorders, and the latter can decompensate and regress to primitive mental states and psychoses.

The somewhat typical character neurotic has learned to adjust to a segment of the outer world that is an upward extension of his childhood environment. He is ordinarily able to create this world for himself, a process that I call *externalization*. All of us use this mechanism, to some degree. We have been trained since childhood to develop certain adaptations and skills that will be useful in certain segments of our milieu. These are vocational, professional, and social skills. In another environment with different customs and mores, and where our vocational or professional achievements are not valued or required, we would feel alienated and probably would develop a character neurosis. It is the extent of the inability to externalize that determines the severity of the character neurosis.

The archetypal master-sergeant illustrates the effects of externalization. He operates efficiently and remains cool in battlelike situations in which the ordinary person would panic. In a peacetime environment or outside of the army he may not be able to function. He may not have the social graces or the technical skills to get along, let us say, in a peaceful urban setting. His background had made him suitable for socially accepted violence. His parents may have beaten him as a child and may have been physically abusive to each other. He has witnessed and experienced violence from early childhood and probably was surrounded by it in the neighborhood where he lived. That is the setting he learned to integrate in his psyche. As an adult he finds such an environment in the army, and he cannot psychically integrate a nonmilitary setting geared toward peace. He externalizes the early violent setting and the internalized adaptive and defensive techniques to deal with that milieu into a segment of reality represented by the military.

One patient illustrates how a character neurosis can develop when the externalized segment of the environment is no longer available.

A business tycoon in his mid-fifties, he had led a frenetic life, working and competing and making phenomenal amounts of money. He ate too much, drank heavily, and got very little sleep. He was a hard-driving hyperactive character, and, as might be expected, nearly died of a myocardial infarction.

His cardiologist made it quite clear that he had to adopt a different lifestyle if he wanted to live. He gave up his business activities, but he was bitter and angry and began to experience waves of anxiety bordering on panic. He felt inadequate and depressed and could not stand just doing nothing. His world had collapsed and he felt totally alienated. He began loathing himself and felt that his retirement from business had introduced him into a world of nonactivity that appeared strange and foreign. His physician insisted that he seek treatment, and he was referred to me.

When I first saw him he was visibly anxious and depressed. He also appeared confused. He focused on his inability to find a niche for himself. His wife had tried to engage him in various hobbies, but he could not muster the interest or skills to pursue them. He had tried playing tennis and golf but he did so poorly that he felt humiliated. He believed that he did not know how to behave at a dinner party. When he was active in business, he did not have time for social frivolities. Now that he did, he felt he could not cope with them. He did not know how. He did not know what to do with free time. The concept of leisure was foreign to him.

He had a striking background. He was born in a tough ghetto. As was the situation with the legendary master sergeant, he was surrounded by violence. His parents were not physically abusive, but their speech was crude and coarse. Still, they valued education, in part because they had so little training, neither one of them having graduated from elementary school.

His peers valued physical prowess rather than knowledge. The area he lived in was dominated by gangs, and their main activity was fighting each other. Because he was smarter and stronger than his peers, he became a leader. He got along well in the ghetto and his name commanded respect and fear. He enjoyed his reputation and power.

Unlike his friends, he did well in school. His teachers encouraged him to go to college, and he managed to get a scholarship. He then went to graduate business school and earned an M.B.A. When he found a job, he traded the jungle of the ghetto for the jungle of Wall Street. He became extremely successful, acquired several companies, and moved to the Midwest, which he made his headquarters. He was extremely competitive and acquisitive, using the tactics of the gang warfare of childhood, but of course at a much higher level.

There was a continuity to his life, from the violence and competitiveness of childhood to the maneuvers and manipulations of corporate warfare. Fighting had become a way of life, but he had also acquired a love for the arts and literature. He developed a keen aesthetic sense, which was reflected in his well-bred, cultivated demeanor.

In spite of his agitation, he spoke in a well-modulated voice with many apt and clever metaphors. There was a poetic quality to his speech. He was widely read and had a large vocabulary, and although he was upset and lamented fate, I found his sessions pleasant and interesting.

After 6 months of treatment, I found that my positive countertransference feelings were undergoing a gradual change. Instead of looking forward to his sessions, I was irritated by his presence. I noted there was a harsh, argumentative quality to my interpretations and observations. I had a chip-on-the-shoulder attitude and wanted to fight with him. The atmosphere in the office was tense, and I experienced it as highly charged.

At first I thought in terms of reactions to painful projections, in that he was putting destructive and angry parts of himself into me. I believe that, to some extent, this did happen, but there had been a marked change in his mode of relating. No longer did he speak like the erudite gentleman he was; instead I detected the "dese" and "dose" of the East Side ghetto. In addition to whatever projections had occurred, he was converting my office into the neighborhood of his birth. He was externalizing the infantile environment into the therapeutic setting and I was reacting unfavorably. I was not only beset by uncomfortable countertransference reactions but I was letting myself fit into the ghetto setting he had created.

Ordinarily, when a patient projects feelings or parts of the self into the therapist, the therapeutic setting is not disturbed. The analyst calmly accepts the projections and the patient's behavior is usually not altered. The therapeutic process is dominated by the transference, which is interpreted. At times, the therapist may feel uncomfortable, especially if he is not aware of being the recipient of projections, but as a rule, this does not create any particular problems. The decorum of the consultation room remains the same, nor does the patient's style change.

My patient had reproduced the tough neighborhood of his past, and he talked as he did when he was a warlord and gang leader. My feelings toward him were part of a stance that was the outcome of his projections. I had become like him and was reacting as if he were a rival gang member or a member of an enemy gang. I had been absorbed by the setting he had constructed and reacted both to projection and externalization.

I finally became aware of these subtle interactions, and my inclinations to argue and fight with him disappeared. This was evident in my choice of words and my general mood. I became more of an observer than a participant. He immediately sensed the change and, with humor, asked me what was wrong. He still spoke with an East Side accent, but not for long. His initial reaction of amusement turned into anxiety. Throughout the months of treatment his mental state had stabilized. He once again became anxious, and his tough, bravado facade crumbled. He felt miserable and begged me to hospitalize him. I explained what I thought had occurred between us and confessed my reactions to the milieu he had created. I interpreted that his anxiety was a reaction to finding himself no longer able to remain in a familiar environment because I had stopped participating. It required at least two people to be able to fight.

I refused to hospitalize him, which in the long run proved to be reassuring. I did not react to his helplessness as a concrete reality, and although his anxiety bordered on panic, he finally began to realize that he had resources that would enable him to survive outside the jungle. His insecurities came to the fore, and he revealed the overcompensatory aspects of his behavior. He had received considerable narcissistic gratification from his business successes and the power he wielded as well as from the admiration of his employees and colleagues. He was famous in the business community. After his myocardial infarction and at the point in treatment when I did not reinforce his attempts at externalization, he lost his narcissistic supplies, which were usually obtained by winning battles.

He discovered, however, that he had other interests that were in tune with his ego ideal, that is, his love of literature. He gradually realized that he could accept himself as he was. He did not have to be a conqueror; the life of a contemplative scholar suited him. This orientation became firmer as we analyzed the basic fears and insecurities that had been covered up by narcissistic defenses.

Toward the end of his treatment, he divested himself of all business interests. He recognized that he did not really like the high-powered life he had led. His wife, on the other hand, could not relate to the quiet, relatively obscure life of the scholar, so she divorced him. He returned to school and obtained a Ph.D. in English literature and is now teaching at a small midwestern college.

CONCLUDING PERSPECTIVES

The borderline spectrum includes various types of character disorders, which are characterized by specific structural problems. The latter are reflected in relationships with the outer world and the capacity to cope with the exigencies of reality. Furthermore, different character disorders vary in how they affect patients' ability to internalize and integrate potentially helpful experiences. This capacity, as will be explored further, has considerable bearing on treatability. Patients in the borderline category are, for the most part, treatable within a psychoanalytic context, but they may present specific problems that differ from those encountered with psychoneurotic patients. The latter also present problems that may be just as difficult to deal with as those presented by patients with primarily structural defects.

To recapitulate, schizoid patients retreat from the world, and in treatment it may be difficult to make connections with them. This is especially true of patients whose ego is based more on privation than deprivation. The patient who has had very little gratification has a poorly structured nurturing matrix, which I have described as an endopsychic registration of satisfactory nurturing experience. Consequently, the therapeutic process does not establish an effective holding environment, and these patients withdraw from treatment as they do from life in general. Interpretations are not nurturing; in fact, the schizoid patient finds them hard to integrate within his psyche, so there is only a minimum capacity for insight.

This does not mean that all schizoid patients are impossible to treat. In many instances these patients may form a bond with the therapist, even though they never had any such bond with their mother, or just a very weak one. As mentioned, there are optimal times during the development of the psyche to make connections and acquire various functions. Bonding occurs in the early neonatal period, but something similar may happen in the treatment setting. This is facilitated by the therapeutic regression, which, to some measure but not entirely, recapitulates early mental states.

The purpose of the treatment of the schizoid patient, as is true of all character disorders, is the acquisition of psychic structure or the correction of ego defects. During the course of treatment the therapist, by being aware of the transference–countertransference axis, learns how the patient is relating to him on the basis of defensive adaptations. By making interpretations the analyst is demonstrating to the patient how his mind works. This occurs in the context of a holding environment.

With the schizoid patient the therapeutic task is to construct a holding environment. The aim of treatment is to achieve an expansion of the ego so that the patient will be able to internalize helpful experiences. The holding environment is not the means to an end; it is the end itself. Its construction means that the patient has made contact with the therapist, indicating that the ego has undergone structuralization by the formation of gratifying introjects. For these patients the therapeutic interaction is primarily a developmental experience designed to compensate for the deficits of their infantile milieu. The analyst supplies a protective setting that permits them to move into the external world.

The patients I have called borderline have made some incursions into the surrounding milieu, but these are inappropriate, maladaptive, and often bizarre. They sometimes use therapy to educate themselves about common everyday activities. They are able to acquire insight, but their capacity to integrate interpretations is limited. They have a better established nurturing matrix than the schizoid group, but it is loosely organized.

They internalize but they are not able to maintain an introject or a mental representation without the reinforcement of the caregiver or the therapist. Often the outcome of successful therapy is an identification with the analyst. They may need to maintain the therapeutic relationship indefinitely in order to stabilize this identification. In other instances they may have to return periodically, and in some cases they may carry an analytic introject apart from therapy. Then they have acquired the capacity to form and hold mental representations without external reinforcement. These patients have achieved what Fraiberg (1969) calls evocative memory.

Patients suffering from character neuroses are able to internalize and are fairly well established in the external world. The therapeutic task is to expand the horizons of reality so they can have more flexible adaptations. Their narcissistic defenses may create therapeutic obstacles.

Narcissistic patients tenaciously cling to their self-aggrandizing defenses, which sustain them. They cannot face their basic feelings of inadequacy. Their self-representation is held together by their grandiosity and they seek admiration in order to support psychic structure. Being admired is their link to the external world. If their narcissistic supplies are depleted, they suffer from psychic collapse, which often takes the form of panic, depression, and loss of identity. They struggle to preserve an exalted view of themselves, and they expect the analyst's cooperation. If they do not receive it, they are apt to terminate treatment.

It is difficult to predict what the course of treatment will be, no matter how well we might understand the psychopathology of a particular character disorder. Furthermore, as repeatedly stressed, there is considerable overlapping among the various entities in the borderline spectrum. Still, there are general patterns that clinicians might anticipate as they become increasingly familiar with this group of patients. In some instances the psychoanalytic method fails, but, often enough, it is the only effective therapeutic approach.

PART II

THE PSYCHOSOMATIC
FOCUS

5

Splitting Mechanisms
and the Treatment
Process

As is true of all elements of psychic structure, defenses can also be arranged in a hierarchic continuum. Denial, splitting, projection, and introjection are placed at the primitive end of this continuum and are presumably characteristic of patients suffering from structural psychopathology. The borderline patient has been described as relying on projective and splitting defenses as well as relating to external objects on the basis of projective identification. Grotstein (1981), Kernberg (1975), and Ogden (1982) have extensively discussed how projective identification is involved in psychopathology, and have made significant clinical contributions.

I believe it is germane to examine these clinical concepts further because by clarifying them, clinicians can learn more about the clinical interaction specifically involved in the healing of ego defects and the acquisition of psychic structure. This is a rephrasing of the question most of us would like to avoid when asked by patients, the question about how therapeutic change occurs. As has been painfully impressed on us, "By making the unconscious conscious" is far from an adequate answer.

Interactions between various parts of the psyche, as well as those between the ego and the outer world, are reenacted in the analytic setting. They require specific technical accommodations, which are based on the clinician's understanding of certain mental mechanisms that are character-istic of a particular group of patients who fit into the borderline category. In this chapter, I will focus on patients who often undergo dissociative experi-ences, that is, deep and painful regressions.

Consequently, early primitive adaptations have to be explored further. Here I should point out that formulations that include projective identifica-tion and splitting mechanisms have become fashionable. As certain concepts gain popularity there is a tendency to be casual and superficial as they are included in various personality and therapeutic models.

Let us now turn our attention to the primitive defenses that have been extensively explored in the study of character disorders.

PROJECTIVE IDENTIFICATION

Projective identification was first described by Melanie Klein (1952). She discussed an interaction between the patient and the analyst in which the patient projects part of the self into the therapist. The therapist, having better psychic structure and greater integrative capacities, would, in a sense, process the patient's projection and cause it to become better organized. The patient then introjects what was projected and makes it part of the self once again. This definition has been amplified, but, in essence, it covers what Klein and her followers discussed.

This concept of projective identification seems somewhat contrived, and what happens in the analyst's mind as it interacts with the patient's projec-tions is unclear. There is almost an anthropomorphic quality to this expla-nation. One mind is working over a piece of another mind and leads to a state of greater organization for the patient's mind. The term *organization*, as used here, does not have much meaning, and how the analyst "processes" is similarly imprecise. Furthermore, identification is a word that also creates some problems.

Projection and identification are concepts that belong to different levels of complexity. Extruding feelings or parts of the self, which in the Kleinian doxology consist of good or bad internal objects, belongs to the primitive end of the spectrum of adaptations and defenses, whereas identification is associated with more complex and secondary-process-attuned mechanisms.

Freud (1915b) wrote that the infant's first response to the outer world was to extrude something that tastes bad, and that this was the prototype for projection. Introjection is on the same plane, in that it is the mechanism on which intake is based. The child does not need to recognize external objects as it uses introjective-projective mechanisms. Schafer (1968) organizes a hierarchy that refers to introjective mechanisms only. He views a progression from assimilation, incorporation, introjection, and internalization. These distinctions gain further importance as clinicians try to understand borderline patients.

Early introjective-projective processes are not really related to introjection and projection, because the latter require some recognition of external objects. Obviously, to project into someone requires the recognition and acknowledgment of that person. Introjection means that something is taken into the psyche and registered. Introjection leads to the formation of an introject. Patients suffering from primitive mental states perceive reality in a dim, evanescent fashion and are unable to acknowledge the existence of someone who may serve as a receptacle of their feelings and parts of their psyche. At most they may feel a need to rid themselves of inner pain in the same manner that Freud described as the extrusion of something felt as noxious.

The term *introjection*, if used to describe the mechanisms of intake of primitively organized patients, would not include the endopsychic registration of a nurturing experience. The maintenance of a percept requires a higher level of ego integration, and the lack of this capacity determines specific symptomatic manifestations. With psychic development, introjection eventually is associated with the construction of introjects, but many patients have not yet reached that level. Schafer suggested that we use different terms to describe these earlier intake mechanisms, such as *assimilation* and *incorporation*. Food is taken in and assimilated, but in the infant it does not alone lead to the formation of introjects or a nurturing matrix. Many other caretaking activities, such as soothing and other types of interactions, are required for psychic structuralization.

Identification, in turn, is an upward extension of introjective mechanisms, but it is considerably more sophisticated. It presupposes a recognition of whole objects, that is, of the entire person apart form its specific function toward the self. There is a merging of the ego ideals of two psyches. Furthermore, the formation of solid identifications occurs at later developmental stages than those associated with projection. Freud places it during the oedipal phase, referring to the superego as being the heir of the Oedipus complex.

In spite of its theoretical inconsistency, projective identification is, nevertheless, a useful clinical concept, especially as it relates to transference–countertransference interactions. It can be conceptualized as an accentuation of ordinary perceptual modes that are constructed at later developmental stages but become modalities for all psychic stages.

This sequence of development of later functions that are incorporated into all psychic levels is true of maturational processes in general. Perception, language, and bowel and bladder control are seldom lost even in states of fairly deep regression. These functions are not significantly affected, although many psychic functions become dominated by primary-process mental operations. Apparently there are no particular parallels between physiological or physical processes and psychological orientations either when patients regress or the fixated developmental phase gains dominance. I am referring particularly to perceptual modalities and various functions that in a large measure have become automated.

Thinking processes can become disturbed as the psyche operates on the basis of primitive mental states. Patients may lose the capacity to hold and form mental representation; that is, evocative memory may be lost (Fraiberg 1969) as well as other internalized adaptations and introjects. These structural alterations are often the basis of borderline psychopathology (see Chapter 3). By contrast, after the sensory system has acquired a certain degree of structure and integration, it remains relatively stable. It can become massively disturbed, as in hallucinations, but this occurs in the context of thought disorders. This emphasizes that the perceptual system functions as an integral aspect of other parts of the personality.

The self is involved in the act of perception as well as in the registration of sensory experiences. How we view ourselves contributes to how we view the world. Thus we put some element of the self-representation into the situation in the outer world that is being perceived. Freud (1925) put it succinctly when writing about the notational function of attention by stating that the preconscious (a significant part of the ego) meets the incoming percept halfway. The ego sends out feelers to examine and interpret a sensory impression. How the psyche is structured contributes to the structuring of external stimuli as they are internally registered. There are no pure perceptions that would mean total objectivity. There is always a structural bias that even determines the phenomenological qualities of sensory impressions.

Reaching out to the stimulus could be considered as the prototype of projection, whereas its registration, even a temporary one as occurs in the system-consciousness, would be a forerunner to introjection. The latter is a far cry from identification.

If projective identification is to have conceptual validity, clinicians have to stress the uneven path of regression and fixation. The capacity to identify is not lost in the regression of some borderline patients. I believe, however, that many interactions that are explained on the basis of projective identification are the outcome of more primitive dissociative phenomena.

DISSOCIATION, PAIN, AND INTEGRATION

In the next chapter I will explore clinical interactions that are characteristic of patients whose egos are fragmented. These patients frequently suffer from psychosomatic problems. The patients I am about to discuss are often afflicted with painful bodily symptoms, but these symptoms are the outcome of a process of self-healing. These are also fragmented patients and they have been raised in an assaultive environment. They are being considered as a separate group because dissociation has adaptive potential as well as painful consequences, and it is part of the healing process. It is especially interesting to note that what these patients describe is similar to some of the clinical phenomena discussed in the *Studies on Hysteria* (Breuer and Freud 1895).

Janet (1929) stressed that hysterics have loosely synthesized egos, which make them prone to dissociation. They can easily fragment and isolate various parts of the psyche from the main psychic current, as Freud (1938) stated. Unfortunately, Janet took a moral position and judged these patients as being weak and degenerate. Freud, on the other hand, remained nonjudgmental and sought to translate the physical symptoms associated with hysteria into psychological terms.

Freud did not emphasize the hysteric's tendency to fragment. Instead he stressed their propensity to resist pursuing the psychoanalytic method, which means to resist free association. He formulated his patients in psychodynamic terms, postulating that inner conflicts succumb to repression. The purpose of treatment was to undo repression and, as has been repeatedly discussed, to make the unconscious conscious. Breuer's ideas were considered mechanistic and nonanalytic and were not pursued further.

I believe, as is true of our renewed interest in psychosomatic disorders, that we have made a 180-degree turn and are back in Breuer's camp without being aware of it. Breuer was thinking primarily in terms of psychic structure. He had not given instinct theory and conflict a prominent place in his formulations, and this was the reason that his ideas were ignored as Freud continued to build the psychoanalytic edifice. Our current interest in understanding borderline patients leads to a revived interest in Breuer's ideas about hysteria.

Breuer believed, as did Freud, that the cause of neurosis was psychic trauma that had not been processed by the ego. Because the patient was vulnerable and nondefended when subjected to the trauma, the tension and anxiety created by it was not discharged. The mind could handle the trauma only by splitting it off and encapsulating it. Thus the trauma is contained in a part of the psyche that is fragmented from the conscious, experiencing ego. Breuer calls this split-off part of the mind that contains the trauma *a hypnoid mental state*. It is out of the sphere of consciousness, but it differs from repression, which emphasizes two systems: the id and the ego. In repression something is pushed out of the ego into the id. The hypnoid mental state emphasizes that a psychic structure, that is, a part of the personality, breaks loose from a previous unity.

Thus Breuer believed that hysterical patients react inappropriately to trauma. He agreed at first with Freud, who stated that the trauma was sexual. Later, Breuer questioned sexual etiology. At the time of the trauma, the patient's affect becomes strangulated because the patient is in a hypnoidal state. Breuer's description of this hypnoidal state is not clear. Presumably, the patient cannot allow himself to experience the anxiety that would be the appropriate response to being traumatized. The trauma and the accompanying anxiety are incorporated into a part of the psyche, the hypnoid mental state, while the patient is in a hypnoidal state. It remains in the psyche as a foreign body. The task of treatment is to bring this hypnoid mental state back into consciousness and to discharge the affect (abreaction and catharsis) that is appropriate to the frightening event, and thus to reestablish the unity of the psyche.

A threatening event (today we would emphasize a generally traumatic infantile environment rather than a specific traumatic instance) is defended against by dissociative mechanisms. The hypnoidal state that Breuer refers to raises several questions. Is the hypnoidal state, in itself, a response to trauma, and does it represent some degree of dissociation? Is it a defense or the product of a breakdown of defenses? This latter question can be directed to splitting and dissociative mechanisms in general, especially as responses to traumas.

When dealing with primitive mental mechanisms, it is often difficult to distinguish what is a manifestation of mental breakdown owing to traumatic impact or a defensive reaction against the assaultive environment. Dissociative processes could signify psychic disintegration in that the ego has fragmented and lost some cohesion and unity. Still, according to Breuer as well as modern clinicians, splitting helps restore psychic equilibrium, and inasmuch as it does, it can be considered a defensive adaptation. A disintegrative process leads to dissociative responses, which in turn lead to some degree of stabilization and prevent further disintegration. Thus splitting can be both a sign of breakdown and a defense against the traumatic factor that is upsetting psychic equilibrium.

Breuer must have had some similar thoughts when he postulated the existence of hypnoidal states during traumatic moments. The hypnoidal state, in which the trauma is pushed aside in order for the ego not to be overwhelmed by anxiety or panic, must also be the outcome of dissociation. The trauma causes further splitting to encapsulate it and strangulate the affect. Then the ego stops acting as an integrated unit; various parts of the ego seem to function independently of each other. In order to reach such a defensive stabilization through splitting mechanisms, the ego already has to be in a state of anticipatory dissociation to be able to defensively dissociate.

The etiology of emotional disorders being attributed to a single traumatic incident is no longer held as valid. Rather, clinicians think in terms of an assaultive environment in which trauma is perpetually present. The child's ego does not achieve any great degree of cohesion in an atmosphere of constant impingements. It remains fixated at fragmented levels and further uses dissociation when overwhelming assaults are inflicted on it. This will be discussed further in the next chapter.

I recall patients who had been frequently, sometimes daily, sexually abused. These children would fantasize being in a pleasant safe setting as they anticipated being violated, and they would get more and more immersed in their fantasy as they were being brutalized. Later in life, as adults, they may or may not have a conscious recollection of being violated. Breuer's ideas about the hypnoidal state is in accord with the concept of repetitive traumas and a generally assaultive infantile environment. The concept of coexisting but nonconnected ego states is explicitly stated in Breuer's hypotheses and has become an explanatory base by which we understand commonly seen psychopathology.

Perhaps the most obvious use of dissociation is found in patients who have been diagnosed as multiple personalities. Those patients were fairly commonly encountered in Freud's and Charcot's time, but recently more and more such patients have been coming to our attention. This seems to be associated with the increased number of patients claiming to having been sexually abused. Whether we are confronted with hysterical fragmentation, borderline decompensation, or even schizophrenia is debatable, but the fact that these patients' personalities are fragmented is unmistakable.

Splitting, dissociation, and *fragmentation* are terms that have been treated as synonymous. Depending on the conceptual viewpoint, they can be considered adaptations or the manifestations of breakdown. In some instances the clinical phenomenon is primarily defensive or predominantly a sign of breakdown. The chief factor is stability. The various parts of the psyche that have become disconnected have achieved some degree of equilibrium and an integration of their own. This is clear in patients suffering from multiple personalities, where each separate personality has a well-developed identity sense and seems to represent a whole person. A few clinicians have questioned whether these multiple personalities are iatrogenic creations; but some split-off parts of the self gain considerable cohesion and serve as defensive adaptations, whereas other parts of the psyche are so fragmented that the patient cannot function.

Regardless of the defensive adaptive qualities of some dissociated states, they are still painful. As will be stressed in the next chapter, unconnected islands of psychic structure are surrounded by lacunae devoid of psychological content, but they are the sites of physiological disturbances that are often expressed as psychosomatic disorders. Lack of unity and cohesion lead to disequilibrium, which is eventually manifested in mental and physical suffering. An integrated psyche restores homeostasis, strengthens the stability of the self-representation, and expands the range of the adaptations of the ego's executive system. To a significant degree the fragmented state is intrinsically painful, and in treatment these patients try to re-create a state in which split-off parts are reintegrated. They also attempt to construct bridges between various psychic levels. The striving for unity can become the main motif of the treatment process, but it may be misunderstood and viewed as a manifestation of an undesirable and perhaps unmanageable regression.

> The patient, a twice-married man in his early forties, reported that his life was a series of contradictions. He could function well professionally, but he was clumsy in sports and socially inept. He believed he had no capacity for intimacy and believed he could not make commitments. Although married, he had no feelings toward his wife, and there had been no sexual contact for at least 2 years.
>
> He stated that he did not know basically who he was. He believed he had a well-established professional identity but other than that, he could not define himself. He did not even know whether he was heterosexual or homosexual, although he had never had a homosexual experience.
>
> He also concentrated on numerous physical ailments and pains. He suffered from asthma, mild hypertension, muscular pains, and frequent skin rashes. More distressing was a feeling of inner agitation, which could intensify to an unbearable degree. He insisted that he could not be soothed, as is true of patients whose distress is prementational (see Chapter 3). He sought relief but he could not find it. He thought of drugs and alcohol, but his religion would not permit him such indulgences. He received some partial relief through constant masturbation.

His childhood was one of material comfort but emotional neglect. His father had been killed in World War II, and he never saw him. The mother apparently had many lovers and would sometimes tease her son by intimating that one of them was his father and asking him to guess who it was. He had been told that his father had died in the war, but his mother's innuendos caused him to doubt whose son he was and who he was.

He was virtually raised by several maids, and there the mother confused him further. She hinted that she was probably not his mother, that he was the child of one of the maids. The question of maternity was even more disturbing than that of paternity. He carefully observed the various maids who took care of him to find if there were any feelings of maternal love for him. He could not find such feelings in them or in his mother. He felt very lonely and afraid.

The mother had very little to do with him. He did not recall ever having been held by her or even touched. He desperately wanted to get close to her, but emotionally and literally she kept her distance.

He had many fantasies about his father. He did not really believe he was the son of one of his mother's lovers, but he was not certain. He was confused. He thought of his father as a large, warm man folding his arms around him. At other times he would become very angry because he had been abandoned by him. He had learned that his father did not have to join the army. He had volunteered, which meant to the patient that he preferred a hero's death rather than taking care of his forlorn son. At the age of 6, he remembers bitterly crying about his loss.

He did not view himself as a whole person. Though he was certain he had parents, emotionally he believed he was an orphan. His parents were viewed as a huge vacuum, which he experienced as being inside of himself. He felt an inner loss and that important parts of himself were missing, such as the capacity to love and being loved.

He recalled that in childhood he felt very sad when he saw other children relating to their parents in an atmosphere of mutual affection. He yearned for such love, tried to be physically close to his mother whenever possible, but she would not respond. He was especially bitter when on a bus she sat with a niece and he had to sit alone in the seat behind them. These experiences reinforced his sense of unworthiness and made him believe that the world was unfair.

His bitterness extended itself to the external world, and he spent many sessions at the beginning of therapy complaining about and citing the experiences where he had felt mistreated and cheated. He indulged himself in litanies of situations in which he was treated rudely, and how he was being manipulated. He believed that people did not like him and found it difficult to tolerate him. His attitude had a paranoid tinge, but he could also feel tenderness toward handicapped persons and pets. He was especially fond of dogs.

He had been hospitalized on several occasions. These had occurred when he had what appeared to be an identity crisis. He would, as happens with Erikson's (1959) Identity Diffusion syndrome, deeply regress to an almost vegetative state. He stopped taking care of himself and literally did not recognize himself. He also had considerable pain, constantly repeating how he could not stand the pain or stand himself. His subjective sensations were dominated by the feeling that he was falling apart. He was given high doses of haloperidol, and eventually he would reintegrate and be discharged.

He also had considerable outpatient therapy with at least five psychiatrists. He did not believe that any of them was capable of soothing him except by heavily medicating him, which took the cutting edge off the pain; but he still did not feel that he was a real person. Apparently, he had frightened his therapists. He had intense bouts of regression, which they tried to control by either hospitalizing him or giving him drugs. They considered him unmanageable with a bad prognosis, and a poor candidate for a psychoanalytic approach because it would stimulate dangerous regressions and fragmentation. They feared a collapse of his ego and a psychotic degeneration.

The patient felt completely misunderstood and believed that his various treatment experiences were mechanistic and unfeeling. He believed that the therapists had no interest in understanding him; they simply wanted to manage his behavior so that they could be comfortable. No one was interested in his comfort.

His treatment took many interesting turns. At the beginning he was extremely anxious that I believe how much he was really suffering. He also wanted to know whether I was interested in him for himself, not because of the fee or whatever professional enhancement I might gain for having successfully treated him. He was, in effect, demanding unconditional love. He continued complaining about his misery and pain and his need to be loved for over a year.

He acknowledged that he wanted to be treated like a baby, but according to him, this was because he *was* a baby. He insisted that I know that he was not acting as if he were a baby. There was nothing "as if" about his infantile status. He was truly an infant. He finally admitted, however, that he was referring to parts of himself rather than the whole personality. Nevertheless, these parts of his psyche could not be related to in adult terms. He had to be treated as a child, but more importantly, he was concerned that I appreciate the gravity of his condition and the extent of his neediness. Apparently, his former therapists tried to interpret his infantile demands as defenses and transference, but according to the patient, their main focus was on medications.

Perhaps patients as primitive as he was are untreatable from a psychoanalytic perspective, and we cannot actually take over the parental role and raise the person as a child when, at least chronologically, he is an adult. Knowing that most therapists would not be able to engage with him at the level he demanded, he felt that I also would be unable to help him. For some reason, however, he believed that he could teach me how to modify my viewpoint so I could adapt the treatment to his needs and then maybe I would be useful.

His main point was that I take what he said at face value, and not try to attribute hidden causes and motives to his thoughts and feelings. At first I was puzzled, because how could I operate as a psychoanalyst if I stopped looking below the surface, which is the modus operandi of psychoanalysis? I felt somewhat reconciled to the psychoanalytic position when I realized that the patient was trying to reveal parts of himself to me and have me stand by as a noncritical onlooker.

As I gradually learned, he wanted me to create a setting in which he could comfortably regress, and this meant that I accept that he was really a baby. His previous analysts were engaged in a power struggle with him. He interpreted that their efforts to provide him with insights that he believed were at much higher levels of sophistication than what he was feeling indicated that they were reluctant to allow him to regress. They were not able to create a supportive matrix that would make him feel sufficiently secure so that he could reveal the most primitive aspects of his psyche. Nevertheless, the therapeutic process was, in itself, a regressive experience, and he felt himself pulled back, as he put it, into frightening and dangerous aspects of his psyche, parts that had been split off but through regression had emerged as dominant. He felt bombarded by primitive feelings and suffered from waves of intense anxiety and panic. His regressions were disruptive, and in some instances he could no longer function. On two occasions he had to be hospitalized, and his analysts concluded that he was too disturbed for analysis.

With these analysts he was repeating a destructive pattern that intensified feeling abandoned and failing once again in his attempts to gain love and succor. These regressive episodes led to an increasing yearning for a caring maternal person. His therapists' emphasis on defenses and conflicts caused him to feel criticized. It was as if they were telling him to grow up and participate in a discourse that was appropriate for an adult. He felt that they did not accept the baby within and that they were admonishing him for his yearnings, which he should have given up many years ago.

They never explicitly made any such statements, but he believed their attitudes and demeanor indicated that this is what they felt.

He stressed that these therapists were wedded to a theoretical system that they could not relinquish; nor could they modify their concepts, which would engender understanding and help them alter their therapeutic perspectives. The patient added that their constricted viewpoints, which limited treatment explorations to higher levels of the psyche, indicated that these therapists had a disdain for primitive feelings and desires. When he inevitably regressed, he did so in the presence of an uncomfortable and confused analyst. The patient felt he had ventured into dangerous territory, a danger created by the therapists' nonacceptance and, at times, what he sensed to be their anxiety.

Furthermore, he eventually understood that these frightening and disruptive regressions were similar to the infantile scenario. Then he would reach out, sometimes with highly charged feelings accompanied by tantrums, but there was no one there to relate to at that level. At the most, his mother would be confused. She would make light of his turmoil and pass it off as a transitory mood that was characteristic of infancy and would stop occurring when he grew up. Undoubtedly she was defending herself against her incapacity to respond. Like the analysts, she could only relate to a higher order of discourse.

I wondered what would have happened if one of the therapists had recognized the repetition-compulsion aspect of the regression rather than considering it unmanageable. Would his understanding and interpretation of the transference have made the regression both manageable and fruitful?

What I learned about these episodes came from the patient during relatively nonregressed periods. I addressed to him the question of interpretation of the repetition compulsion. He answered promptly and said that he did not think it would have helped; it would have only disturbed him further. This made me ponder because I firmly held to the thesis that the interpretation of the transference, insofar as it was a reenactment of an infantile struggle and traumatic situation, was an essential feature of the psychoanalytic curative process. Perhaps his previous analysts did not understand what was happening, but even if they did, they were still rendered helpless to function effectively as analysts. I was facing a similar dilemma. The patient had been able to teach me how important it was not to drag up discourses that bypassed his needs.

I had to accept that the baby parts of himself were real and should not be treated in the abstract, that is, as regressive defenses. He insisted that they were primary and an intrinsic aspect of his self-representation. Could I analyze a baby? To some degree, analysis requires that we make contact with those parts of the patient that are capable of introspection and self-observation, and babies do not have these capacities. Still, this patient was extremely perceptive and had considerable understanding of psychological processes and mechanisms. During regressed states he had to lose these later acquisitions in order to experience himself as an infant.

There are different types of regression. As discussed, most regressions are partial and involve some degree of splitting. Patients usually retain an adult part of the psyche even when they return to primitive mental states. These elements are the mainstays of the self-observing ego, which was first described by Sterba (1934), and they participate in the analytic process. The more cohesive and integrated the ego, the greater likelihood to have an effective self-observing ego during regression, and the more manageable and therapeutically constructive regression can be. The regressed state, in these instances, is a dissociated state containing coexisting adult and infantile components. It is interesting that the propensity to use splitting mechanisms is enhanced in an ego that does not primarily use such defenses.

I believe that these regressions point to the fact that there is much more to understand about dissociative processes. They are not just the manifestation of psychopathology or limited to primitive adaptive defenses. They are also involved in higher mental operations and involved in creative activity. Well-integrated egos can tolerate ambiguity. Contradictory ego states can exist side by side and eventually can reach higher states of unity and synthesis. The simultaneous coexistence of primary- and secondary-process operations characterizes some regressed ego states as well as the creative process.

By contrast, my patient was not able to maintain an observing ego during regressed states. If he brought such elements into his mental field, it would immediately lose its primitive qualities, and he would no longer be regressed. His splitting was different from the dissociation I have just discussed, a difference that is proportional to the degree of psychopathology.

In severe psychopathology all the split-off parts of the self are divorced from the psychic stream, and only one particular psychic constellation exists. There is a rigid adherence to that ego state that cannot be relaxed without completely losing it or without an ensuing confusion or chaos. Thus the personality is rigid, constricted, and has a unidimensional quality. Therapists have to deal with the patient at the level of the dominant, split-off part. They are, in fact, relating only to part objects rather than to a whole person.

Such patients are concretely oriented because they lack the fluidity characteristic of mentational activity. Because contrasting parts operate on a solo basis rather than participate in an interaction with opposites, there are no gradations, no gray areas that are the outcome of the neutralization of polarities. The world is viewed rigidly from just one perspective.

With many borderline patients this means the loss of the intrapsychic focus and, often, a concentration on somatic factors. The concrete outlook on reality dominates as the awareness of internal processes is split off. In some patients this awareness never develops because they have not acquired the cohesiveness that is required for introspection. To be able to acquire an intrapsychic focus—that is, to understand that there are inner processes responsible for emotional and behavioral aberrations—presupposes the recognition of the multifaceted aspects of psychic structure. One level of the personality is making observations about other levels; this requires more than just a single psychic state unable to relate to other states and incapable of self-scrutiny. Rather than splitting, some patients suffering from character disorders have never reached a state of cohesion that can later fragment. The patient has always been fragmented and presents only a limited part of the self to the world at a time. To repeat, there are different types of regression, and not all dissociative states are the same. These distinctions are important because they determine what is therapeutically efficacious.

Returning to the patient, I did not believe I could actually be his parent. I had been sufficiently instructed not to make any interpretations although my instincts propelled me to do so. I had understood that he had to experience such states and that I, by explaining them with words, would have forced him out of the regression. I did not know how to fulfill my analytic function. I decided to simply be an observer.

His regressed states were similar to those described in the next chapter. He would begin by moaning as if he were in pain. I recall asking him if he were having painful feelings and he replied that he was suffering intensely all over his body. His moaning became louder and louder until he was finally screaming and crying. Amidst his babbling and keening, I could detect an occasional word such as "mommy" or a phrase like "I want my mommy." It was unclear but it definitely sounded like the screams of an infant. There was a poignant and violent quality to the primitive verbalization of his yearnings. These supplications were followed by even louder screams such as one might expect from a person who is being tortured. He acted as if he were being sadistically beaten. He might spend the whole session wrestling with such intense and dangerous feelings. At the end of the session he felt better and believed that he had made progress.

I noted that when I asked him whether he felt pain he answered my question and was not disrupted by it, as he would have been had I made an interpretation. I concluded that I could make comments and remain in his frame of reference and level of discourse. This meant that I had to confine myself to remarks directed to his actions and feelings. I could ask him to expand on what he was feeling or to repeat something that had been so indistinct that I could not hear it. I was limiting our interaction to such exchanges, aimed at sharpening his communicating to me and making it possible to understand him better. This was a surface, phenomenological approach. I could also point out to him shifts in his attitude and the varying degrees of tension he experienced. He was receptive to my attempts at monitoring his pain and trying to assess how he was feeling.

Some of these sessions could be quite loud, and he was able to fill the office with an all-pervasive tension. It was also painful for me to see him suffer so intensely and there was a strong urge to do something to help him feel better, that is, to snap him out of his disruptive regression. This was a countertransference problem that I had to control acting upon. In any case, I was able to reassure myself that he was trying to work out some important problems.

Later the patient brought in material that helped me understand the essence of his regressions and what he was hoping to accomplish. He was putting himself back in the time frame when he was most aware of his painful yearnings for maternal love. Insofar as he had not bonded, or because whatever bond he had with a nurturing caregiver was so weak, his psyche never achieved stability or synthesis. He constantly complained that he was not a whole person, that parts of himself were missing. Those parts should have contained representations of caregivers and endopsychic registrations of nurturing experiences. Ordinarily they would have been incorporated and integrated into the psyche and become part of the ego fabric that gives structure and cohesiveness to all psychic systems, especially the self-representation.

During regressed ego states my patient was desperately trying to incorporate these missing parts. I asked myself what there was to incorporate if it had never existed. This was too absolute a viewpoint. Though the patient had never achieved a comfortable cohesiveness of the personality, he still had some caregiving introjects and elements of a nurturing matrix. They were defective, however, and split off from the core ego. This made him feel that something vital was missing. While regressed, his screaming and pain were manifestations of his tortured attempts to take in these fragmented and defective parts of the psyche. This literally hurt, but he was attempting to repair and appease the hostile, abandoning, and destructive maternal introjects by making them part of himself.

When he yelled "I want my mommy," it was followed by "Please, please don't leave me." As I came to understand him better my hearing also became more acute. He often wailed "Come back" and "Don't hurt me." At first these words were hardly audible, as they were drowned in animallike grunts and screaming. At times there was a rhythmic, repetitive tone to his utterances, as if he were ululating a weird chant. He would occasionally clap his hands, keeping time with the beat as he punctuated this eerie rhythm with crying and sobbing. Then he might loudly and explosively exclaim "Why have you left me?" and have a tantrum as he violently sobbed and kicked his feet and beat the couch with his fist as he lay on his stomach. He was reenacting feelings that would have been appropriate to the stage of childhood in which he was ignored and neglected, a time when helpful nurturing relations should have led to the acquisition of psychic structure, developmental progression, and differentiation and synthesis of the psychic apparatus.

To integrate painful experiences is in itself acutely painful. At first, it is comparable to the oxymoron *poisonous nurture,* as was poetically described in Hawthorne's (1950) short story, "Rappaccini's Daughter." He felt destroyed by what he was incorporating, and it is also interesting that he suffered from all types of bowel symptoms and was diagnosed as having colitis. One internist believed he had a variety of ulcerative colitis, but this was not pursued by the patient, even though during his regressions in treatment his bowel symptoms intensified.

He had to survive the destructive effects of incorporating defective parts. By bringing them into the mainstream of the psyche, the defects, in a sense, are healed, a process that Melanie Klein (1935) described as occurring during the reparative phases of the depressive position. How this healing occurs remains largely unknown, but my patient always felt much better after such painful sessions and reported that he felt enhanced as a person.

His somatic symptoms persisted, however, and he finally developed a peptic ulcer that responded well to medication. Following the treatment of this ulcer, he had no somatic symptoms for at least 6 months, but then his diarrhea and cramps returned. He is still in treatment and periodically he continues to regress during his sessions.

Similarities between the process illustrated by this patient and Breuer's concepts are summarized below. As discussed, Breuer believed that when a patient experienced a traumatic event, the trauma was encapsulated in a part of the psyche that was then split off in what he called a hypnoid mental state. The therapeutic task is to recover these split-off hypnoid mental states and to reintegrate them into the main psychic structures. Breuer stressed that this reintegration occurred through abreaction and catharsis and that once the affect is discharged, there would no longer be a split-off state. It becomes decathected and rejoins other mental structures. This process of synthesis and integration, however, is secondary to the discharge of strangulated anxiety.

Breuer viewed the distress his patients, particularly Anna O., suffered to be manifestations of the discharge of anxiety. The tension and pain Breuer witnessed while the patient was in a hypnotic state were the expression of a disruptive affective state, anxiety bordering on panic. Afterward, there would be considerable relief and a reintegration of character, but the latter was not stressed. This sequence was the essence of the curative process.

Matters are not as simple as Breuer depicted, nor, with the exception of the traumatic neuroses, do discharge phenomena play a vital role in therapeutic resolution.

Both Freud and Breuer believed in the traumatic etiology of emotional disorders. Consequently, their ideas about abreaction and catharsis are consistent with the treatment of the traumatic neurosis. If all neuroses are conceptualized as a type of traumatic neurosis, then it makes sense that discharge phenomena would be an essential feature of the treatment process. Freud, however, distinguished the traumatic war neuroses from the traditional neuroses, but as with Breuer, the mechanisms involved in the production of psychopathology were in many respects similar. The repetition compulsion and the reliving of a traumatic incident are similar events. The repetition compulsion consists of the repetition of infantile traumatic constellations, whereas in the abreactions of the war neuroses, a traumatic situation is reconstructed and lived over once again with the purpose of mastering it. Both war traumas and infantile traumas (Freud 1920) have to be mastered if therapeutic resolution is to be achieved, and this involves discharges of psychic energy. Trauma, both psychic and physical, still plays a central role in classical psychoanalysis, but it is also an important factor for the understanding of patients in the borderline spectrum.

With our increased emphasis on structural factors, psychoeconomic concepts and tension-discharge hypotheses recede into the background. My patient's turmoil was not a manifestation of discharge of anxiety. As he constantly emphasized, it was the outcome of his attempts to regain lost, damaged parts of the self.

The internalization of defective psychic elements is intrinsically painful, as is the healing process. To introduce faulty structure into various ego systems, including the self-representation and the ego's executive system, is a disturbing experience, but as mentioned above, it is meant to be restorative. At first, as was true for my patient, there is an even greater lowering of self-esteem. Besides the pain, he felt that being in pain was in itself a humiliating experience, as was the open expression of his neediness. When he assimilated his abandoning introjects, his sense of unworthiness intensified. As the feeling of being abandoned became further integrated, his conviction that he deserved to be rejected increased. This attitude of being bad and undeserving had been with him ever since he could remember, but during regressed states it became incorporated in his pain. As we were able to reconstruct these psychic events we pieced together a picture of a mind filled with reproving and disdainful personages who did not want to have anything to do with him. They were not inadequate and incapable of helping. They simply did not want to give him anything that would promote psychic growth and self-esteem.

He had no narcissistic supplies. His self-representation was not bolstered by either internal or external object representations. He also felt, as does the typical borderline, unable to function at the simplest, most pedestrian level, although he continued doing quite well professionally. He had often lamented that no one had ever taught him anything or paid him any respect, as he quoted a well-known comedian.

SOMATIC DISRUPTION AND HYPOCHONDRIASIS

The patient was afraid that his internal milieu had caused somatic damage, as was evidenced by his bowel disturbances. This psychosomatic component became a dominant element of his emotionally disturbed condition.

Again, he felt incomplete, but this now included an incomplete somatic apparatus in addition to lacunae (see Chapter 6) of the psychic apparatus. It is not exactly identical to splitting because he was not missing parts of his soma, but he explained that his bowel was not working as a synthesized unit. Rather, it was disjointed, asynchronous, and in a constant state of turmoil. He viewed it as part of a disturbed equilibrium, and, as stated, he insisted that it was reacting to the neglect that it had suffered. He was assigning a human status to the gastrointestinal tract, with the same feelings and anguish he usually felt.

I do not wish to imply any etiological significance to his ideas nor to identify them with Kleinian formulations, which sometimes confuse theoretical postulates with fantasies. What I have described are the patient's fantasies, which are end products of psychic processes rather than their causes. Nevertheless, his fantasies are important and are relevant to our explorations of the treatment process and to our understanding of how disruptive regressions have the potential to gain higher levels of psychic integration and, in this instance, somatic integration as well.

He had a querulous, hypochondriacal attitude. Besides his bowel, he complained about many other physical infirmities, as is true of many patients within the borderline spectrum. Meissner (1988) especially focuses on the hypochondriacal borderline patient. The patient had frequent headaches, and at times he feared he had a serious neurological illness because he was often physically depleted, and he believed that he was suffering from a progressive muscular weakness. He was continually in and out of doctors' offices.

Because he had suffered from the "blows" of maternal omission, he was internally damaged, but more importantly, his visceral organs had not received the "attention" they needed in order to mature properly. His narcissistic injuries and depletions included the soma as well as the psyche. Through his hypochondriasis and visits to a horde of medical specialists, he was trying to make up for the lack of nutriment of infancy, which had affected everything inside of him. His hypochondriasis was a reaction to the fear that he was in fact somatically damaged, but it was also a restitutive attempt to spotlight what had been neglected in the past. He had been fed and all of his physical needs had been taken care of, but except for an occasional maid, no one really cared if he were getting proper nutrition or if his bowels were regular. He was emphasizing that no one cared even though someone was taking care of him. No one cared for either his body or his mind.

Another patient, a young professional adult, stated that she was suffering from a "hypochondriasis of the mind." She believed that her analyst had misunderstood her in that he felt that she had much more cohesiveness to the self-representation than she believed. She had presented a picture of an "as-if" character, much in the same fashion as Deutsch (1942) had described. She was emphasizing that she was a true as-if character, that she did not really have an identity of her own. This was in contrast to a pseudo–as-if character, in which the patient's identity is repressed or split off for defensive purposes. The as-if characteristics are superficial qualities designed to hide the essential identity sense. The therapist did not agree with the patient. He believed that whatever as-if qualities she attributed to herself belonged in the defensive category.

There was a considerable difference between the way the patient viewed herself and the analyst's perception of her. These evaluations referred to the structure and boundaries of the self-representation. She did not see herself as a distinct person; rather, she felt that she made herself subservient to other persons, particularly her husband. She could shove her feelings and opinions into the background and adopt as her own what was sometimes forcefully presented to her. The analyst, on the other hand, believed she had considerable strength of character, and that her submissiveness was defensive and sometimes more of a complicity with, rather than an abnegation of, her true self. She seemingly let herself be bested simply to maintain the peace.

It was the differences of these two viewpoints that defined the hypochondriasis of the mind. In a sense, she complained about her mind in the same way that the previous patient focused on his bowels. She was in no way as vociferous as that patient, but in her own quiet way she had, during one period of treatment, devoted considerable psychic energy to making observations about her lack of structure, in essence the same type of complaints many patients direct to somatic systems.

There is a continuum between the psyche and soma, the soma representing the periphery of the psyche. Ego boundaries can be considered as an interface between the internal world of the mind and the external world of reality. Freud wrote, "The ego is first and foremost a body ego . . ." (Freud 1923, p. 26). Thus, from this statement, it would seem the soma is also an interface between the inner mind and the outer world.

Both patients believed that essential parts of themselves were missing. The first patient was trying to integrate painful parts of the self in order to feel like a whole person. His fragmentation and lack of coherence extended to the soma, which was also experienced as unintegrated and split off from the rest of his character and body. The patient who believed herself to be an as-if character did not view herself as having a self-representation of her own. These orientations were manifested in the first patient by hypochondriacal preoccupation and somatic symptoms, and in the second patient by a description of a hypochondriacal attitude toward her mind. To some extent, this patient felt she had no mind, that is, she had no mind of her own. She had simply borrowed someone else's mind, a mind which was not well integrated with the rest of her character. Her analyst continued to believe that this mind-fragmentation was primarily defensive, but there were elements in her early life that would have encouraged splitting defenses, such as her relationship with her mother and a serious childhood illness.

Besides being a manifestation of somatic fragmentation, hypochondriasis can also represent an attempt to gain cohesion. The regressions of the patient I described were characterized by internal explosive pain, a reaction to the disruptive process of integration. Hypochondriasis can represent a painful similar attempt to integrate somatic systems with each other and the psychic apparatus.

Freud (1911) viewed hypochondriasis as a stage of the psychotic process. As libido is withdrawn from the external world it cathects the soma, the periphery of the psychic apparatus, on its introverted path. This halting of libido as it hypercathects various organ systems is experienced as hypochondriasis. Then it travels further into the interior, leading to megalomanic states. The manifestation of psychoses such as delusions are reactions to the libido's attempts to direct itself toward the outer world, to repair the "rent of reality" as Freud stated. He added that hypochondriacal and megalomanic stages can, in some instances, be only momentary, so much so that they may not be detected.

If the patient does not move beyond the hypochondriacal stage, there may be no manifest psychosis.

It can also be compared with anxiety, which Freud (1926) described as the core of the psychoneuroses. Anxiety was conceptualized as a danger signal that stimulated defensive operations to reestablish repression and psychic harmony. These defenses were attempts to gain unity, which had been disrupted by intrapsychic conflict. The effectiveness or noneffectiveness of these attempts determined the severity of the neurosis.

In an analogous sense, psychotic stabilization could be considered an attempt to defend the psyche against the painful disruptive aspects of hypochondriasis. The process is more complex because of the question of which is the most disruptive: the psychotic attempts to make contact with the external world, or the pent-up state of hypochondriasis. Hypochondriasis could be considered in some instances as a defense against psychosis.

Furthermore, Freud's model does not work for many psychotic states, such as those characterized by schizoid withdrawal. In these instances there do not seem to be any restitutive attempts to reestablish contact with reality. Libido remains withdrawn. Freud's model was specially constructed for paranoia.

I do not wish to generalize. Although hypochondriasis often is a defense against psychotic breakdown, it need not always have that function. I am stressing its propensity to maintain some degree of psychosomatic cohesion and to prevent further fragmentation. Hypochondriacal disorders are found in many personality types and do not, by themselves, define the degree of psychopathology.

I have also witnessed patients whose hypochondriasis intensified during treatment and represented attempts at reintegration similar to the painful explosive feelings my patient had while in regressed states. In fact, that patient's hypochondriasis became more acute during treatment and was a manifestation of attempts to achieve synthesis and unity. This could become a circular process in which the integrative process itself becomes disruptive and leads to further dissociation.

Disruptive somatic states and hypochondriasis can be traced back to disturbances during the prementational stage, as will be further elaborated in the next chapter. They are the outcome of defective soothing and painful nursing. Hypochondriasis, however, is at a slightly higher level than defective soothing and prementational agitation. The organ systems that are the targets of hypochondriacal preoccupation are involved with intake and elimination. Though these somatic tendencies are present at birth and have intrauterine prototypes, their being felt—that is, when they acquire perceptual representation—brings them partially out of the somatic realm. As sensory experiences they become part of an interaction with the outer world. They are upward extensions of basically somatic disruptions, but they become involved in an object relations context. Thus hypochondriasis becomes a mode of relating that helps maintain psychic synthesis.

As is true of many psychic processes, hypochondriasis, which is initially a somatic prementational phase disruption, is a manifestation not only of attempts at integration but also of disintegrative phenomena. This has already been discussed in reference to splitting mechanisms and dissociative phenomena. The role of hypochondriasis and other types of somatic disruptions has to be evaluated during treatment, and the therapist has to determine where they fit in the context of the therapeutic interaction of the moment. As stated, they may be indications of a striving for self-healing or they may refer to the opposite, a further ego disintegration and a loss of psychic synthesis as the psyche continues to fragment. Clinicians have to make both qualitative and quantitative distinctions to assess the therapeutic interaction.

The therapeutic interaction can become confusing, and the same fragmentation that is occurring within the patient's psyche can spread to the treatment relationship. The analyst may lose his orientation and narrow his perceptions to a split-off part, perhaps missing its constructive qualities; or the opposite may occur and the analyst may believe that the patient is making progress, whereas in fact he is further dissociating.

This is especially true when the analyst is caught in the middle of the vicious circle I mentioned; that is, the regaining of the missing part of the self is so painful that once it reenters the main psychic current it again causes cleavage; and the psyche, instead of achieving cohesion, fragments further. What is extruded becomes even more difficult to reintegrate, and this continues in an increasingly painful crescendo. Each session becomes more painful than the previous one, for both patient and analyst. Analysts often absorb the patient's pain and believe there is no constructive purpose to what is happening. They also react as if their professional self-representation is losing its cohesion. In other words, they feel fragmented as therapists, and their patients are not helping them regain cohesion.

This may sound strange, that is, attributing an obligation to patients to help their analysts from fragmenting as therapists. Nevertheless, in any successful therapeutic venture there is a reciprocal interplay that maintains a therapeutic momentum. This constitutes a positive feedback sequence that enhances the self-esteem of both the patient and therapist. Understanding leads to further understanding and eventually to higher levels of emotional cohesion.

Because of these interactions, encountered in the treatment of patients who belong in the borderline spectrum, many such patients have been considered to be untreatable; and indeed this is often the case. Nevertheless, if the analyst and patient can recognize that some of the pain experienced in the consultation room, instead of being disruptive and leading to an impasse, can be a manifestation of a healing process designed to establish cohesion, then it might be possible to successfully treat that patient. The analyst has to be able to look beyond the chaos and misery that surrounds him. He must not lose his therapeutic perspective and give in to the feelings of hopelessness that threaten to destroy the treatment setting.

A 19-year-old adolescent provides an example of how complex and confusing the treatment interaction can be and how it can degenerate into a nonproductive and even destructive relationship. Again, this was a situation in which fragmentation was a dominant aspect of psychopathology.

From the first session the patient bitterly complained that he was falling apart. He had seen three previous therapists, and after a short time they all had insisted on hospitalization. He lamented that he had no friends, no joy in life, and was totally unable to function. He was a college student and had managed to pass all his courses, although his performance was, at best, mediocre. He emphasized how hard everything in life was for him, and that if he did manage to complete a task, it was at a very great expense.

He seemed to be an example of the typical borderline patient as described in Chapter 4. The world was too complex for him. What was pedestrian for others was an overwhelming task that he had to struggle to accomplish. As he repeatedly stated, he did not have the adequate tools to deal with the problems that were inundating him. He felt that he was not put together well enough to face the trials and tribulations of everyday living.

In spite of his distressed attitude, he was remarkably coherent in his assessment of his previous therapists. When his therapists had suggested hospitalization he felt completely misunderstood. He viewed the suggestions that he be hospitalized as total rejections because they could not stand him. Whatever insecurities he had, which were accompanied by the anguish of hopelessness, only intensified as he was confronted with the prospect of hospitalization.

To his therapists this seemed strange. They had expected that he would feel some relief in a hospital setting because there he would get the care that he needed to help him "pull himself together." The patient told each of his therapists that they did not appreciate the depths of his distress. At first this seemed paradoxical, because they were recommending institutional care as they would for any very seriously disturbed patient. He later revealed that they did not understand that he was so disturbed that he would not be able to benefit from what the hospital staff and setting could offer him.

His mental state was further aggravated by severe attacks of asthma, which on several occasions caused him to be hospitalized on medical wards. In each instance his allergist called for a psychiatric consultation, and the patient was medicated. He was put on both alprazolam and haloperidol, which he bitterly resented. When discharged, he gave up the haloperidol but continued the alprazolam. He managed to see a psychiatrist who put him on a tricyclic antidepressant, and to this day he continues seeing this psychiatrist to monitor the medications.

Apparently what had happened to his therapists was exactly what he concluded. His analyst talked to two of his previous therapists, who still had strong feelings about the patient. They felt extremely frustrated as they continued witnessing his deteriorating condition. They believed that he was fragmenting on a daily basis, and they were powerless in their capacity to help him. They could not just stand by as their frustrations and agitation increased, so they recommended an inpatient setting, not so much to get him off their hands as to get him into a facility that could contain him. The settings they had provided obviously could not.

In addition to lamenting the sorry state of his psyche and soma (asthma), he began treatment by questioning its validity. He wondered whether psychotherapy or psychoanalysis could help him. He had already seen two analysts and he was no better; in fact, he was worse. He spent at least 3 months debating whether he should continue, and that question kept recurring after 3 years of treatment. He wondered whether some other approach might be helpful, although he kept lamenting that he was beyond help because he never received help or adequate care during infancy. In spite of the content of his material, his tone was less vociferous, and he acquired a modicum of comfort from the therapeutic relationship.

The treatment survived some very stormy moments, and it nearly underwent the same fate as his other therapeutic experiences. His therapist felt frustrated, as everyone else had, and apparently for the same reasons. With the patient, he also wondered if psychoanalytic psychotherapy was a wise choice, and the constant questioning began to irritate him. He felt that his professional competence, or rather the extent of his expertise, was being challenged.

In time, and after having received some supervision, he tried to view the patient's material as having some constructive potential. This attitude was somewhat reinforced by the information the patient had given him regarding his response to the efforts to hospitalize him. The fact that he felt his therapist had lost hope meant that possibly the patient was looking for someone who would not lose hope, which further meant that perhaps there was some hope. This was a solacing thought, which helped the therapist through a period when he was beginning to believe that treatment was a futile endeavor.

This glimmer of hope caused the therapist to view the patient's lamentations and tortured moments in terms of their adaptive potential, if any could be found. He told his patient that, rather than both of them simply witnessing his mental disintegration, perhaps there was some purpose to his feeling so terribly disrupted and in pain, both mentally and physically. The patient was silent for about a minute and then began sobbing and crying. This was quite different from his usual tense behavior. He cried quietly and seemed to be feeling more deeply than when in the throes of agitation. He now indicated where his previous therapists had failed him. They were trying to get him to feel better and rid him of painful ego states. They did not allow him to experience these early states of primitive agitation in their presence. They believed that as long as the patient felt the way he did, they were failing him, whereas the patient believed the exact opposite. He had to have a setting in which he could allow inner tension to emerge, and this would not be in a hospital where efforts would be made to give him relief, most likely through medications.

This patient indicated later in treatment that he was trying, like the patient previously described, to reintegrate lost parts of the self. I will not pursue this topic further or explore childhood antecedents. I wish instead to emphasize the enormous technical difficulties analysts have to face when dealing with patients who feel fragmented both mentally and somatically.

Therapists are faced with a paradox, paradoxes being very common occurrences during the treatment of patients in the borderline spectrum. The patient creates an atmosphere of painful failure, feelings that are the manifestations of attempts at self-healing. The curative process, that is, the striving to achieve cohesion and integration, is experienced as explosively destructive. The analyst believes he is witnessing a disintegrative process and does not want to be a participant. As he finds himself being drawn in to the patient's turmoil, he feels he is not providing him with a helpful interaction and attempts to counter what he considers to be a deepening disintegrative process. Increased somatic distress and an intensification of hypochondriacal complaints only serve to create further chaos.

The feeling of failure pervades the consultation room and, as mentioned, leads to a destructive chain reaction. Although these patients vociferously complain about their lack of cohesion and the misery they are experiencing, they are basically trying to reestablish unity through that pain. If analysts accept their lamentations at face value and also view them as phenomena, then they lose their healing potential.

The patient often blames the analyst for their disruptive state and the lack of therapeutic progress. I recall a patient who blamed me for all the misery she ever had experienced. On the surface, this was absurd because I was being held responsible for her distress in the years before she had ever been in therapy. The patient I am discussing also took his therapist to task for having created his distress. At one level both patients were correct.

The therapist's nonrecognition of the positive adaptive aspects of the symptoms and his exclusive concentration on their destructive qualities only served to accentuate their disintegrative features. It was this accentuation that the patient was referring to when he accused the analyst of being the source of his misery. To some extent, the analyst's focusing on the negative obliterated the positive, and the patient experienced this change of balance as an intensification of emotional imbalance that accompanies fragmentation. Thus the analyst's reaction produces an increment that the patient views as an iatrogenic creation, which leads to further havoc and an antitherapeutic, confusing perspective.

If the analyst does not perceive this negative feedback sequence and therefore does not act to break the cycle, this leads to a situation that may interfere with the patient's attempts at reparation, making the analyst the traumatic source. It was a traumatic infantile environment that was initially responsible for the lack of emotional development and the formation of a fragmented psyche. Ordinarily, because of the repetition compulsion, the traumatic infantile environment is re-created in the consultation room. If the analyst cannot perceive the patient's restitutive efforts, then he has unwittingly allied himself with destructive rather than constructive forces. Not only has he accepted the projections of the repetition compulsion, but he has also, on his own, so to speak, introduced an antitherapeutic perspective. This becomes increasingly chaotic because the analyst believes he is trying to be helpful and to save the patient from an uncontrollable regression, whereas in fact any active attempt to alleviate inner pain is counterproductive and is viewed unconsciously or even consciously by the patient as a traumatic impingement.

Patients may also be unaware of what is happening. If they remain in treatment, they eventually recognize their efforts at self-reparation, but the meaning of their behavior may be in the realm of unconscious strivings, and the analyst's ignorance can have devastating effects on the stability of the therapeutic interaction.

In these circumstances, analysts may find themselves flooded by disruptive countertransference feelings. They are faced with the paradox that therapeutic efforts become part of a damaging trauma. Their usual defense is to blame the patient for the negative turn of events. Their condemnation of the patient is more often covert than overt. They are likely to make formulations about the untreatability of this very difficult group of patients.

Indeed, this is a very difficult group of patients, but, as is true of most patients found in the borderline spectrum, closer understanding of the interplay of structural defects and the analyst being able to expand his vision beyond the obvious disruption the patient presents can, in some instances, lead to a helpful therapeutic experience. If clinicians adopt an attitude that stresses the primacy of structure, as Althea Horner (1991) does, it becomes possible to view from a broader perspective various phenomena that had been diagnosed as malignant regressions and to harness them to achieve higher levels of psychic integration and cohesion, an upward progression from a psychopathologically fixated and fragmented ego state.

6

The Concrete Patient,
Massive Trauma, and
the Psychosomatic Focus

All of the patients who have been discussed in previous chapters have had depriving and traumatic infantile environments. They have suffered varying degrees of privation and deprivation, as Winnicott (1963b) has described. Therapeutically, they pose specific and difficult problems that have to be understood in the context of structural psychopathology if therapy has any hope of achieving some degree of resolution.

The patients I am about to describe have also had very traumatic childhoods, even more traumatic than those just described, if such comparisons are possible. Many of the patients I will discuss have been physically assaulted and sexually abused.

Clinicians are confronted with an ever-increasing number of patients, especially women, who report episodes of incest and other types of sexual abuse during childhood and adolescence. Freud (1896), at one time, believed that the cause of hysteria was seduction during early childhood, around the ages of 3 or 4. The child, usually a girl, played a passive role as she was approached by an older person, usually the father. Freud also discussed an older male child, around the age of 7, being the active seducer but later suffering from remorse and guilt feelings. He would develop an obsessive-compulsive neurosis. Freud further believed that this child had also been the passive victim of sexual abuse at an earlier age.

Later, as is well known, Freud (1905a) changed his mind and instead believed that when patients were discussing childhood sexual experiences, these were not actual experiences but fantasies, often wish-fulfillment fantasies. This did not mean that sexual traumas did not occur or did not produce neuroses; rather, he was challenging the universality of such occurrences.

Recently, Freud has been attacked for having given up his so-called seduction hypothesis. He has been criticized for believing that his patients were reporting fantasies rather than facts. Presumably, then, the cause of all emotional problems is a childhood sexual violation. This would mean that every patient who seeks psychiatric consultation or psychotherapy has been a victim of sexual abuse, which is a blatant absurdity. Nevertheless, a large number of patients claim that they have been sexually assaulted, and in numerous instances it has been possible to verify these claims. The question arises as to why there has been such an increase in the number of patients who allege that they have been sexually mistreated, particularly in the past decade. These are often highly concretely oriented patients.

Perhaps the situation is the same as that which occurred with homosexuality. Clinicians doubt that there are more homosexuals today than a generation ago. It is believed that with a more accepting and tolerant environment, they have come out of the closet. They do not see the need to hide their sexual preference. Similarly, victims of sexual abuse, especially after hearing about other such victims, feel encouraged to reveal their traumatic backgrounds.

The situation, however, is not that simple. Many of these patients are defensive and afraid of revealing what went on in the family. As children, these patients were threatened not to discuss or admit that there had been incestuous relationships. Regardless of the tumultuous atmosphere that characterized family interactions, these traumatized patients need to maintain the familial balance, and no matter how much they are suffering, they do not want to disrupt it.

Nevertheless, many patients openly discuss their childhood or adolescent sexual experiences. I find it especially interesting to note that some patients who have been in treatment for many years recently have begun to remember instances of sexual abuse.

A middle-aged woman who had been in treatment for 15 years and who had never reported such an incident began to remember an episode with an uncle who enticed her at the age of 6 into kissing his penis. I state "began to remember" because, at first, she was highly uncertain as to the reality of this incident. As she concentrated on the past, the memory of that experience became clearer and more distinct. She then further remembered other situations in which this same uncle had her masturbate him, an activity that lasted until she was 8 years old. Although she had been in treatment for many years, the material was especially meaningful and represented a breakthrough in the analytic process.

Therapists may wonder why it took so many years for such material to emerge. They may note that the climate is especially propitious in that more and more such incidents are being openly discussed. They may even wonder if this is a histrionic reconstruction and, as Freud surmised, based more on wishful fantasy than on historical truth (Spence 1982). The fact that it represented a breakthrough would not be particularly relevant, because psychoanalysts know how powerful fantasies can be and what far-reaching and sometimes devastating effects they can have when they come to the surface.

Clinicians also know that traumatic memories can be deeply repressed. In fact, as discussed in Chapter 2, it was such an insight that led to the discovery of psychoanalysis. Consequently, some patients may have to struggle for many years before they can get in touch with such memories. The calm acceptance by the external world, rather than its shocked rejecting reaction, may encourage the uncovering process. The milieu may have been the variable that permitted what had been repressed to emerge.

The aforementioned patient is in many respects different from those whom I will soon discuss. To begin, she was psychologically minded and was able to free-associate with relative ease. Her parents were unstable people, but they provided a fairly secure and safe setting. It was not an environment in which she was bombarded by disruptive external stimuli. Her mother was able, to some extent, to provide her with a protective shield.

It was not a sufficiently secure environment, however, to protect her as much as she needed to be protected. She was raised in what she called a noisy atmosphere but not a turbulent and highly disruptive milieu. She had a large extended family—aunts, uncles, cousins, and grandparents— and in her early childhood some relative or relatives lived in her household, including the uncle she believed had "seduced" her. To some extent, she had internalized aspects of her early environment that caused her to feel constantly agitated.

SOMATIC PROCESSES AND PSYCHIC INTEGRATION

Patients who fall within the borderline spectrum are frequently agitated, and, as has been discussed, their inner disruption stems from prementational levels. Attempts at soothing often involve somatic processes, which are manifested by psychosomatic symptoms and a concrete perspective.

In Chapter 5 I discussed hypochondriasis, which can be considered to be a link between the psyche and soma. Hypochondriacal preoccupation serves as a defensive organizer. Focusing on the soma has a binding effect and maintains a type of integration and integrity.

Hypochondriacal symptoms are the manifestations of a particular type of psychic integration that involves object relationships and, at the same time, is associated with withdrawal or a partial withdrawal from the external world. As Freud (1923) stated, the ego is first and foremost a body ego, meaning that the interface of the ego and the outer world that contains the soma as the skin is the periphery facing reality. The mind is somewhere behind the soma. Hypochondriacal preoccupation and psychosomatic symptoms are located at this interface. Insofar as patients' preoccupations are at the borderland between the internal and external world, they are directed toward both the inner and outer, representing a focus toward reality and the inside at the same time. Thus somatic fixations have the qualities of both object relations and withdrawal from object relations *qualities*.

As discussed in Chapter 5, both hypochondriasis and psychosomatic phenomena become means of communication, directing the ego toward the external world of object relations. As stated, these are secondary defensive functions.

Whatever degree of stabilization is achieved by somatic dysfunctions is still the outcome of psychopathology based on splitting mechanisms that may be the result of defensive regression or the lack of development of integrated and synthesized ego states. The psyche is fixed on a transitional area, the interface between the inner and outer world, and although these are somatically based object relations, these patients are, in an emotional sense, frozen. Affective exchanges are confined to reactions about somatic turmoil. Object relations revolve around a narcissistic axis. Thus the capacity to become truly involved with the external world is limited.

Focusing on the body draws attention away from the mind. These patients are concretely oriented and show no appreciation of the concept of psychic determinism. Understandably, this would make them difficult to treat in a psychoanalytic frame of reference, and in some instances, initially attempting psychoanalysis is a fruitless if not ludicrous approach.

It is as if psychopathology creates a Cartesian dualism. Rather than a smooth continuum between somatic activities and mental processes, the mind and body are split off from each other. This is another type of dissociation, which emphasizes different parts of the psychic apparatus. Ordinarily, clinicians think of the splitting of various parts of the mind, whereas with concrete and psychosomatic patients I am stressing a separation of the psyche from the soma.

To be more accurate, I am still discussing a splitting of various parts of the mind, but the parts involved include that section of the psyche that contains somatic representations. Again, clinicians have to determine whether this division of the mind is the outcome of defective development or regression. The former would be characterized by an extremely rigid, concrete orientation, whereas the latter would be found in patients who might have reached a level of integration that permits a significant degree of psychological mindedness and therefore makes them more amenable to psychoanalytic treatment. I will soon discuss this type of clinical interaction.

I believe that concreteness and dissociation of the somatic parts of the psyche from the psychologically oriented mind is often found in patients who seek and cling to biological theories of etiology of emotional disorders. These patients forcefully resist any explanations that refer to intrapsychic etiologies. For these patients, all disturbances are the outcome of somatic processes and have to be understood on a somatic basis. However, the soma is viewed as being outside the self, so they feel that the sources of their difficulties also reside in the external world. They refuse to accept an intrapsychic contribution to their problems, thereby abnegating any responsibility for the production of emotional dysharmony. Many psychiatrists reinforce these patients' concreteness and dissociation by stressing biological sources and totally ignoring intrapsychic elements.

The reinforcement of a characterological defect may help alleviate symptoms, but it may also lead to a state of frustrated hopelessness. I have seen several patients who have had every drug imaginable and their conditions had only worsened. Finally, in desperation they sought psychotherapy. Unfortunately, in some instances, because of their concreteness, psychotherapy was also ineffective, but there have been other patients who were able to relate and to improve in a psychoanalytic context.

As mentioned in the Preface, psychoanalysts are not finding many patients who are psychoanalytically treatable. Furthermore, it has been stated that patients are no longer as interested in being analyzed as they had been in past decades. They want symptomatic relief but do not care to become involved in self-examination. This attitude is in keeping with their concrete orientation, which is supported by many elements of society, especially biologically oriented psychiatrists as well as other physicians. This implies that the surrounding world makes a contribution to the production of structural psychopathology, which, in turn, determines whether a patient is analyzable.

It is difficult to believe that cultural influences are etiological factors in the causation of structural defects. The converse, however, is more plausible; that is, that the population of patients within the borderline spectrum contributes to the shaping of the current milieu. Concretely oriented patients would produce segments of society that are concretely oriented. Then these segments would reinforce and justify the rigid concrete positions these patients hold. There is a reciprocal relationship between the culture and certain character configurations, which has cast shadows on the value of the psychoanalytic method.

STRUCTURAL DISCONTINUITY AND THE PSYCHOSOMATIC FOCUS

Nevertheless, in spite of the patient's concreteness and focus on somatic symptoms, it is sometimes possible to engage such a patient in a psychoanalytic relationship.

I will begin this section with a clinical example.

The patient, a middle-aged professional man, was pushed into treatment by his wife and friends as a last desperate attempt to save his life. He was severely depressed and was suffering from a life-threatening regional ileitis (Crohn's disease). At the time he entered treatment, he was unable to work and was severely debilitated. He was about 50 pounds underweight and so weak that he could hardly climb stairs. He was extremely thin and emaciated.

His therapist found that gathering information about him was a tedious task, because he was cryptic and usually gave monosyllabic answers to questions. Furthermore, he seemed to totally lack an intrapsychic focus. His attitude was concretely oriented, and he looked for the causes of his difficulties in the outside world or in somatic processes rather than considering the possibility that something inside, that is, in his mind, might be a factor in the production of his emotional and physical problems. He was typical of the group of patients I referred to in the preceding chapter.

The analyst felt discouraged about the prospects of being able to analyze or otherwise help him. In the third session, he discussed free association with him and suggested that he use the couch. He did not believe that the patient understood a word he said, but he was glad that the patient did not object to lying down on the couch. In fact, the patient seemed eager to be on the couch.

He did not free-associate; instead, he instantly fell asleep. His analyst was surprised, but he had no inclination to wake him up. He let him sleep through the entire session. At the end of the session, he awakened him and gave him his schedule for the following week. The analyst anticipated that the patient would not return, feeling that he was wasting his time, as would be in keeping with his practical and thrifty outlook. On the contrary, he was eager to get his appointments and seemed obviously pleased with his therapeutic experience.

For several months the patient said nothing except the usual amenities at the beginning and the end of the session. He slept throughout the rest of the session and found this sleep refreshing, whereas otherwise he suffered from insomnia and could not get any rest. The analyst's office was the only place he could sleep and relax without medications. Furthermore, for the first time he could remember in many years, he began to dream.

He felt better in all aspects of his life. He could now work part-time, had regained considerable strength, and his depression was lifting as he discontinued all medications. What was most remarkable was that a barium enema revealed that there was no trace whatsoever of an inflamed bowel. His regional ileitis disappeared and has not returned in over 20 years.

Gradually, the patient began to talk as he told his analyst the dreams he had while he slept in the office. Some of them were frightening in that he dreamed of monsters and other threatening figures chasing or attacking him. Nevertheless, he was proud of his new-found capacity to dream, and though the act of dreaming could be uncomfortable, he felt better because he saw himself more as a whole person. He believed it was important and helpful to perceive and experience feelings, impulses, and parts of the self that were lost to him as he was swallowed by depression, and his bowel seemed to express his inner chaos and destructiveness.

Before proceeding further with a discussion of how this patient's inner structure required precisely what the analyst provided, I wish to discuss how colleagues reacted to the presentation of this case. The analyst presented the first months of treatment when the patient was almost totally silent. He was immediately attacked for "allowing" the patient to sleep. He should have intervened and interpreted that the patient was resisting free association and withdrawing from the treatment by preventing himself from experiencing transference feelings.

The therapist protested that the patient had a transference, a positive transference, manifested by his eagerness about keeping his appointments and his dependence on them. The therapist further asserted that he strongly believed that if he had prohibited him from sleeping he would have lost the patient. Some of his colleagues agreed with him but added that rather than letting the patient continue in this travesty of analysis, it would be best to confront him to determine whether he wanted or did not want to be analyzed. Analysis had become an end in itself.

The patient's concrete orientation and his misery and moribund state would have made such a confrontation meaningless. The patient indicated that he was naive about analysis and he sought it, as he would seek a new miracle drug, because he was told to do so on the assumption or hope that it might help him, perhaps save his life. His initial orientation, as revealed in his history, was almost exclusively somatic. He intensely focused on his bowel problems and physical incapacities and showed no propensity for introspection and insight.

Everybody in the seminar group agreed that the patient desperately needed help and that paying attention to his emotional problems would be useful. They questioned whether the analytic approach was feasible, that is, asking him to lie on the couch and to free-associate, especially because he would rather sleep than free-associate.

A patient once stated that the aim of treatment was not symptomatic remission but the fostering of autonomy, which might, in turn, lead to symptomatic resolution. We can apply these criteria to the treatment of my colleague's patient. Regarding the formal accoutrements of analysis, the patient lay down on the couch when it was suggested, but instead of talking he remained quiet and fell asleep. The analyst did not attempt to interpret the meaning of this behavior, partly because he did not know what it meant, but neither did he make an effort to try to understand it, as by questioning the patient or asking him to at least discuss why he wanted to use all of this expensive time merely to sleep. The analyst intuitively felt that if he had pursued such tactics, the patient would have found them destructively intrusive. Most likely, he would not have been able to say anything that would clarify the situation, and perhaps he would be sufficiently disturbed that he would flee from treatment. Nothing would be gained.

Both the therapist and I believed that, especially with regressed and borderline patients, the principal analytic task is to create a setting in which the patient can comfortably regress. To let this patient sleep comfortably represented the construction of such a setting. To have interfered with this regression would have been antianalytic. True, the patient was not free-associating but he was behaving autonomously in that he was doing what he apparently felt he needed to, and this was confirmed later in treatment.

The therapist was accused by his colleagues of encouraging the patient to act out by not stopping him. As we later learned, the patient was finally able to fulfill even the most rigid requirements of analysis; he was able to free-associate and developed a full-blown transference neurosis. Obviously, this would not have happened if he had run away from treatment.

Winnicott (1955) has emphasized that the treatment of borderline and psychotic patients requires management before analysis is possible. He was one of the first analysts who believed that these patients needed a support system, a holding environment, something that they lacked in infancy. The patient found a place where he could sleep without sedatives, a sleep that was restorative. He had been able to construct a safe haven, an effective holding environment. He could allow himself to be vulnerable and regress because he viewed the therapeutic setting as protective. But there was more to his early treatment than just the construction of a setting that the patient could trust.

By sleeping, he was in fact fulfilling the goals of even the most classical analyses if those goals involve making the unconscious conscious, an endeavor that Freud (1912) constantly stressed. Prior to treatment, the patient seemed to have no concept of an unconscious mind. As stated, he was concretely oriented and incapable of viewing mental phenomena from a psychological perspective. His approach was mechanistic and he could think only in terms of external sources to explain why he felt as he did. It seemed as if he were totally out of touch with his unconscious. He acted as if he operated only on the surface, as if he did not have an unconscious, and knew nothing about unconscious motivation.

Sleeping and dreaming produced profound changes in his mode of relating. His dreams indicated that he had an unconscious and that he was capable of getting in touch with it. He could now distinguish the inner world of the psyche from external reality and recognize that the sources of his pain and misery resided within himself, within his psyche. He was no longer as concrete nor as fragmented as he had been.

His previous psychic configuration has to be distinguished from splitting mechanisms, which have defensive functions. The patient was not reacting defensively. His concreteness and disjointed psyche were characteristic of his personality makeup and not a manifestation of splitting defenses. They were manifestations of faulty and traumatic development, but as such, they did not represent specific defensive reactions. Because he had faulty psychic structures, he had to construct defensive adaptations in order to be able to relate to the vicissitudes of external reality. In a sense, he was defending himself against ego defects, rather than the splitting of the ego itself being a defense. I believe that many borderline patients who seem to be using splitting and projective defenses (Grotstein 1981, Ogden 1982) are in fact demonstrating a basic psychic configuration, as has been discussed.

This patient suffered from psychic discontinuity. He had no smooth continuum from primitive, unconscious primary-process structures to higher, reality-oriented, secondary-process ego organizations. He demonstrated a particular type of fragmentation in which various parts of the psyche were isolated from each other, islands without connecting bridges. This is still a split psyche, but the spaces between various psychic structures assume greater significance in the production of emotional disturbances than has been assigned to them. They are particularly important in the production of psychosomatic symptoms, as has been discussed and will be discussed further.

I have discussed elsewhere (Giovacchini 1979) a patient who somatically illustrated a similarly fragmented or a disjointed and discontinuous psyche.

The patient, a young adult, would suddenly and unexpectedly scream, twist his neck, and writhe as if he were experiencing intense pain. He would then continue free-associating without referring to this strange outburst. During one session he had about 20 such episodes. Some were so violent that he appeared to be having a grand mal seizure.

I finally called attention to this bizarre behavior and conjectured that, perhaps, he was warding off a blow that he was expecting from me. He indicated that he did not believe it was related to an interpersonal experience. Rather, he felt that something, a feeling or impulse, deep inside him was struggling to emerge. He referred to a Van de Graaf generator, which consists of two vertical electrodes with spheres on top. A current is sent through one of the electrodes until it reaches a certain potential, at which point a spark jumps across an empty space onto the other electrode. He also discussed a machine in a science fiction movie in which a scientist would somehow transmit raw feelings, such as anger or lust, and through the machine they would be "refined" and elevated to the status of logical and, perhaps, abstruse thoughts. On a final occasion some of the fuses within the machine are damaged, and as the scientist feeds his feelings into it, it explodes.

These are graphic descriptions of a psyche that has no intermediary links or bridges between lower and upper levels of the psychic apparatus. These bridges are similar to transformers, psychic transformers, that process and modulate raw impulses as they move upward from primary-process to secondary-process operations. It is interesting that this patient had many dreams of collapsing bridges or of bridges just hanging in empty space without shores at either end.

This so-called empty space or lacuna requires further elaboration. Is it really empty? My colleague's patient had regional ileitis, a serious somatic disorder, alongside a concrete orientation that seemed to be the outcome of a lack of communication between the id and the ego, an inner lacuna between different psychic levels. When he was able to make contact with his unconscious, he no longer had regional ileitis. In other words, when he no longer had an inner lacuna, he was free of his somatic disturbance. Is it possible that, mentally speaking, the regional ileitis was related to these empty spaces and that it represented a psychic representation of the lack of connecting bridges?

Lacunae and emptiness point to the lack of psychological content rather than to total emptiness. I have described a prementational phase, a beginning stage of emotional development (Boyer and Giovacchini 1967, 1980, Giovacchini 1986), as discussed in Chapter 3. Disturbances of this stage can be detected in later psychopathology, and the data indicate that such disturbances are accompanied by somatic disturbances. Inasmuch as the prementational phase precedes psychological representation and the formation of psychic structures, it can be thought of as the center of a psychosomatic focus. The empty spaces that characterize psychopathology are somatically organized and devoid of psychic content. They occur as fixations on the prementational phase, a phase that has undergone an incomplete or defective development on its journey to the construction of psychic systems.

This defective development leads to what might be considered a lopsided psyche. I realize I am indulging in imprecise imagery, but I find it useful in making clinical assessments. When dealing with borderline and other severely regressed patients, clinicians are often struck by the lack of an orderly, sequential emotional development and the chaos arising from a lack of cohesive inner organization. Many of these patients are uncoordinated and physically clumsy, a somatic manifestation of psychic disjointedness.

Another patient, a woman in her early thirties, depicted her psychic structure in dreams. These are representational dreams that emphasize the architecture of the mind rather than id–ego compromises symbolically expressed. The latter elements are not necessarily excluded from these dreams, but they are simply not dominant. Freud (1900) referred to Silberer's "functional dreams," which illustrated various psychic activities. The dreams I am discussing here are similar to these functional dreams, but they encompass wider expanses of the psychic apparatus and their interconnections.

This patient dreamed of a group of islands surrounded by infested waters. Some of the islands also had small swamps and cesspools full of rotten vegetation and decaying carcasses. The patient would find herself on an island that was in the center of this archipelago but she wanted to cross over to an adjoining one. There was no way of doing this except to swim over because there were no connecting bridges. She would not get into the water because it was so virulent that it would kill her.

For example, in one dream the island was overrun with rats, and she felt cornered because she could not escape to another island. She would awaken in a state of panic. But the themes of danger, lack of connections, and feeling trapped were constant in all of her dreams.

When she had such dreams, she felt totally unable to function. She felt trapped in her house, being able to leave only for her sessions. She was in a constant near-panic state, which was not affected by medications. At times, her distress assumed paranoidlike proportions, although her feelings were not as systematized as is seen in a full-blown paranoia. She might feel that she was so loathsome that her husband might want to kill her and for a few minutes she could believe that he was actually plotting her murder, but these moments were short-lived.

She also felt that she suffered from multiple personalities, although this belief was, in some measure, stimulated by some articles she had read in a popular psychology magazine. She was referring to different mood and behavioral states that fluctuated widely during the course of the day. They did not have the organization or cohesiveness required to label them as separate personalities.

In fact, she felt severely disorganized and described herself as being scattered. She did not have the subjective experience of feeling herself as a synthesized whole. In this mental state she tended to polarize her surroundings and persons in terms of good and bad, although most of them were in the bad category.

It was interesting that she viewed her body as a bad object. The soma became the enemy as she suffered from innumerable physical difficulties. She complained of aches and pains all over her body, which often localized in certain joints that were diagnosed as being arthritically inflamed. She also had intense migrainelike headaches, and she occasionally had rashes on both forearms, which were thought to be allergic. The rash itched intensely and reminded her of a festering sore, exuding pus. It was not, but the colors in the rash made it appear as if it were. She also had severe gastrointestinal symptoms—cramps, nausea, vomiting, and diarrhea—to the extent that her internist referred her to a surgeon.

The patient's reaction to her illnesses was terror. She felt overwhelmed by her body and was afraid she was going to die. She thought of her body as being polluted and, in her fragmented way, feared that it was determined to kill her.

It was interesting to note how she had personified the soma as if it were not connected to herself. She also believed it was the source of all her difficulties and, as she put it, it was tearing her apart.

I was particularly impressed by her descriptions of festering, pus-producing sores and her polluted body. Her body might have been represented in her dreams by cesspools and polluted *bodies* of water. Her soma seemed to be suffering from the same putrid decay as was found in the pools and the sea surrounding the pools. The fright she felt in the dreams of falling into the sea was similar to the terror she experienced when she feared that her body was going to swallow her up. In fact, she had difficulty breathing, perhaps a bronchospasm that made her feel as if she were drowning.

The sea determined that the lands it surrounded were islands. It represented the lacunae that I have discussed and was responsible for the psyche's fragmented state. As these dreams graphically illustrate, lacunae are not empty spaces, as was represented in the space between the two spheres of the Van de Graaf generator my patient described. The patient with Crohn's disease was conceptualized as having an intermediary space between the unconscious and conscious, an area that contained a psychosomatic focus, an area of turbulent somatic activity rather than a psychic vacuum. Similarly, this patient had many spaces between the islands of her mind but they, too, were not empty. They could be conceptualized in the same way as they were with the man who slept on the couch. They might be devoid of psychic content, but they contained all sorts of virulent matter, a pictorial representation of the turbulent, disruptive somatic processes that were expressed in her numerous symptoms and illnesses. Again, we can think of these premental, or better stated, nonmentational, states in terms of a psychosomatic focus.

It is possible that some physical disturbances that have been considered to be psychosomatic might be associated with the fragmented psychic organization I have just described. Of course, psychosomatic illnesses cannot be so simply explained; there must be many complex variables involved in such complicated processes. Nevertheless, the characterological constellations of such patients must have some relevance.

The patients I have described, those with a psychosomatic focus, do not characteristically employ splitting and projective defenses. Their general psychic status quo is that of a split or fragmented self, a basic rather than a defensive organization. Again, this is not absolute, and the patient whose dreams I described used projective defenses, as evidenced by an inclination toward paranoid thinking.

I now wish to point to another group of patients who primarily use projective and splitting defenses as a reaction to uncontrollable inner and outer trauma, which, like an earthquake, causes fissures and cavities in the psychic apparatus. They undergo tremendous stress, which tears them apart as their basic unity is destroyed. Splitting and projection are defensively used to introduce some order into what otherwise would be the total disintegration of psychotic collapse. These defenses produce an orderly disintegration, permitting the ego to split to a certain degree but no further.

In many ways these patients resemble the patients previously discussed. They may also present disjointed psychic states with lacunae and a lack of connecting bridges. This organization, however, represents a regressed psychic state, a defense against overwhelming trauma and painful inner feelings. These patients' backgrounds and infantile worlds have been unbelievably cruel, disruptive, and sexually abusive compared with those of other groups of patients.

Many of these patients are reputed to be suffering from multiple personality disorders, indicating that there has been a highly organized splitting or dissociative reaction to the early abusive behavior. I will not discuss multiple personalities per se, because I have never seen such a patient, but I have encountered patients who have been brutally abused, and whose psychopathology revealed badly damaged egos on the verge of collapse manifested by unbearable waves of terror and acute psychic pain.

The following vignette illustrates a peculiar combination of states of inner emptiness that are experienced as extremely painful and disruptive.

The patient, now in her fifties, had spent a good portion of her adult life in mental institutions. At times she was diagnosed as schizophrenic, but most of the time her reality testing seemed intact and she did not exhibit the bizarre thinking of a thought disorder. Rather, she was extremely agitated, most of the time verging on a state of panic.

Medications might temporarily help, but she usually developed a tolerance to the new drugs that were constantly prescribed. She would be hospitalized when she was helplessly nonfunctional and could no longer sustain herself in the external world. I found it odd that after she was discharged she did not seek, nor did anyone suggest, psychotherapy. She was simply maintained on a drug regimen, which eventually led to another hospitalization. A psychiatrist, a relative of hers in another city, insisted that she contact me for psychoanalytic treatment. Though she could have violent and turbulent reactions, she could also be unusually compliant, so she arranged an appointment.

When I first saw her, she was acutely agitated. She found it difficult to sit quietly, and she would pace back and forth in a small area of my office. She wrung her hands and frequently wiped the perspiration from her brow with her handkerchief. Before we started to look into her background she asked me, in a desperate voice, for a glass of water. I had no water in the refrigerator, so I put some ice in tap water and gave her a glass. She took a short, quick sip and then dipped her handkerchief in the water and continued wiping her brow. Then she took the ice from the glass and wrapped it in the handkerchief and once more rubbed it against her brow and temples. This was not always a gentle movement. Occasionally she struck the ice against various parts of her head and face with sufficient force that it must have been painful, and, in fact, she sometimes winced after such a blow.

Her speech was as agitated as her behavior. Her flow was rapid and the tone of her voice was tremulous. She pleaded with me not to make any demands of her because she was afraid she would collapse.

During the main part of the first session she presented herself as a helpless, panic-stricken infant. In the last 10 minutes, however, there was a dramatic change in her demeanor. She became querulous and challenging. What made me think that I would be able to help her? No one had ever been able to make her feel better, not even the most powerful drugs in the world.

She then barraged me with a series of questions regarding my qualifications and experiences with difficult patients such as herself. She also had a typewritten sheet describing various situations that might occur between patient and therapist, and in each case she wanted to know how I would react. She was asking about the limits of my tolerance. Apparently my responses were moderately satisfactory in that she was willing to continue our relationship.

Her background was so horribly traumatic that it seemed unbelievable. To this day, I wonder about the balance between fact and fantasy, but in view of her vulnerability, anxiety, and rage, there must have been considerable fact interwoven with the fantasies. She reported that as far back as she could remember, around the age of 3, she was brutally beaten by both her mother and father. She also had memories, presumably dating back to age 7, of a group of people dressed in black robes standing in a circle with her in the center, bound hand and foot. The men in the group approached her one by one and stuffed their erect penises in her mouth, almost choking her to death. Then the women would beat her across the abdomen with leather thongs. When discussing this presumably satanic ritual, she screamed, cried, and convulsively sobbed. At one point she actually fell off the couch and started coughing and choking as if she were drowning.

Her infancy was described in terms of one horror after another. Between the ages of 6 and 16, she was repeatedly raped by her father and then beaten by her mother. The mother frequently participated in these sexual violations by pinning her daughter so her father could enter her with the least exertion. She recalled many instances when her parents, on the maid's night out, would be gone for many hours, leaving her alone but chained in a dark closet. There were other occasions when she claimed that she was kept in that closet for days at a time.

During her adolescence her father drowned in a boating accident. Because he was an alcoholic it was assumed that he was drunk. Her mother is still alive, living the life of a grand dame in an expensive style. She is also an alcoholic and can be counted on as sober only before lunch. Before passing out at night she tends toward violence, and the servants have to protect the furniture. This family is quite wealthy, a factor, I believe, that kept the parents from being committed.

Although the patient was practically nonfunctional, she managed to live alone in an apartment. She also had considerable musical talent and was able to practice long hours. On occasion she would make public appearances. It was hard to reconcile the image of virtuosity with the helpless, tearful panic states that characterized most of her behavior in my office or on the telephone.

During the first year of her treatment, she presented herself primarily as a terrified woman. She vehemently accused me of hating her, and of feeling that she was a vicious worm that should be stepped on and crushed. She would feel worse after each session, and frequently she would go directly home and spend the rest of the day screaming. Partly, this was because she actually felt physical pain—sharp, jabbing pains throughout her whole body and hot flashes that made her feel she was being burned alive. Even more disruptive was her mental anguish. She stressed a pervasive and invasive sense of emptiness that reduced her to a state of "agitated nothingness" and caused her to disparage herself emotionally and physically. As with the previous patient, she despised her body. Furthermore, she felt herself to be a completely worthless person who should be eliminated from this world as expeditiously as possible. She was able to project these attitudes in the transference and was frightened that I would attack her.

I had to be very careful with my interpretations. If I remained silent, she despaired because I was abandoning her and would not talk because I loathed her. If I made interpretations, she would accept them only as criticisms and attacks. For example, if I tried to correct some distortion about my feelings, then I was indicating I had no respect for her judgment and capacity to perceive. This was even true of her most negative and disruptive feelings and attitudes, which she attributed to me. I might be feeling quite cheerful and grateful to her because I believed I had learned something from her that was clinically useful. Then, she might misperceive my mental state and insist that I could not stand her presence and wanted to kill her. Calmly, I would point out that since she perceived the entire world as blatantly destructive, it was not surprising that I, as part of the world, be experienced in the same fashion. She immediately took what I said to mean that she was so stupid that she could not distinguish her feelings from her perceptions. I had no faith in her judgments and evaluations; therefore, I loathed her.

Eventually I became aware of feeling some irritation. Everything I tried to do was, from her viewpoint, an attack, whereas I was trying to be helpful. I could understand her lack of trust and her anticipation that she was the target of external destructive forces, but her accusations were beginning to wear me down. I felt there was nothing I could do for her that would not be misconstrued as an attack.

I finally decided that I would try to interpret on another plane than that which focuses on projections of internal reactions to the infantile milieu. I wanted to go one step beyond her feelings, because I was not able to get her to accept their transference significance. She believed they were realistically based, and this could be viewed as a transference psychosis. As gently as I could, I pointed out that she had difficulties in availing herself of potentially helpful experiences. Before I could go on, she barked that I saw her as defective. Although she thought this was true, she felt I was being sadistically cruel in shamelessly confronting her with her senseless handicaps.

Inasmuch as everything I said or any experiences she had were viewed as an attack, her orientation was paranoid, and clinicians know how futile it is to directly confront paranoid patients. The traditional paranoid splits internal objects into good and bad and then projects the bad objects into the external world, which is then filled with persecutors.

My patient's paranoid phenomenology did not have the fixed delusional rigidity of paranoid characters or paranoid schizophrenia. Her infantile world was in fact persecuting and assaulting, and she has incorporated these experiences as hateful introjects. Her view of the world, however, was less based on projections and more determined by generalizing the infantile environment, to include the current setting, a process I call externalization (see Chapter 4). In other words, she viewed reality as an extension of her early environment. Actually, up until puberty, there was little to distinguish infancy from adolescence, presumably because her parents continued to attack her. Thus it was understandable that she would generalize these experiences to practically all contemporary interactions, leading to a paranoid stance. However, the impact of the external world was the predominant factor in shaping her attitudes, rather than internal forces distorting her view of the world. There were such distortions, but they received tremendous support from repeated traumas.

Borderline patients have suffered assaultive traumas and abuse; and to understand the manifestations of psychopathology it is useful to assess to what degree the impingement of reality contributes to distortions created by hateful introjects. There is a reciprocal interaction, an interplay, between internal and external forces. Insomuch as external forces dominate, the psyche is more severely disturbed in terms of structural defects and fragmentation. This can be stated as the obvious sequence: the greater the trauma, the greater the damage.

What was most striking was her sharply contrasting moods. To repeat, she could be submissive, compliant, and almost totally self-obliterating. On the other hand, she could be contemptuous, mandatory, to some degree even arrogant, to the extent that I felt controlled and immobilized. Apparently she had succeeded in projecting her helplessness into me. In any case, there seemed to be little connection between these ego states, and for a long time I found them unpredictable.

After 3 years of treatment, she admitted that I was really trying to help her, but because of her vulnerability and lack of trust, she could not accept whatever I had to offer. She recognized, with my help, that she was operating within the context of a vicious circle. Consequently, she had organized her life around a core of anger, and behaviorally she was overwhelmed by the manifestations of splitting mechanisms.

Affects have a binding function (Giovacchini 1975a, 1990), as discussed in Chapter 2. Anger in particular gives structure to internal chaos that is the outcome of an amorphous ego organization. This patient's early life was filled with violence, and her chief adaptive modalities were infused with anger. She could, to some measure, soothe herself by being angry, in that such an ego state helped overcome her feelings of extreme vulnerability. It also helped fill a feeling of miserable emptiness.

To attack was better than being attacked, and this was finally realized as it occurred in our sessions. In fact, this was the first observation or interpretation that she was able to accept. As described earlier, she would often begin her sessions in a whimpering fashion, emphasizing her helplessness and weakness, and then, toward the end of the session, she would abruptly change and viciously attack me for being useless, unempathic, and sadistic. This sequence was pointed out to her, and, uncharacteristically, she elaborated that anger was a pacifier and also furnished her with a protective robe.

This is an example of an interpretation that has a minimal threatening potential. It refers to a general movement in the analysis, a description at the phenomenological level of macroscopic aspects of the patient's behavior. As such, it is a nonintrusive comment and therefore difficult to view as assaultive. Of course, paranoid patients can view any phenomenon or statement as an attack, but it is much more difficult to do so when interpretations do not make reference to feelings, defenses, or parts of the self. It was not giving meaning to behavior either; rather, it was simply a description of certain shifts of ego stances such as shifting from a passive to an assertive attitude (see Chapter 12).

She again emphasized that she was struggling against painful emptiness, and when anger failed her she felt as if she were falling apart. This is where splitting mechanisms entered the picture, something that happened fairly frequently at the beginning of treatment.

Her ability to proceed from passive vulnerability to active counterattacks was evidence of some ego strength. By being angry she was protecting herself as well as filling a painful inner void. Over the next several years she learned that she did not have to murderously retaliate to survive the dangers of the traumatic external world of the past, which at times was represented by the analytic setting. Being active and aggressive became equilibratory experiences.

In the past, anger had become involved in a self-destructive cycle, a vicious circle. She began this cycle by contemptuously depreciating practically everybody. For example, in the transference she used me as a target, but first she would go into endless detail how corrupt, stupid, and insensitive were various analysts she had met socially. If a psychiatrist became involved in a scandal that made the newspapers, she would cut it out and gleefully show it to me. She had a sizable collection of such clippings.

Although such revelations made her feel momentarily triumphant, they eventually caused her to become even more depressed and miserable because she felt desperately isolated and her painful inner emptiness intensified. As a consequence, her anger would increase because of the rejecting, corrupt surrounding world, and, in turn, she would react with further feelings of helplessness and emptiness, the final outcome being painful splitting experiences.

In conclusion, instead of being protective and adaptive, anger had been one of several factors that prevented her from receiving and internalizing potentially helpful experiences such as the therapeutic interaction. This maintained fragmentation and discontinuity and led to an intensification of her feelings of emptiness.

EMPTINESS, PSYCHOSOMATIC RESOLUTION, AND FRAGMENTATION

I have emphasized how spaces within the psyche devoid of psychological content—psychic lacunae, as I have called them—often become the locus of somatic disruption, a psychosomatic focus. The patient I have just discussed stressed how painful such emptiness could be, often causing her to feel that, psychically speaking, she was disintegrating.

My patient, both in the consultation room and in her apartment, usually in the evening, would feel "as if she were falling apart." At times she had the experience of feeling outside herself, an intense feeling of depersonalization. Simultaneously she felt dead, but this in no way deadened her pain. On the contrary, she would moan and scream. When I witnessed several such episodes, both in my office and on the telephone, I was struck by the bizarreness and animallike nature of her crying, moaning, and grunting. At first, I also found these episodes distressing because I surmised that she was going through a disruptive splitting experience in which she was losing what little psychic unity she had. Later, I learned that there were other meanings and purposes to this behavior.

After 4 years of treatment, she admitted that when I was with her, either at the office or on the telephone, she usually felt better after such outbursts, provided I did not interrupt them. I was prepared for this disclosure because of other patients I had encountered and whom I described in Chapter 5. These were, as discussed, attempts to achieve integration.

During these quests for cohesion, these patients are able to form connecting bridges between various parts of their psyche as they reintegrate lost and split-off parts of the self.

A fragmented psyche can be viewed as a loose organization with many empty spaces between various parts of the self. Again, we are faced with lacunae and a lack of psychic continuity. The latter can be associated with psychosomatic symptoms and the feeling of painful emptiness. To fill up this emptiness can be a painful experience, as discussed in Chapter 5.

The therapy of patients suffering from psychosomatic symptoms can have painful moments, not only when the patient is undergoing states of ego disintegration. They can also occur when the patient is attempting to reintegrate lost, traumatized parts of the self in order to achieve psychic cohesion, as discussed in the previous chapter, but here I am referring to episodes when the patient is not particularly regressed. This striving for unification, that is, to no longer be fragmented, has a significant influence on the course and persistence of psychosomatic symptoms.

McDougall (1989) has wondered about unexplainable changes that are related to the appearance or disappearance of psychosomatic symptoms.

Patients in psychoanalytic treatment sometimes become asymptomatic for no apparent reason. The patient who had regional ileitis is an example of a dramatic remission of a potentially life-threatening disease. His improvement could be correlated with increased psychic cohesion from a discontinuous state in which there was little connection between the unconscious and conscious, a severe type of fragmentation. In other patients it is difficult to understand what has happened within the psyche to explain why psychosomatic symptoms have disappeared.

A 23-year-old single male first saw me in the spring. When discussing the schedule he alerted me that he would have to be gone for a month toward the end of summer. He had such severe allergies that he had to leave the city to seek a ragweed-free environment in the Southwest. Besides his hay fever he told me about many symptoms and character traits that indicated he was a schizoid personality as described in Chapter 4. For the most part he felt alienated and he withdrew from the external world.

He was, at times, concretely oriented, but there were many sessions in which he demonstrated keen intuition and a capacity for insight. He related that he had many different facets to his personality that operated independently of each other. Like the other patients described in this chapter, this patient was psychically fragmented and his behavior was determined by the discontinuous aspects of his character structure, but he was not particularly disconnected from his unconscious, as occurs in many concretely oriented patients. Nevertheless, he did not feel as if he were a well-put-together, whole person. He felt isolated and complained about loneliness and the lack of emotionally meaningful relationships.

He often felt hopeless because he believed that he did not fit in the current milieu. He did not believe he had the social skills required to move comfortably in the surrounding world, and he despaired of ever learning them because of being psychically damaged. He also believed that he was physically unattractive and no amount of therapy could change that.

Actually he was a rather plain-looking person, short and with a somewhat stooped posture. He was not particularly appealing but he was not at all as ugly as he claimed. It was true, however, that it was unlikely that anyone would spontaneously reach out to him.

Nevertheless, as the months went by I found him less lugubrious and more open. At first he would hardly talk, and I felt myself struggling to keep the therapeutic dialogue flowing. By the end of the second year of analysis, he spoke quite freely and was quite engaging. As I found myself becoming immersed in his material I realized that he had never taken a leave at the end of the summer, as he had announced during our first session.

I wondered about his hay fever, so I asked him why he did not leave for the Southwest at the end of two summers. He replied that since he began analysis, he no longer had hay fever, an allergy that he had had for over 10 years. Racking my memory, I was not able to point to any psychodynamic shifts that had occurred between the spring and summer of the first year of therapy. I attributed this partly to the length of time that had elapsed between the disappearance of his allergic symptoms and my awareness of his improvement.

I was both disconsolate and amused because the analyst is often the last person to learn about the patient's improvement. I should have asked him why he was not leaving for the Southwest that first summer. It simply had not occurred to me. Still, he did not volunteer anything and it would seem that being rid of such a chronic and unpleasant condition as hay fever might have been worthy of comment. When I confronted him with his noncommunicativeness, he had nothing to say. He did not find it unusual that he had not commented about the disappearance of his somatic symptoms. In fact, he did not think much about it himself. I regretted that I had lost the opportunity to study this interesting turn of events about a psychosomatic phenomenon. I felt that 2 years later the material was too stale to allow reaching any meaningful conclusions.

The analysis continued for 6 more years, and he had no further somatic symptoms. He had made significant improvements. Vocationally he had discovered that his mind was capable of a keen understanding of computer concepts, and various companies eagerly sought his services. Apparently he was considered somewhat of a genius in this area. He also started a relationship with a former beauty queen and eventually married her. What was most striking was that he was low-keyed about his accomplishments. In fact, he did not even consider them to be accomplishments. This was striking in view of his attitudes and insecurities at the beginning of treatment when he viewed himself as inadequate and so ugly that no woman would want to have anything to do with him, especially a beauty queen. Now he saw nothing unusual in his marrying such a comely person or in that he was a very special person in the world of computers.

I do not believe it is relevant to discuss what occurred in the analytic interaction. I simply want to call attention to certain character configurations that might have been associated with his recovery from hay fever and which might be considered unexplainable if we remained in a psychodynamic context. In any case, because of the passage of time, it is not possible to reconstruct the unconscious currents that might have been involved with somatic processes that reestablished the integrity of the immune system.

What was most impressive about this patient was his low-keyed reaction to fundamental changes and improvements in areas that had previously been highly disturbing. He had dreaded the onset of the ragweed season, and he bitterly lamented his inability to have a heterosexual relationship because he was so unattractive that no woman would have anything to do with him.

Furthermore, other than possessing a basic core of inadequacy he had felt as if he had no identity sense. He had a dream early in treatment where he was flying over different European countries, beginning with the one from which his parents had emigrated. He left his head there, letting it parachute to earth. He left his arms, legs, and body in other countries. In conjunction with this dream, he stressed how scattered and disjointed he felt.

His orientation had reached a degree of concreteness that made me wonder, at times, whether he was psychotic. He described a fragmented psychic state but he believed that what he lacked was certain hormones and anatomical structures that would bind him together. He was literally attributing his sense of fragmentation to somatic defects, which he insisted were due to a poor genetic endowment.

He also viewed his hay fever as the consequence of a lack of unity and as a manifestation of the disjointed functioning of the respiratory system, which he believed was operating independently of the other elements of the breathing apparatus. Inasmuch as the nasal mucosa and other sites involved in hay fever were not under the control of the respiratory system, these regions would, according to the patient, "go on a spree," that is, react in a wild, uninhibited manner manifested by the symptoms of hay fever. A fragmented part of the self or soma would not be subjected to regulatory and modulatory influences that are characteristic of a state of cohesion and unity.

When he first started treatment, everything was considered a calamity. In spite of being withdrawn, he was constantly agitated. He was tense and anxious and he would cause others to withdraw from him because they found themselves absorbing his disruption (see Chapter 3). I recall that at the beginning I was not exactly at ease during his sessions. I did not look forward to them and was sometimes relieved when he occasionally canceled a session. Undoubtedly, I had absorbed some of his agitation.

As so often happens under these circumstances, the patient begins to feel somewhat soothed. After several months he was no longer as intense as he had been. In retrospect, I now believe that he was gradually beginning to achieve some degree of cohesion, that he was no longer as fragmented, and that he was not as agitated or hyperactive. He had achieved a modicum of calmness. He still had a long way to go, as attested to by his many years of analysis, but he may have achieved a sufficient amount of unity that was reflected in the soma.

If we view the soma in the same way we conceptualize the psyche, we may again think in terms of cohesion and fragmentation. As the patient described, his upper respiratory apparatus was not in synchrony with other somatic processes, and the hay fever represented a disruption of a somatic homeostatic balance. To paraphrase Freud (1938), there was a split from the main somatic currents. Relatively quickly, that is, before much unity occurred in the psyche, there was a comparatively early readjustment and cohesion at the somatic level. I suspect that at the first hay fever season the patient was feeling fairly comfortable during his sessions, because to some extent the therapeutic setting had established a holding environment.

I have given many clinical examples of fragmentation in this and the preceding chapter. As I have generally emphasized, faulty psychic structure is characteristic of concretely oriented patients and others who belong to the borderline spectrum. The patient just presented differs markedly from other patients I have described in that he did not experience painfully regressed episodes as he was trying to establish some degree of psychic and somatic integration. Quite to the contrary, his symptoms quietly disappeared, whereas other patients were loud and bombastic as they painfully struggled to bring lost parts of the self back into the main psychic current or to gain some relief from disruptive somatic disturbances.

I believe that in some measure these contrasting phenomena can be ascribed to different infantile backgrounds. This patient was, for the most part, neglected by his caregivers. His mother was a frail, depressed woman who was anxious when trying to nurture her son. The father left the house when the patient was 3 years old, so he hardly knew him as a child. As an adult he occasionally sees his father and views him as a passive, ineffectual person.

His infantile environment was characterized by what I have called errors of omission, as contrasted with errors of commission (Giovacchini 1979a). The former refers to neglectful, incompetent caregivers, whereas the latter corresponds to an assaultive, violent atmosphere that characterizes the childhood of fragmented patients I have described who were massively traumatized. Obviously, when dealing with clinical phenomena, clinicians cannot make hard and fast distinctions. There is usually considerable overlapping, but there are clinical examples that will emphasize one element of their background, particularly massive trauma. The patient I have just discussed stressed the incompetence and frailty of his background and downplayed assaultive intrusions. He described periods of understimulation and abandonment rather than disruptive impingements from the external world. He described a low-keyed setting rather than an atmosphere of uncontrollable and dangerous violence.

I believe that these qualities of the infantile milieu are responsible for how patients react differently to both regressed episodes and attempts to achieve psychic and somatic integration. The patients hitherto described emphasize how painful it was to reintegrate lost, trauma-encapsulating parts of the self, whereas this patient experienced a quiet internal rearrangement and synthesis as he was freed from a psychosomatic disability.

There are significant differences in the character structure and types of fragmentations that characterize these two types of patients. Whatever the psychic structure of massively traumatized patients, the early assaultive environment battered away and undermined the basic foundations of the mental apparatus. These patients had to construct splitting defenses, no matter how fragmented their personality may already have been, in order to survive. The patient suffering from hay fever did not have such horrible and violent experiences. He was, as was also true of his mother, fragilely put together. There was a general lack of cohesiveness, not as a response to repeated assaults but as the consequence of a generally depriving environment, one that failed to meet his basic needs. In retrospect, it would not be surprising that he would gain some unity and synthesis when he was able to react to the holding-environment aspects of the analytic relationship.

Clinical explorations reveal that there are different types of splitting mechanisms. Kohut (1971) wrote about horizontal and vertical splitting, obviously a spatial or geometric distinction. A closer look reveals that *horizontal splitting* is simply a rephrasing of the familiar process of repression, which basically is not a dissociative phenomenon associated with a fragmented psyche. *Vertical splitting* refers to ordinary fragmenting processes. The geometric perspective, as emphasized by such adjectives as horizontal and vertical, adds nothing to our clinical understanding of emotional development and psychopathology. In fact, these formulations give the false impression that they explain different types of dissociative phenomena just by drawing lines through the psychic apparatus.

Freud (1923) drew a horizontal line, although it was slightly slanted, through his model of the mind to indicate the repressive barrier. This was merely a graphic depiction and was not meant to be taken literally. It also emphasized a dynamic interaction between different parts of the psyche, primarily the id and the ego, and did not indicate that there is any disturbance of the unity of the mind when repressive defenses are active. According to Freud (1926), the aim of all defenses is to achieve repression in order to maintain cohesiveness. The only exception is splitting itself, which is designed to prevent further fragmentation.

I have stressed that lack of psychic unity can be the outcome of faulty development or a defensive, as well as a disintegrative, reaction against massive trauma. There is a reciprocal relationship between these two states in that the less organized the psyche is, the more it will fragment when traumatized, as might be expected. These distinctions are important for the understanding of psychopathology and the problems therapists have to face when treating these patients.

PART III

THE THERAPEUTIC PROCESS

7

The Holding

Environment

As discussed in the Preface, the literature dealing with conceptual systems underlying primitively disturbed patients is voluminous, but there has been relatively little written about the treatment relationship, especially with concretely oriented patients. Recently, Kernberg and his associates (1987) have written what is essentially a handbook for the treatment of borderline patients. Roth (1987) has written a similar book that deals with the more general aspects of psychoanalytic treatment, a book that contains considerable wisdom. However, neither of these volumes specifically examines the dynamics of the therapeutic interaction in a fashion that is consonant with our recently gained perspectives about psychic development, structural psychopathology, and disturbances in object relations. In other words, our concepts about technique and the so-called metapsychology of the psychoanalytic process and its modifications have not kept pace with the theories and hypotheses postulated about the wide variety of patients who present us with primarily characterological problems rather than intrapsychic conflicts.

Viewing the psychoanalytic interaction from a broader perspective may cause clinicians to reconsider their attitudes about the rules and definition of psychoanalysis. Heretofore, psychoanalysis has been strictly defined and distinguished from other forms of treatment such as supportive psychotherapy or even psychoanalytically oriented psychotherapy, treatment approaches that supposedly have more modest goals than "pure" psychoanalysis.

Today the situation has drastically changed. Although these attitudes have not completely disappeared, many older as well as younger analysts and other mental health professionals have done a 180-degree turn. Those who in former days would have been called heretics for attacking or even questioning Freud now find that it has become fashionable to do so. Freud, as a person and as a clinician, has been discredited by several authors.

The wholesale discrediting of Freud is no less ridiculous than having elevated him to godlike status. These are ad hominem positions designed to protect or to attack psychoanalysis. But the validity of a system of thought has to be examined on the basis of its merit rather than on the personality of its discoverer. No one ever thought, for example, to judge the theory of relativity by impugning Einstein's marital experiences.

These criticisms have caused mental health workers to question the efficacy of psychoanalytic treatment. Opponents of psychoanalysis, as they stress biological etiologies and pharmacological treatment regimens, emphasize how fruitless the psychoanalytic approach can be. In many instances their observations are correct, if these very disturbed patients are subjected to the requirements of a formal, classical psychoanalytic setting.

As stated, treatment has to be tailored to meet their needs. As discussed in previous chapters, these patients are concretely oriented, so they cannot immediately accept the principle of psychic determinism. They are also needy, and the analyst has to be able to provide, from the very beginning, a modicum of support. Simply stated, the analyst has to be able to reach out to the patient and give him something rather than make demands.

These patients are not able to conform to rules that are beyond their level of comprehension. Furthermore, their sense of identity is so poorly constructed that they cannot adapt to a structured setting that is beyond their level of organization. They do not have sufficient stability of psychic structure to enable them to maintain internal regulation and balance. To demand this type of control by conforming to the formal requirements of analysis at the beginning of treatment is therapeutically unrealistic.

By *formal requirements of analysis*, I am referring to expectations as well as explicit instructions. Concerning the latter, analysts ask their patients to free-associate, lie down on the couch, and sometimes to abstain from certain activities. This will vary as therapists make "contracts" with their patients. Regarding the former, analysts expect patients to be psychologically minded and to express themselves verbally rather than revealing themselves through their behavior.

ACTING OUT AND THE THERAPEUTIC INTERACTION

Freud demanded that his patients have the capacity to express themselves verbally rather than act out impulses in the outside world or the consultation room. What constitutes acting out, however, is not a closed issue. As is true generally of the therapeutic interaction, clinicians have to think of the object relationship quality of the analytic process. What one therapist may label acting out could be considered by another analyst to be a form of communication or an adaptive technique. Acting out has to be viewed on a relative basis rather than just unilaterally as a resistance and perhaps a contraindication to analysis.

To illustrate that the analyst often decides that a patient is acting out rather than that the patient's actions are intrinsically characteristic of acting-out behavior, I recall the following vignette.

The patient, an unmarried woman in her middle twenties, had had what she called unpleasant experiences with several therapists. She directly told them that she wanted to be analyzed, but before accepting her request they had to take careful histories, and then they would conclude that she was too impulsive, with a propensity to act out.

True, she seemed flighty and had what might be considered a "spaced-out" quality, but there was nothing spectacular in her behavior; she was not promiscuous, antisocial, or addicted to drugs. At the most, she displayed, on occasion, histrionic and melodramatic behavior with some affective lability.

Her former analysts did not take her wish to be analyzed seriously. One of them stated she was too immature to understand the complexities of the analytic process. I was somewhat confused because although she did, indeed, appear frivolous and infantile, she would occasionally make a statement that indicated she had profound insights about the analytic process. For example, she detected subtle changes in a friend who had been in analysis for many years, whereas others felt he had made no progress whatsoever because he was still highly dependent and indecisive. She commented that no one recalled or knew him at the beginning of treatment when he was totally nonfunctional and fragmented. She admitted that he still had symptoms, but claimed that the essence of analysis was not symptomatic or surface improvement; rather it involved internal changes such as an increased sense of security and autonomy based on getting in touch with lost parts of the self. There was nothing academic in the mood accompanying these statements. In fact, she had read practically nothing about psychoanalysis and her outlook in general seemed naive.

She was extremely upset about her last therapist. He had asked her to lie on the couch and instructed her to reveal her thoughts and feelings by free-associating. The patient, a versatile actress, frequently interrupted her discourse with childlike exclamations. She spoke in a baby voice. Her analyst became critical and impatient and confronted her by saying, "Is this the way for a grown-up woman to talk?", whereupon she got up and left his office. She never returned, feeling rebuked. He believed she was acting out and "too sick" to be analyzed.

At the beginning phases of her treatment with me, she occasionally used her baby voice. Instead of being critical, I found this infantile way of communicating fascinating because it represented a barometer of an infantile ego state by which I could judge which developmental level was foremost. When she realized that I was receptive to her infantile, regressed mode of communicating, she stopped expressing herself as a child and resumed her adult demeanor. Her previous analyst had labeled her behavior as acting out and a defense against internal exploration, whereas I felt she was simply getting in touch with infantile parts of the self.

It does not matter how we classify her reactions. It is important, however, how we respond, whether we accept her behavior as a revelation of an infantile ego state or whether we confront it as an unwelcome resistance that has to be expeditiously curtailed.

Ideally, we would like to have our patients free-associate. Thus they gradually reveal ego states and primitive organizations that characterize fundamental psychopathological configurations. It is often true, however, that when patients are capable of this type of communication, they have resolved the obstacles to free association and worked through fundamental conflicts that inhibited both modes of communication and adaptive techniques. To be able to free-associate is a goal of treatment rather than a precondition.

Our treatment approach has to focus upon defective characterological patterns. In some instances, this means that the patient might not be able to free-associate because of certain basic constrictions and ego defects. These patients, however, reveal themselves by various modes of relating rather than exclusively by words. As I have discussed, these communicative modes should not be summarily dismissed as resistance and acting out.

PSYCHIC DEVELOPMENT, THERAPEUTIC OUTCOME, AND THE HOLDING ENVIRONMENT

Inasmuch as the clinical focus is on structural factors rather than psychodynamic conflict, the aim of therapy is directed toward the acquisition of psychic structure and the gaining of further cohesion of the psychic apparatus rather than the resolution of intrapsychic conflict. Again, I have to emphasize that these are not mutually exclusive goals; they can supplement each other. It happens that patients who belong in the borderline spectrum suffer from structural defects and the therapeutic process has to address them. Does this mean that analysts have to modify their techniques and otherwise introduce parameters, as Eissler (1953) suggested?

I will discuss technical maneuvers in the next section as they are associated with the analyst's general perspectives regarding the treatment of patients. I do not believe that the treatment of borderline patients requires any gross deviations from what has been considered standard analysis. As discussed in Chapter 2, there are important differences in the therapist's attitude, rather than specific technical deviations, that are germane to the analysis of this group of patients.

Freud (1926) assumed that psychoneurotic patients had reached fairly high levels of ego integration. The analytic task is to reestablish a better balance between fairly integrated psychic systems. The ego, in response to an anxiety signal, sets in motion certain defensive processes in order to reestablish equilibrium. This defensive response, to some extent, hampers the functioning and harmony of the psychic apparatus. Still, there is a basic unity to the personality, even though it is not functioning at its highest potential. The goals of treatment do not especially involve changes in or accretions of psychic structure.

By contrast, patients in the borderline spectrum do not have the cohesiveness that has been attributed to psychoneurotic patients. These patients demonstrate different types of fragmentation, as has been discussed in Chapters 5 and 6, which specifically affect the treatment process. Because of their concrete orientation they are not usually able to free-associate. Frequently, they refuse to lie down on the couch because they feel too vulnerable and they are not yet able to trust the analytic setting. Their fragmented egos do not permit them to make connections with the analyst or the process.

Whether these dissociated psychic states are primarily the outcome of an inadequate infantile milieu or a response to massive trauma or, as is usually the situation, a combination of both, these patients have particular difficulties in adapting to the surrounding milieu and relating to external objects. They reluctantly enter an analytic relationship because they anticipate rejection and assault. In view of past experiences, they are suspicious and mistrustful. Because they are usually functioning as part persons, they cannot wholly immerse themselves in a project or a relationship. They do not have the unity of the psychic apparatus for such accomplishments. Although they may be extremely dependent, they cannot allow themselves to express their needs because they lack trust and security, and if they have been extremely traumatized, they do not know the meaning of gratification or how to achieve it.

Rather than seeking an analytic relationship, which to so many borderline patients is incomprehensible, they pursue magical solutions that are more in keeping with their primary-process orientation. This can be a quest for a miracle drug that will "cure" them or for an omnipotent therapist who has all the final answers. Patients suffering from character disorders are largely responsible for the popularity of psychopharmacology and biological psychiatry. These approaches and perspectives fit well with their concrete orientations and their incapacities to achieve succor at the interpersonal level.

Thus, defects in psychic development are prominent. As has been repeatedly stressed throughout this book, some of these patients can become engaged in a psychoanalytic relationship in spite of the obstacles just mentioned and regardless of their severe structural problems. If the analyst can provide the holding environment Winnicott (1958a, 1963) described, then it may be possible to treat these patients from a psychoanalytic perspective.

The analytic relationship recapitulates early developmental phases, but the holding environment provides what was destructively lacking during infancy. This relationship leads in the direction of unity and cohesion, the mending of a disjointed, fragmented personality. It is as if the course of early development is diverted into other nontraumatic pathways.

The analytic environment does not produce a corrective infantile setting. The gratifications it provides are suitable for both infantile and adult needs. In fact, the holding environment helps the psyche developmentally advance to a position in which it is possible to be gratified (Bollas 1987, 1989).

Most discussions of the therapeutic interaction are draped in such generalities as I have just stated. The clinician might agree that the establishment of a holding environment is a favorable situation for the treatment of needy patients. This is an obvious truism. One could ask, however, whether this is an esoteric endeavor wrapped in the charisma of gifted therapists who do not, or need not, know how they manage to construct such a setting. Their depth of understanding and intuition leads to appropriate actions and reactions that help patients develop trust and, in some instances, construct dependent needs that their fragmented egos could not previously structure. The ordinary clinician, however, needs a more explicit description of the holding environment and how to make it a supportive matrix so that a therapeutic interaction is possible.

As is true of most technical maneuvers, there are no specific instructions that the clinician can follow in order to conduct psychoanalytic treatment. As to the holding environment, the situation is somewhat similar, but there are a few concrete characteristics of this environment that enable us to deal less in generalities and divest it of its esoteric aura. What is most important for the construction of this supportive matrix is what the analyst does *not* do, rather than what he does.

Unlike what happened in the infantile milieu, analysts are not intrusive nor do they give the patient the impression that they value some material more than other material. In some instances we have to abandon our reliance on free association for several reasons. First, many of these patients are unable to get in touch with their unconscious because of the fragmentation of psychic structure. As discussed, their vulnerability and lack of trust will not permit them to lie down and relax sufficiently so they can relinquish conscious control. Furthermore, setting up a rule, even the basic rule (*Grundregel*), as Freud called it in his technical papers, is painfully reminiscent of early traumatic assaults.

This does not mean there are no rules. A complete laissez-faire setting would most likely lead to chaos. The therapeutic setting has to supply structure, especially for patients who have very little structure of their own. This need not, however, require setting up rigid rules, making contracts, or constructing explicit boundaries. These activities are often referred to as confrontations, which I will refer to later.

Clinicians are, for the most part, conveying attitudes to their patients. They also indicate, overtly or covertly, that they have expectations of their patients, which might be more than the patient can integrate. If many patients are not even able to be gratified, how can they internalize complex attitudes and expectations that refer to much higher levels of development than they have achieved? Analysts have to ask themselves what are the most nonintrusive conditions they can create and still be able to work comfortably with patients. I am referring to fragile, vulnerable, and fragmented patients who exhibit the many borderline qualities that have been discussed.

To repeat, I am stressing what analysts must not do or demand if they wish to construct a holding environment, which most clinicians agree is essential for the treatment of borderline patients. What should they supply in a more active and positive sense? Again, there are no specific directions; what is to be discussed is intrinsic to the analytic setting. Winnicott stressed the constant reliability of the analytic session as well as its determinable duration, that is, the end of the hour, which provides limits and structure. Gitelson once wittily remarked that if there are two persons in a room, it is best that only one of them be anxious. He was emphasizing the calming, nonanxious aspects of the holding environment.

Little (1990), in writing about her analysis with Winnicott, describes many incidents in which Winnicott's supportive presence and actions kept her from having a total breakdown. He was able to contain her psychotic anxieties, and this sometimes meant he literally had to hold her to prevent her from striking him. She was describing unique aspects of their relationship, which perhaps cannot be generalized to the treatment of other patients suffering from characterological disorders. This implies that all holding environments have unique features based on the patient's particular background, ego defects, and needs.

I have described a process that I refer to as externalization, which I believe occurs in the psychoanalytic treatment of patients who have had traumatic backgrounds (Giovacchini 1979a). Within the transference context patients project feelings and parts of the self into the therapist; they also try to re-create the traumatic infantile milieu in the analytic setting. Viewed as a scenario, the analytic interaction contains both the significant characters of the patient's life as well as the setting in which interactions take place. As is true of the nurturing relationship, with its foreground of nurture and its background of soothing, this scenario can be viewed in a similar fashion. The analytic setting acquires the general atmosphere that pervaded the infantile milieu, such as assaultive violence or indifferent neglect (McDougall 1985). It is this general atmosphere, the background setting, that I consider to be the product of externalizing processes.

I have described clinical examples of externalization elsewhere (Giovacchini 1979a). Here I wish to demonstrate how the holding environment can be formed by interactions with the externalized infantile milieu, and that in many ways this process is similar to the correction of transference distortions. As with transference, patients have certain expectations of their analysts, which are reflections of how they were treated in the past. Many of these expectations concern general attributes pertaining to the therapist, such as appearance, comportment, tone of voice, mode of relating, and inferences about his weltanschauung. These traits refer to the analyst's personality, which to some extent has to be *oppositional* to the infantile milieu as it is externalized into the treatment setting. They then become incorporated into the fabric of the holding environment.

As stated, the concept of the holding environment may seem somewhat vague. Clinicians view it as a supportive matrix that engenders trust. As such, there is nothing specific or definitive about it. I am proposing, however, that the effects of the past have to be dealt with in the therapeutic interaction beyond simply revealing them or understanding them in their conflictual or defective structural context. *These therapeutic responses are reactions to attempts at externalization, and they define the holding environment.*

Thus the holding environment has to stand in sharp contrast to the traumatic past. I will describe these events further in Chapter 9 when I discuss the psychoanalytic paradox. Here I wish to stress that the analyst does not deliberately attempt to create a corrective scenario to undo the effects of assaultive or neglectful caretakers. The therapist's reactions are spontaneous and often a response to his own inner needs. Hence, by establishing comfortable settings for patients, therapists are also providing themselves with a calm, workable environment.

If patients, on the other hand, predominantly externalize, that is, succeed in converting the consultation room into the battleground of their childhood, then neither the analyst nor the patient can maintain a functional degree of emotional equilibrium. The understanding analyst needs to do something to counteract the traumatic effects that were pervasive in infancy and childhood, but this response is by no means a mere contrivance.

Analytic responses will vary depending upon the unique aspects of patients' backgrounds and the specific features of their psychopathology. This means that there is no general holding environment. It will vary and is dependent upon the patient's inner needs and the analyst's personality as it becomes enmeshed in an interaction designed to achieve psychic cohesion and synthesis. The therapist's inner orientation has to be in tune with the patient's inner requirements and protective adaptations, which leads to certain spontaneous reactions that establish a therapeutic base.

A case example illustrates how one analyst had to create a setting that was vastly different from what the patient's parents provided.

The patient, a schizoid adolescent, was the youngest of nine siblings and thus viewed himself as an afterthought. His physical needs were well met, but he had practically no emotional bonds with anybody. He generally felt uncomfortable and was socially ill at ease. He kept to himself and had no friends, either male or female. He believed that his parents, his father especially, related to him only in an intrusive fashion. They sarcastically rebuked him for being passive, socially clumsy, and backward. He felt they were pushing him, but not because they were concerned about his welfare; rather, they experienced him as an embarrassment.

In the first session of therapy he was unable to say anything spontaneously. He was extremely withdrawn and volunteered nothing. At the most, he answered some questions, but his responses were monosyllabic.

The therapist felt as if he were pulling teeth. It was hard to determine how uncomfortable the patient was, but the analyst definitely felt perturbed. As he learned more about the patient, he began to feel he was behaving like an intrusive parent. Consequently, the analyst asked the patient if he would like to lie down on the couch. There he could be alone with his thoughts and feelings and not be subjected to intrusive questions. If he wanted to share his thoughts, the analyst would be nearby and would be glad to hear what he had to say. Still, nothing would be required of him.

To repeat, the analyst was uncomfortable, and this occurred before he knew anything about the patient's background. As an analyst seeing a patient for the first time, he felt he had to interview him, and this meant that he had to get the patient to come out of his shell, at least a little bit. This was the analyst's professional orientation, but it was not in tune with establishing a therapeutic orientation.

The therapist's asking the patient to lie on the couch was a response to his own discomfort. His professional modus operandi was not consonant with the patient's needs. His role as interviewer was inappropriate. The setting he had constructed was antitherapeutic because it was at least phenomenologically similar to what the patient's intrusive, sadistic parents had constructed, although the analyst was not aware of these surface similarities.

Nevertheless, by reacting as he did, the analyst was laying the foundations of a holding environment. He had created an atmosphere that was vastly different from what the patient had known at home. The patient was allowed to withdraw without being attacked, and in fact the analyst tried to make his withdrawal as pleasant as possible.

To repeat, the analyst started to feel discomfort very early during the first session. He began to understand that analytic exploration was perceived as traumatic and that this could have been the outcome of childhood sensitivities and vulnerabilities—as indeed turned out to be the case. The patient was not, however, projecting parental imagoes into the therapist, or, at least, that was not the way the analyst viewed it. He was not yet the receptacle of the patient's projections. The situation was different from that which occurs in a transference–countertransference interaction. In fact, the patient was withdrawn and removed from any contact with his therapist. He reacted as if the world were dangerous, including the treatment setting, but there was nothing unique about any relationship. The analysis was the same as any environment, intrusive and incomprehensible.

The analyst's actions resulted in a setting that was the antithesis of the infantile milieu; this setting was the holding environment. Later, within this setting, the patient would be able to project elements of the past as well as primitive parts of the self and become involved in an analytically useful transference. Again, I emphasize that the analyst did not offer his patient an alternative to a formal interview because he had made a formulation and then acted on it. He knew that to continue in an orthodox fashion would be unproductive and perhaps fatal to any therapeutic endeavor.

For several months the patient lay on the couch during each session, saying practically nothing. Nevertheless, he seemed comfortable and the therapist felt no need to push him to talk. It seemed that the patient had gained considerable composure and was no longer as awkward, clumsy, or vulnerable as before. He seemed to have gained some structure, and this was reflected in his attitudes and curiosity about the external world.

Heretofore the analytic atmosphere was quiet (indeed, literally so) and nonintrusive. After about 6 months the patient began to ask an occasional question, usually something about dress codes. He seemed to be totally ignorant as to what modes of dress were appropriate for certain situations, locations, and seasons. For example, he wondered if shorts were acceptable at a prom. At first the therapist found this naivete incredible, but then he remembered this was a person who never ventured outside the house except to go to school. The patient began to ask many similar questions as well as to expand his range of topics. His questions continued, however, to refer to such pedestrian matters as how to make a telephone call and ask a girl for a date.

Though analysts often do not answer questions because they want to explore the meaning and motive behind the question, the therapist responded spontaneously and with enthusiasm. Without any deliberation, he would have found it unthinkable not to directly address the question, and at the time he did not consider whether his reactions were nonanalytic. He was convinced that if he remained silent or countered with a question, there would be no treatment relationship. He also felt that because the patient had been uncommunicative, anything that came from him assumed great value and had to be acknowledged. More important, he looked forward to the questions and wanted to engage or be engaged by his patient in discussions about how to relate to the external world. The patient was showing interest in his surroundings rather than exclusively withdrawing from them. To the therapist this represented an advance in ego integration, indicating some acquisition of psychic structure. The nonintrusive holding environment he had constructed permitted the patient to make tentative explorations into an external world that had become somewhat less frightening and demanding.

The holding environment had changed. The atmosphere in the consultation room was no longer quiet. There was an actual and lively interchange between patient and analyst. Although the matters they discussed were pedestrian, they were of great interest to both of them. Again, this environment was the antithesis of another segment of the infantile milieu. His parents did not relate to him. They did not cultivate his curiosity or encourage his explorations. They either withdrew from him or directed their interests elsewhere. There was no interest in him in this depressed large family. He was raised in a low-decibel atmosphere, whereas his treatment was noisy and at a high-decibel level.

Maintaining the auditory metaphor, the beginning months of treatment were conducted in a low-decibel, nonintrusive fashion. This created a comparatively safe setting, but it did not recapitulate the emotional neglect and abandonment he had experienced at home. The analyst made it quite clear that he was there and that he was available to the patient. He was quite eager that the patient keep his appointments, and if there were any reasons why either one of them could not make a session, the analyst was eager to arrange another time and was meticulous in doing so. He conveyed that he wanted to see the patient and that he valued their time together. The therapy had been successful in creating various types of holding environments, low-decibel and high-decibel, which were at variance with different aspects of the traumatic past.

These early interactions set the stage for later transference projections that could be dealt with in a more traditional analytic fashion, that is, by interpretation and the transference reenactment of traumatic past constellations through the repetition compulsion.

There are some patients who cannot live in any environment that is significantly different from what they experienced in childhood, and this includes the treatment setting. Otherwise they feel, as one patient stated, "like fish out of water." They have learned to adapt to their traumatic experiences and they seek or create similar situations in their everyday life because they know how to deal with them. In these instances, patients in therapy project both destructive and abandoning introjects into the therapist, thereby establishing usually a negative transference; and, at the same time, they externalize the traumatic infantile environment into the consultation room. Clearly, these would be impossible analytic relationships because all these patients would be doing is re-creating the world of their psychopathology. They would not be encountering novel experiences that could be potentially helpful and have integrative effects.

Nevertheless, there is more involved than living out psychopathological constellations. This would require a totally compliant analytic setting. The analyst would have to allow the patient to externalize, and he would have to assume the transference role that the patient has assigned to him. This, of course, would clash with the therapist's professional self-representation.

Though patients may create an atmosphere in which their analysts have been made into the monsters of their childhood, the analytic setting cannot survive under these circumstances.

Some patients may not be able to exist in any other setting than one that is pervaded by noxious childhood elements. Consequently, they do not permit a relationship to be established. The analyses of many severely traumatized patients flounder before they begin, because patients are too anxious or frightened to be receptive and accept that their analysts really want to help rather than harm them.

The patient is not the only person who may sabotage the treatment process. Frequently the analyst cannot stand the position that has been forced upon him. The patient expects to be attacked, and analysts do not view themselves as sadistic persecutors. That is why they find paranoid patients so difficult to treat. Patients in the borderline spectrum are usually not as organized in their anger as is the traditional paranoid; rather, they more openly reveal their helplessness and vulnerability.

Therapists are further frustrated because they are aware of their patients' neediness but are unable to reach out and help them. These patients have either never bonded with another person or else formed such weak bonds that they are unable to make any meaningful attachments. Thus, as stated, they can only repeat the failures of the past in a similarly constructed setting. These analysts might not be able to contain their frustration, and perhaps direct it toward their patients as anger or subtle attacks. This reinforces the patient's projections and propensity to externalize, and hence both the goals of treatment and the construction of a holding environment are lost sight of. The therapeutic setting collapses, often enough because of the analyst as well as the patient.

The analyst's unwillingness to be an accomplice of the traumatic past can also be beneficial to the treatment process and the construction of the holding environment. Because the patient cannot integrate a benign relationship, the therapist is viewed in terms of the patient's needs, but he does not accept that role. These analysts do not challenge their patients' images of them as uncaring and brutal, but they indicate through their attitudes and feelings that they are truly invested in their patients' welfare. At first, patients may not recognize this positive attitude because it is not in the realm of their experiences, but in time they become aware of differences in the interaction that they may not, at first, be able to define. The awareness of these differences gradually contributes to the construction of a holding environment, as was evident with the patient discussed in Chapter 6 who, after a long time in treatment, admitted that I was trying to help her even if this was a futile endeavor.

Neither the patient nor the therapist may recognize this type of asynchrony, that is, the dissimilarities according to which patient and therapist view the analyst. The analyst clinging to his resolve to provide a helpful setting may be gradually integrated by the patient and, to some extent, become internalized. This helps provide a therapeutic base that is vastly different from the destructive foundations of childhood and infancy.

The holding environment can also be described in terms of its intensity. This can be seen in the clinical situation I referred to as high-decibel, a compensatory reaction to the low-decibel home atmosphere. With patients who cannot accept relationships or interactions that differ from those of childhood, there is an intense need to defend themselves against people reaching out to them in a benign fashion. The patients presented in the previous chapters illustrate how vehement the rejection of potentially helpful experiences can be. The adolescent patient did not actively resist relating at a high-decibel level, but his lack of intensity was associated with a childhood setting that was markedly different from that of these other patients, and these differences determine the types of holding environments that might be therapeutically effective.

In essence, patients who resist being helped do not know what help is and therefore cannot integrate such experiences into their fragmented egos. The young man I have just described also had very little cognition of a potentially helpful external world and the variety of relationships that it might offer. He had a lack of supportive introjects that would elevate self-esteem and promote explorations of his surroundings. The internal world of many patients, usually fragmented, also possesses hostile, destructive, uncaring introjects. As discussed in Chapter 3, they have encapsulated traumatic experiences, which causes them to violently oppose anyone who approaches them. They are wary and untrustful and often attack their therapists for their presumed ineptness.

There are occasions in which the therapist might respond with equal or greater force and overcome the patient's opposition to either forming or maintaining a therapeutic relationship. Some of these patients eventually become engaged and form a treatment alliance, but these alliances may be tenuous, and even a slight aggravation or trivial event can cause a paranoid regression. Under these circumstances the analyst may have to create an intense holding environment, not in terms of decibels but as an opposing force to the patient's denunciation of the treatment process and of the therapist as a helpful person, and to being seen as intrusively dangerous.

Clinicians occasionally hear of dramatic moments in treatment, turning points that rescue the therapeutic relationship and set it back on the path of further development. The dynamic interplay of these interactions can often be explained in terms of a specific type of holding environment that is characterized by its intensity. As mentioned, these are relationships that have had some positive elements, but because of some altercation the patient has regressed to a destructive state that threatens to disrupt the treatment process.

On the surface, the analyst's behavior may appear to be far removed from establishing a holding environment. It may seem idiosyncratic, based on disruptive countertransference feelings, and nonanalytic. It may also seem similar to the patient's expectations of the analytic setting based on the externalization of the infantile milieu. There may be a countertransference contribution, and phenomenologically there can be similarities to the tyrannical aspects of the childhood setting. Although the analyst may appear demanding and intrusive, his intentions are directed toward saving the treatment and are based upon benign countertransference feelings. Consider the following case example:

A businessman in his middle thirties had seen several analysts before he settled in with his current therapist. His description of former therapists had many paranoid elements. According to the patient, they all disliked him; it was only their arrogance and greediness that caused them to accept him as a patient. He believed that some of them disliked him to the extent that they wanted to harm him. He had intense feelings, but his life in general was not particularly filled with persecutors. There were several associates he did not like, and they were not fond of him. If they could put his career in jeopardy they would, but he was not particularly concerned. He was suspicious and wary, but he did not consider these attitudes unusual because of the highly competitive environment he lived in. He was successful and undoubtedly generated considerable envy in his less successful and less talented colleagues, some being older than himself.

The patient believed that his achievements were the outcome of only his efforts and skills. He emphasized that no one had ever supported or encouraged him. His wife was only interested in his income and never even acknowledged his aptitudes and accomplishments. No one praised him or even told him that he was doing a good job. He knew he was, because his work led to tangible results and was measured in financial gains, which were considerable. He also had been promoted to a top and invulnerable position.

He stressed how everyone tried to exploit him and had no interest in his welfare. His father had also been very successful, far more successful than the patient. He had acquired an empire and was given, or demanded, godlike reverence. Everyone bowed to him, probably out of fear or the expectation of favors awarded to sycophants. Toward his son he was disdainful. He never gave him a word of approval. If the son did well in school or sports, nothing was said, but if he failed at some endeavor, his father would mercilessly revile him. He constantly compared the patient's achievements with his own.

The patient remembered with poignancy and vehemence how he had embarked on a project that would have led to an award. He was competing with peers for this prize, and it seemed likely that he was going to win. He was well ahead of his colleagues in the competition. When he mentioned this at home in an ebullient mood, his father did not respond. He remained silent and morose. The patient felt both angry and depressed, and consequently he slowed down in the pursuit of his project.

Furthermore, he hit a snag, one that his father could have helped him resolve. He did not know he was involved in an area in which his father had considerable expertise. He learned about it when he lost the contest and his father ridiculed him for his failure, emphasizing how inept he was, whereas he, his father, could easily have solved the problem that was impeding his progression to victory. The bitter irony of the situation was reinforced by the fact that what the father said was true. He had, in fact, solved many similar and more difficult problems in the course of his work.

The patient felt betrayed by his father. He believed that he had deliberately withheld the information that he was an expert in the area that was perplexing the patient because he wanted him not to succeed. In the past he was resentful of his father and felt constantly beaten down by him, but from then on he saw his father as the enemy who could not be trusted. He believed that he had to be totally self-reliant and never expect anyone to help him. Nevertheless, he was angry at the world and intensely resented that he would have to make his way in the world without any support or encouragement. He felt bitterly lonely and depressed, and he longed for a relationship that would provide him with succor and comfort.

The previous analysts were unempathic, according to the patient. He viewed them the way he viewed his uninvolved, arrogant father. He reacted to the present analyst in a different fashion. He was impressed by his easygoing, nonanxious demeanor. He also felt that this analyst was genuinely interested in him and that he asked intelligent and meaningful questions. For about a year, the patient continued to feel quite positive about his treatment to the extent that he was mildly idealizing the therapist.

In view of his background, the clinician might question the patient's capacity to sustain a positive relationship. Apparently he must have been able to reach out for and receive some affection, most likely from his mother. He also mentioned an older brother with whom he had a good relationship.

He was able to idealize, but he was unable to attach himself to an idealized person. This had happened several times in school. He recalled a young gym instructor he admired while in elementary school, and although he was fairly competent as an athlete, this instructor paid no particular attention to him. The patient could not capture his interest. In business graduate school, something similar happened. He was unable to go beyond the usual student–teacher relationship with a professor he held in high esteem because of his personal charm and professional expertise. He recalled how disappointed he had been when he realized that he was just another student for this teacher.

He compared college with his family. He went to a large university, with many students in each classroom. Therefore, he received very little if any individual attention. His family was also large in that he had eight younger siblings and the one older brother whom he respected. He had, as he stated, fairly distant relationships with his numerous brothers and sisters. He pictured his mother as a baby-producing factory.

Because of his busy schedule, he frequently had to change appointments, and his analyst did the best he could to accommodate him. On one occasion the therapist, because he forgot to note an appointment, double scheduled. This patient and another patient arrived at the same time. The analyst was embarrassed and confused and had to make the difficult choice as to which patient he would see. He reasoned that the other patient had to travel a great distance, whereas the businessman patient was located fairly close to the office. Therefore, the analyst chose the other patient. That evening the patient left a message on the telephone answering machine indicating that he was canceling all future appointments. In contrast to his usually pleasant demeanor toward the therapist, his voice was cold and hostile and he emphasized that he could no longer trust the analyst. He had, in fact, terminated the treatment.

The analyst became quite upset. He recalled how pleasant it had been to work with this patient in spite of his bad experiences with previous therapists. The patient valued the treatment and felt that he had a special relationship with his analyst. Now, because of a stupid error, it seemed as if everything was going to collapse. The incident appeared flimsy in proportion to the patient's intense reaction.

In view of his history, it is understandable that the patient reacted as he did, although the intensity of his response did not seem appropriate. During childhood he felt like a displaced person, and with the exception of his older brother, he believed that no one even acknowledged his existence. He had built a foundation of trust with his analyst, who turned out, according to the patient, to prefer another patient, as evidenced by sending him away. He had protested that the other patient had been given his session, but the patient's sessions varied from week to week because of his erratic schedule.

The analyst was aware of the patient's sensitivities and regretted the incident. He even wondered whether he had unwittingly participated in the externalization of the patient's family constellation by making the appointment error. Had he been caught in the repetition compulsion? He was trying to understand what had happened, and he felt reasonably certain that by choosing the other patient he had re-created a continuing childhood trauma. The patient had succeeded in believing that he represented something special to the analyst, and now he was bitterly disappointed. He was abandoned for a sibling and no one cared. In the past his mother had left him with each new birth and the father never had been available. His older brother had helped him develop a minimal capacity to feel loved, which made the pain of rejection unbearable.

The therapist felt extremely sad about the patient's resolve to terminate treatment. He also believed that the patient was exacting revenge by canceling his appointments, a reaction to his being "canceled." The analyst was also amazed at the complete Jekyll–Hyde transformation.

These feelings impelled him to take some action. He could not sit still and do nothing. He wanted very much to continue the treatment. Consequently, he called the patient and requested that before taking any precipitous action, they should have a session and try to understand what had happened and to explain the intensity of his feelings. The patient remained cool and aloof and kept repeating that the damage had been done and he could never again trust the analyst. There was a paranoid fervor to his words, but the therapist did not recognize the futility of trying to reason or argue with such firmly rooted beliefs, which, on account of their intensity, had to have considerable projective elements. On the contrary, he felt himself being drawn into the discussion as he tried to persuade the patient to return to treatment. Finally, in an uncharacteristic fashion, the analyst lost his temper. In a fairly rough voice, he told the patient that he would not put up with such nonsense. The patient knew his appointment times and he had better keep them or else. Then, he hung up.

The analyst was surprised and shocked at what he had done. He also wondered what he could have possibly meant when he shouted at the patient that he had better keep his appointments or else. What could he have been threatening? As he gradually became aware of the depth of his response, he conjectured that he was simply emphasizing how much he cared for the patient and could not bear to lose him.

The patient kept his appointments, but he continued to be angry. As time went by, his reactions could be understood as negative transference and as reactions to disappointing idealizations. All of his feelings were related to various aspects of the infantile milieu. He could not sustain his idealization of the analyst indefinitely. It was the rapidity of the emergence of the negative transference that had been startling. The patient must have been ready to get in touch with his anger, and all he needed was some provocation as occurred when the analyst scheduled two patients for the same session. How much the patient might have contributed to the therapist's error through his frequent requests for changes of time remains a moot question.

Several years later, the patient reviewed what had occurred when he had threatened to terminate treatment. The negative transference and sibling rivalry had been analyzed and partially worked through. In spite of his tremendous anger and hostility, it got through to the patient that his analyst really cared for him and was interested in his welfare. Although the patient was obsessed with the thought that he had been abandoned for someone else, the analyst's uncharacteristic and intense reaction acquired meaning for him and eventually became a significant memory.

The analyst, without any awareness, was the total antithesis of the patient's father. The father would have ignored and depreciated his son while stressing his own superiority. By contrast, the analyst was, to some measure, expressing his neediness in that he needed to preserve the therapeutic setting, whereas the father had to sustain his narcissism by having a vulnerable and needy son. Eventually the patient was able to perceive that his analyst held him in high esteem and that the therapist's interest and attitudes toward him had helped construct a holding environment that would be able to survive the impact of his violent rage.

From the beginning, the treatment process had been set in motion because of the construction of a holding environment. The early setting caused the patient to feel that he was at the center of the stage. He felt secure in the analyst's emotional investment in him, and undoubtedly this sense of security contributed to the weathering of the patient's intense rage and prevented the collapse of the treatment relationship. During this time, however, the holding environment was not threatened by the patient feeling denigrated and abandoned because someone else took over center stage. The patient knew that his analyst had other patients, but he was able to push this perception into the background. For the most part, the holding environment caused him to feel special, as if he were an only child.

Suddenly this serenity was shattered. The past crept into the present, and the double scheduling acted as a catalyst. The emotional awareness of another patient being given preference caused cracks in the structure of the holding environment. The patient could no longer maintain an only-child image, and all the disruptive feelings of childhood overwhelmed him.

The analyst's intense reaction, in addition to his previous idealization, eventually restored equilibrium so that treatment could continue. In essence, the analyst had succeeded in once again creating an only-child holding environment. This time, however, he was demonstrating an active, intense investment in the patient, a diametrically opposite attitude to the father's arrogant indifference.

WORKING THROUGH AND THE REPETITION COMPULSION

If asked what is the essence of the therapeutic process, most analysts would reply that working through is the chief element of analytic resolution. As I have discussed elsewhere (Giovacchini 1986), do we really know what working through means? Freud (1914b) stated that it involves remembering rather than the patient acting out impulses through repetitive behavior. Rather than being discharged through actions, impulses reach the level of conscious awareness, where they can be dealt with at higher, rational levels of psychic integration. The unconscious becomes conscious and the irrational is handled rationally.

Freud's ideas are related to his concepts of psychopathology as a conflict between different parts of the mind, that is, between forbidden unconscious impulses and higher, inhibiting ego and superego levels. The structural defects that have been discussed throughout the book require more complex formulations of the therapeutic action. Simply making the unconscious conscious is not enough to achieve psychic harmony and growth. The working-through process has not been given much attention in the context of structural psychopathology as it is unfolding during the treatment interaction.

Some of Freud's patients, especially those in the *Studies on Hysteria* (Breuer and Freud 1895), had dramatic moments in treatment. An insight suddenly opens up new vistas and the patient has a different orientation toward both the inner and outer world. The insight has been integrated as a consequence of working through.

Although clinicians do encounter such moments during the treatment of patients, they are relatively rare occurrences. In a similar vein, changes in the patient are seldom marked or obvious. In many instances they are not even noticeable. The working-through process is slow and gradual and often silent. Furthermore, within the treatment setting there may be little evidence that the analysis has had any effect. It is always gratifying for a therapist to hear from a relative or a colleague who may be treating a spouse or a friend of the patient how much for the better that patient has changed.

The converse also occurs; that is, the patient and analyst know there has been improvement, but others do not agree. In fact, they may feel that the patient's condition has worsened rather than improved. From the relative's viewpoint this may be true in that the patient's needs and adaptations have changed and the equilibrium of the object relationship becomes disturbed (Giovacchini 1958, 1961). Internal changes are not necessarily associated with improved relations, especially if the relationship is based on psychopathological needs.

These relatives complain about the lack of progress. I recall a patient's mother who called me frequently asking about the progress of her 38-year-old son. She complained that nothing had been worked out. She was intrusive but felt justified in asking because she was paying for the treatment. I had to call to her attention that if you ask a mother once a week whether her child has grown taller, she will not have noticed any growth. Such judgments can be made only over longer periods.

Freud also wrote about the slow, gradual pace of working through, especially during mourning (Freud 1917). He emphasized how countless memories of the relationship with the lost love object had to be worked through. In this case, it meant decathecting the ambivalent attachments to that person. The ultimate purpose of this process is to assimilate the positive elements of the relationship into the psyche, perhaps expanding the sense of identity or enlarging the repertoire of the ego's executive system. The lost love object as a discrete entity slowly disappears as it is psychically absorbed.

In a general sense, something similar occurs in treatment and can be considered an aspect of the working-through process. The patient creates a scenario in the consultation room that, in a modulated fashion, re-creates the traumatic environment. With the analyst's help, he decathects the noxious elements of early relationships and incorporates whatever positive qualities existed. Even the most disturbed patients must have had some, though minimal, positive experiences or else they would not have survived psychically and physically.

These formulations retain elements of the psychoeconomic hypothesis, which has generally been pushed to the background when discussing borderline patients. Still, the psyche requires energy in order to function and to attach itself to persons and address tasks in the external world. In working through, certain types of detachments from the past are required, which can be referred to as decathecting processes. This formulation is not based on a tension-discharge hypothesis.

Still, detachment from traumatic experiences does not tell us much about working through. Actually, we are dealing with a tautology. In essence, I have stated that overcoming psychopathology by divesting it of psychic energy defines working through, but this removal of psychic energy from its psychopathological attachments is inherent in the concept of working through. It tells us nothing as to how this comes about, of the processes and structural changes that make this possible.

Working through has to be discussed in several contexts. It has to be brought into focus with the repetition compulsion, externalizing processes, and the holding environment that has just been discussed. Levels of psychic development also have to be included inasmuch as the therapeutic aim is to reach higher developmental stages and states of ego integration. These structural accretions occur as the patient achieves greater autonomy and freedom from the constrictions of the traumatic past.

In the preceding section I gave examples of how patients try to externalize, which means that they want to create a scenario that is modeled after the infantile environment. The holding environment, which is the scenario the analyst constructs, is oppositional to what the patient strives to externalize. The patient's efforts to create a scenario can be thought of as the setting in motion of the repetition compulsion, but in an expanded sense.

Freud (1920) described the repetition compulsion in terms of overcoming certain threatening feelings and situations. The patient perceives danger, and the repetition of the traumatic dangerous event represents an attempt to achieve resolution, that is, to convert passive vulnerability into active mastery. This certainly happens, but more is involved. Patients with character problems seek to create a setting in which they can survive. This is both a repetition of past traumatic constellations and an attempt to create a more comfortable environment. From a therapeutic perspective this view of the repetition compulsion contains negative and positive elements.

The holding environment blends with the positive aspects and is oppositional to the negative elements. These interactions occur within the framework of the working-through process, which seeks to expand the patient's range of adaptations and to provide a safe external world. Freud (1924a,b) stressed that the main problems in severely ill patients involved conflict between the ego and the outer world. The working-through process strives to relieve this conflict by internal changes that increase the patient's range of adaptations. This leads to greater flexibility that permits the patient to become engaged with wider segments of the external milieu. It also frees patients to wander into areas that were previously unavailable because they did not know how to cope with them or because they generated anxiety. The following vignette illustrates how the working-through process operates in effecting internal changes that affect relations with the outer world that are mediated by the holding environment.

The patient, a retired army noncommissioned officer, a man in his early forties, sought treatment shortly after he had been discharged. All he had known was the military. His father was a regular army officer, and the patient's childhood was spent in different barracks. After he graduated from high school, he enlisted. Now, being thrust into a civilian environment, he was bewildered and anxious. He was still comparatively young and he did not know where he fit in the scheme of things. His adaptive techniques were geared toward military, not civilian, life.

He felt he was frequently overwhelmed with anxiety and depressed. These symptoms began while he was still in the army, where he sought psychiatric help. He was given antianxiety and antidepressant medication. These drugs were not particularly effective. He was dissatisfied with himself as a person and believed he needed more than what the army was able or willing to supply. He felt he needed psychoanalysis, and he was particularly chagrined when the first civilian psychiatrist he saw recommended supportive, brief psychotherapy. Nevertheless, this psychiatrist referred him to an analyst who began treatment without any preconceived notions, as Freud (1913) recommended.

His mother presumably suffered from a manic-depressive psychosis, which caused her to be periodically hospitalized. He described his father as a strict disciplinarian bordering on the tyrannical. As an adolescent he felt cowed by him and did not believe he could do anything to please him. He knew that as long as he worked hard at after-school jobs and newspaper routes, his father would be moderately receptive. The father did not value the patient's excellent academic record, believing that scholarly success was unmanly and a waste of time. All that mattered was hard work, thriftiness, and self-discipline. The patient wanted to go to college, but neither parent supported him. They refused to help him so he joined the army out of desperation and to separate himself from his family. He worked hard in the army, was very good at following orders, but showed very little initiative and had no ambition to advance himself into the officer category. His father, who finally became a colonel, did not encourage his son to apply to Officer's Training School.

The patient did not think much about his circumstances. He drifted along, had a few casual affairs, but never married. He seemed content with the security the army offered and felt he was fairly well adjusted. His superiors were satisfied with his performance and, in some instances, gave him the license to do as he saw fit because he was quite competent.

Leaving the army changed everything drastically. He was suddenly placed in a competitive world in which his military skills had very little relevance. His pension provided some security but it was meager in the face of the increased expenses of civilian life. More important, he did not have an organized sense of identity that fit with the exigencies of the nonmilitary world.

In treatment he presented himself as helpless and vulnerable, and he desperately pleaded for help. He had deteriorated to a condition in which he was functionally paralyzed. Before starting treatment, he was hospitalized in a Veterans Administration hospital for 3 months. He moved to Chicago because an old army friend had promised him a job working as a mechanic in his garage, but he did not particularly relish the idea of being a mechanic.

Other than revealing his anxiety and asking for guidance, he found it difficult to be spontaneous. His early sessions were filled with long periods of silence. He admitted that since leaving the army he was subjected to too much freedom, and he did not know how to handle it. Previously, decisions were made for him. Although it led to some tense moments, the analyst remained nonintrusive and nondirective. He was genuinely interested in the patient's thoughts and ideas, and he would ask questions to get the patient to go beyond his initially cryptic descriptions. The patient responded to these questions, but he seldom went beyond the topic to enter areas that may have been extensions of what was asked.

It became apparent that he was treating his analyst as he might have reacted to a commanding officer. He was more than properly respectful and usually responded to or addressed his therapist as "Sir."

It was obvious that the patient was repeating the past with his father as well as his army career in the consultation room. As it became abundantly clear later in treatment, he was intensely afraid of his father and he had apparently suppressed all spontaneity, to the extent that he could not allow himself to have an idea of his own. Passive acquiescence was, however, a defensive adaptation. He had externalized various defensive techniques that permitted him to move safely and securely into a constricted external world, that of the noncommissioned officer.

The repetition compulsion was also operating, although it seemed to be moving in the opposite direction from what Freud (1920) had described. He did not appear to be converting an experience of passive vulnerability to active mastery. In childhood it seemed that he had collapsed into a state of passive surrender to protect himself from a harsh, tyrannical father. The repetitive aspects of his behavior were related to defensive adaptations that he had had to construct in order to survive in what he perceived as a dangerous environment.

His compliance, however, was not just a simple surrender. During childhood and in the army, he had built up a private domain in which he had explicit values. He felt scorn and contempt for his father's ideas, which followed certain aspects of military tradition. He believed that his father and other commissioned officers were basically stupid, crass, and often ridiculous. The patient knew how to manipulate them and how to get things done, which eventually turned out to his advantage. He compared his approach to Machiavellian strategies.

In fact, he was quite well educated, although he had no formal schooling beyond high school. The army posts to which he was assigned had excellent libraries, and he read extensively. He had read most of the classics and was well versed in modern literature. He also had a particular interest in philosophy, but he kept his scholarly pursuits secret. Occasionally, evidence of his scholarship or intelligence would break through, but he was able to cover it up retrospectively; if this happened in front of a superior officer he could apply it to the performance of a task or the solution of a problem. He considered himself to be their superior, at least in knowledge, intelligence, and cleverness.

Though he was passive and let others dominate him, he felt that he was in control of most situations and had actively mastered a milieu that could be treacherous and dangerous by having armed himself with a knowledgeable, agile mind. He was able in this fashion to actively protect himself from what was potentially dangerous. He was satisfied even to the point of smugness with his ability to manipulate and reduce others to being his puppets. These elements of his orientation and behavior represent the repetition compulsion that is covertly, rather than overtly, manifested. His silent attitudes determined his modus operandi and caused him to feel safe and secure.

After discharge from the service, the repetition compulsion could no longer function because it was not appropriate to, nor could it be effective in, the civilian milieu. He recognized that there were many intelligent and educated persons whom he might not be able to manipulate and who might defeat him. He felt weak and vulnerable as a mechanic, without prestige or the ability to command respect. In the army he was respected by noncommissioned officers of lesser rank and had the admiration of superior officers who relied on him. As stated, he kept hidden his contempt for them. His civilian status did not permit him to use the adaptive techniques that operated within the context of the repetition compulsion.

When he entered therapy, he had already lost the repetition-compulsion mantle of protection. He was helpless in a world in which he was devoid of adaptive techniques. He had been reduced to, and had regressed to, a borderline state (see Chapter 3). He was now externalizing the early world of childhood without any defenses. He was acting like a helpless child facing a dictatorial, demeaning, and dangerous father. Any effort he might make toward helping himself achieve autonomy or seeking adaptations in keeping with his intellectual capacities would lead to immense anxiety and possibly panic. Later in treatment, he explained that he was afraid that his father would kill him. He had numerous dreams and fantasies of being attacked, beaten, and threatened with castration.

His analyst knew immediately that he was not talking with the traditional master sergeant and that the patient in no way viewed life as the typical mechanic might. In spite of the patient's anxiety, the analyst was able to converse with him and learn a good deal about his attitudes, scholarship, and philosophy of life. The analyst made it quite clear that he was puzzled as to why the patient had not aimed his sights higher than settling on being a mechanic. He had sensed his potential and was exploring with him what possibilities were available. He went so far as to suggest vocational counseling. The patient had not yet told his therapist about his self-schooling. Nevertheless, he was pleased, as he later revealed, at his analyst's interest in having him seek vocations that belonged, as he put it, to "higher echelons." The analyst raised the question of formal schooling, and the patient was both pleased and frightened.

The therapist had intuitively addressed the patient's basic fear, that of being destroyed if he sought activities or expertise in areas that were outside his father's domain or value system. True, he had been rebellious and rejected what his father dictated, but he did so in a covert and unnoticeable fashion. He seemed to comply by remaining in the army, but he never tried to climb to his father's officer level. His father was satisfied, because basically he did not want his son to be his equal or to surpass him.

Although the analyst's attitudes and suggestions proved eventually to be helpful, the patient was at first confused. In the midst of his confusion, however, he began to feel less anxious. Clearly, he was seeking protection; he needed someone who would help alleviate his intense feelings of vulnerability and helplessness. He wanted to be rescued.

The analyst did not directly respond to his pleas for help, which were, in part, due to his feelings of weakness and inadequacy. Instead, he addressed the patient's strengths and potentials, and this, as stated earlier, was initially confusing for the patient. On the other hand, he was confronting the source of the patient's fears, which were associated with feeling unprotected. The patient was externalizing the early environment, in which he felt that any striving toward autonomy would be met with his father's murderous retaliatory rage. The analyst was encouraging him to explore areas that the patient felt would cause his father to kill him. This was frightening but also reassuring, because it meant that the analyst was receptive and would not, like his father, want to kill him if he achieved in areas that he himself chose. Still, he felt very much exposed.

The treatment process involved a blending of the externalization of the early environment, the repetition compulsion, and the holding environment. The active mastery components of the repetition compulsion were no longer effective and protective once the patient left the protective setting that the army provided. He wanted therapy to give him the protection that he could not get in childhood. At that time, he had turned to his mother, but she, for a variety of reasons, was not able to stand against the father. In treatment he initially presented himself as a vulnerable child and had externalized the threatening environment his father had created to the civilian milieu, which included the treatment setting. The therapist, in turn, created a holding environment that counteracted the patient's perception of his father as his potential murderer, although he did not know this at the time. The patient's fears stemmed from his introjected father.

The working-through process was the outcome of the interactions of externalizations, the holding environment, and the repetition compulsion. To summarize drastically, the analyst's acknowledgement of the patient's scholarly achievements, as well as his encouragement to pursue them, helped modulate his anxiety. He took night courses in business administration and accounting. He complained of his ineptness and his inability to function and emphasized that he could never succeed. These feelings were often presented in an intense, anxious fashion, and he rebuked his analyst for not being sensitive to his deficiencies. He also was upset because he felt the analyst did not appreciate the depth of his depression.

This was the outcome of an interesting interplay between an attempt to externalize his frightened, vulnerable self in the treatment interaction in the context of a paternal transference. As occurred in childhood, he viewed the father as wanting to kill him for any achievement. Emphasizing his vulnerability and inadequacies served to reassure the father imago as it was projected into the analyst that he was not going to transgress his father's prohibition to be autonomously successful.

The repetition compulsion was also operating. Although he protested that he was only a weak, incapable person, he privately knew this was not the case. He was at the head of the class, and when he took his accounting licensing examination he had the highest score, which was published in the newspapers. Once again he was secretly defying his father, an active rebellion against the vulnerable position his father's murderous rage had placed him in. Thus the treatment process involved the repetition compulsion, the infantile defenses against its exposure, and the holding environment, which permitted the patient to reveal both the repetition compulsion and the compensatory feelings of inadequacy. The patient was able to compare his infantile view of his therapist with the attitudes that the therapist expressed and the confidence he showed in the patient's capacities to achieve positions that went beyond the mechanic's role he had initially accepted. He was finally able to understand that his past was coloring his view of the treatment, but the holding environment had been effective in correcting the distortions of transference projections. He continued operating within the framework of the repetition compulsion, but he was no longer keeping it secret. He could talk about his achievements and his ambitions, as he pulled further and further away from what he called the military mentality.

The main synthesizing element that led to working through was the feeling of being protected, which I believe is more or less true of any holding environment. I also believe that with many patients it is more important than being able to be dependent. These two feelings are, of course, related. Obviously, a patient cannot allow himself to be dependent without a feeling of trust and of being protected.

This patient, after 5 years of treatment, had succeeded in working through the damaging and inhibiting effects of what had become the internalized father. His interactions with his father had been repeatedly interpreted within the transference context as the purpose of the repetition compulsion had been focused on. As stated, the initial holding environment made this possible as it enabled the patient to reveal strivings and accomplishments. In the past, their revelation would have been terrifying.

He still felt afraid that his father would kill him, but not because of his civilian achievements. His father had been dead for many years, but the remnants of his introject were nevertheless active. They were manifest, however, at a higher developmental level than previously.

He married 4 years after he started treatment when he was beginning to admit that perhaps he could be competent. Within this context of life circumstances he began having dreams that, at the manifest level, were filled with oedipal material. He had many fantasies of his father wanting to castrate him because of his heterosexual endeavors. He had a moderate sex life while in the army, but there were never any relationships in which he became emotionally involved. Now he had made a commitment and achieved intimacy, and had become the father of two children.

It was interesting how his previous feelings of inadequacy and vulnerability were no longer connected with strivings for autonomy, which involved mastering the exigencies of the outer world. They were not related to basic survival. It seemed that as he progressed in his analysis, anxiety and conflicts that were associated with early ego levels had moved up the developmental scale and had reached the oedipal level. There was no evidence in his history or during the first 5 years of analysis of conflicts related to the Oedipus complex. At this juncture his material became markedly sexual. From having presented a borderline perspective reflected in his confusion and feelings of inadequacy about dealing with the civilian world, he now sounded like one of Freud's early patients who were labeled as hysterics, their material being predominantly erotic. He focused on the fear of castration and told many stories in which it had been prophesied, usually by a witch, that the protagonist will be killed or meet some otherwise tragic fate when he reached maturity. No matter what is done to protect the hero, he nevertheless perishes or meets his inexorable fate. In therapy he had the same feeling that he could not escape what had been preordained. He believed that his father would not let him achieve manhood, but this was related to a heterosexual orientation.

To stress oedipal issues, he occasionally mentioned incestuous feelings toward his mother and tried to associate them with his lack of intimate involvements with women while in the army. On the other hand, he could not imagine himself feeling attracted to his mother. He saw her as a devouring monster who, rather than being protective, was a threat, as the father was. From a realistic viewpoint, he did not feel cowered by her, because she was so disorganized and helpless that he did not believe she could do much to harm him. During infancy, he did not know how he had experienced her.

Regarding working through, the technical issue arises as to whether earlier, preoedipal phases had been resolved, so that now the task was to deal with the oedipal phase. Two questions have to be discussed: (1) What does resolution of preoedipal phases mean? and (2) Where was the oedipal conflict when the patient was facing preoedipal problems?

Regarding the first question, the obvious answer is that *resolution* refers to the analysis of conflicts associated with pregenital developmental stages. These conflicts have been discussed in terms of externalization of anxiety-laden states of helplessness and the compensating aspects of the repetition compulsion. In classical psychoanalytic theory, analysts would have made formulations about intrapsychic conflicts concerning the fear of annihilation associated with aggressive strivings and defenses to contain that fear. Resolution would refer to the emergence of anxiety as defenses were analyzed in the transference context. In the case discussed, the projection of the malignant father imago was minimal; rather, the patient viewed the analyst as a benign father, which permitted him to reveal his helpless and compensatory aggressive strivings. The patient then began to understand that he could be aggressive and that rather than his being destroyed for such strivings, the benign father he had wished for in childhood approved of his endeavors.

This formulation does not go far enough. It directs itself to intrapsychic rearrangements. The vicissitudes of psychic structure are not included in this type of conceptual understanding. Nevertheless, something must have happened to the patient's character, as evidenced by the shift of material into sexual areas. This seems to be the outcome of changes in psychic integration such as occur with further characterological synthesis.

It would seem that the patient made a developmental advance moving from a pregenital to an oedipal phase. In the first 5 years of analysis, there had been practically no sexual material in his associations, fantasies, or dreams. The change that then occurred was indicative of a movement toward phallic or genital psychosexual stages. This would definitely be a structural accretion. Presumably, the patient had been fixated at an early pregenital phase, and the working-through process led to a reactivation of a developmental impetus.

This forward progression appears to answer the question as to where Oedipus was before its manifestations reached the oedipal stage of development. His characterological problems kept forward development immobilized and oedipal issues had not yet been structured. He had not faced issues of commitment and intimacy that connected with oedipal feelings; he was much more involved with the immediate issue of survival.

When dealing with psychic processes, clinicians cannot make absolute pronouncements. The mind can be viewed as a series of hierarchically structured layers. With the exception of the severest forms of psychopathology, such as extremely regressed psychiatric patients, most patients have at least vestiges of higher developmental phases, such as the oedipal phase. These may only minimally contribute, however, to the general organization and operations of the psychic apparatus, which is dominated by earlier, pregenital orientations and adaptations.

Still, character structure cannot be viewed as absolutely lacking in the structures and developmental phases that are aspects of the human condition. This is important to note because it supplies clinicians with a ray of hope. Even though higher elements of the psychic apparatus are poorly constructed, there is the possibility, through analysis, to achieve further development and reconstruction of what is psychopathologically underdeveloped. Although this therapeutic task may be difficult, it is easier than creating psychic structure de novo, that is, to construct structures that were not previously there. In most patients there is at least some base, some foundation upon which to build further.

The patient just discussed may have also been illustrating another mechanism besides moving forward in the developmental continuum. The sexual material may not have been entirely oedipal, although it manifestedly appeared to be. It may have been due to the erotization of primitive—that is, preoedipal—psychic processes. As the analysis was involved with the interplay of infantile vulnerability and the defensive repetition compulsion, these experiences within the therapeutic framework might have become erotized. As has been discussed in previous chapters, affects, including sexual feelings, have a binding and synthesizing function. Sexualizing both anxiety and the various elements of the repetition compulsion could represent a striving for greater psychic integration.

What is from a manifest viewpoint an oedipal configuration lends itself well to the expression of this patient's, and many other patients', basic conflictual orientation. Within the context of faulty psychic structure and adaptations that are limited only to a particular segment of the external world—in this case, the military—the attending conflicts can be molded into an oedipal form. To repeat, they are not oedipal in that they do not belong to a higher developmental phase; they have similarities to the Oedipus complex in that they represent struggles between aggression and anxiety. There is an inherent conflict regarding aggression when it is associated with a certain degree of destructiveness toward persons who seem to stand in the way of active mastery and accomplishment.

This patient's repetition compulsion, as discussed, concerned functioning in a masterful, active fashion. Casting this in oedipal terms would convert these strivings into an aggressive, dominant stance toward the father, which in the legend means killing him. The retaliatory fear of castration, which frequently came up in the patient's material, is an embellishment of his anxiety about revealing his accomplishments. As stated, he was afraid his father would kill him if he found out about his scholarship and his hopes that it would lead to a satisfying job and gratifying relationships. He was fearful of his father's vengeful jealousy, which in the Oedipus complex is expressed as the urge to castrate the son.

Again, when dealing with the human psyche, nothing is absolute. Although I believe that the sexual material is, for the most part, the outcome of erotization of pregenital elements, this does not mean that oedipal material was not also a factor contributing to the patient's associations. Furthermore, in an analysis there are shifts between different developmental levels, and as patients make progress, the same material may represent higher levels of psychic integration, whereas initially it is associated with more primitive constellations. This patient continued with manifest oedipal material, which became the central core of the analysis.

8

Psychic Structure, the

Transitional Space and

the Analytic Introject

Classical analysis emphasizes shifts in conflictful configurations. As the superego becomes less rigid, the ego is better able to reconcile itself with what had been ego-alien id impulses. Freud stressed the psychodynamic elements underlying psychopathology, and that with analytic progress there would be energic displacements as secondary-process blended with primary-process elements. Basically, analytic treatment very much involved redistribution of psychic energy, making what had been consumed in maintaining repression available so that higher levels of psychic functioning could be achieved. Feelings and impulses that have been banished to the lower recesses of the psyche cannot gain access to the main mental stream. This lowers the functional capacity of the psychic apparatus because it does not have access to all parts of the self.

In this model the curative process concerns regaining these banished parts, but again this is conceptualized in terms of psychic energy. The psyche, once the repressive barriers have been lifted, can then include greater amounts of primary-process energy in its energic reservoir. It remains, however, under the control of secondary-process regulation insofar as the personality is in tune with both internal and external reality.

The above formulations can, in part, be used for our understanding of the therapeutic process involved in the treatment of patients suffering from characterological defects if clinicians focus on psychic structure rather than forbidden or ego-alien impulses. In discussing the psychoneuroses, Freud wrote about the acquisition of psychic energy that is being consumed by intrapsychic conflict; whereas with borderline patients, clinicians are focused on regaining lost parts of the self. As has been discussed, split-off parts of the self are integrated into the main psychic stream.

There is a fundamental difference, however, between the goals of treatment of psychoneurotic patients and of patients who belong in the borderline spectrum. Although both groups of patients are involved in expanding their psychic horizons by regaining either energy lost in maintaining a psychopathological equilibrium or split-off parts of the self, the borderline patient is also striving to gain *new* psychic structures. As stressed in previous chapters, these patients have to set the developmental drive once again in motion and seek higher developmental levels. Our concepts of the treatment process have to include spatial concepts as we view the personality in terms of a structural hierarchy. The mental apparatus has to be studied in terms of its breadth and depth. This places a greater emphasis on its structural integrity, which can be explored in a microscopic as well as in a macroscopic fashion.

The term *microscopic* refers to psychic structures and systems. The structures include internal objects as well as functions, and self and object representations. Psychic systems encompass functions that are related to the general operations of the psychic apparatus, such as perception, ego-executive activities that involve internal and external adaptations, and interactions with the outer world. Introjects consist of internal object representations and include the functional significance of that person, such as the maternal introject consisting of both the mother as a person in her own right and as a nurturing modality.

The *macroscopic* viewpoint of the psychic apparatus stresses gross orientations, particularly developmental levels. The developmental spectrum that has been found most useful in the treatment of borderline patients was discussed in Chapter 3. Unlike Freud's focus, it is not primarily concerned with energic factors; it deals mainly with the internal and external adaptations that occur as various developmental phases participate in determining how the patient will react to the vicissitudes of the external world. The macroscopic approach permits the clinician to examine spatial qualities, that is, relationships between various developmental levels as well as how various psychic systems and introjects interact with others. During the treatment of patients suffering from structural problems, different developmental phases are called into play as the patient struggles to overcome the constriction and fears of childhood that painfully impinge on his psyche and in many instances emotionally immobilize him.

Winnicott (1953) introduced the concept of the transitional space, an extremely important area of psychic development. This space is responsible for some of the highest human achievements and, indeed, for the very humanity of the mind. It is the place in which illusion, playful fantasy, and creativity originate. Although I have discussed the development of the transitional space elsewhere (Giovacchini 1979a, 1986) it is germane to repeat some of the fundamentals involved in the construction of this geometrically visualized landmark that is so meaningful in the creation of a fully human being.

The reader will recall from the discussion in Chapter 3 how the transitional space enables the child to enter the world of external objects, that is, how to distinguish the outer from the inner world. The child finally recognizes what is fantasy or illusion and to distinguish these from external events and experiences. Patients with characterological problems have not reached the transitional stage of development, or they have constructed a defective one. Thus *the task of therapy is to help the patient construct a transitional phase and pass through it, or to repair a damaged and defective one.* The latter task is directed toward assuring that the transitional space acquires the functions that are characteristic of its operations, functions that have either never been attained or been defectively distorted so that they impede further development and lead to various maladaptations. Many of the manifestations of psychopathology can be explained by problems in the formation of the transitional space or defects in its structure.

For example, as discussed in Chapter 3, the formation of the transitional space is associated with the construction of a nurturing matrix. There is a reciprocal interplay between the formation of what is essentially an introject, the nurturing matrix, and a space that brings parts of the internal world into reality. The transitional space, which protrudes into the external world, extends the psyche's boundaries. As the external world reacts appropriately to the child's "omnipotence," as Winnicott (1953) states, the nurturing matrix becomes more firmly established. The assurance that one's needs will be met creates a foundation of security and self-esteem that emboldens the child to move into and explore the external world, and to experience it as a familiar and friendly place. The psyche is propelled into a positive feedback sequence in that successful forays into the environment, as exemplified in play and experimentation, strengthen the feeling that nurture is forthcoming and gratifying. This leads to optimism and self-confidence.

Many formulations about the transitional space and phase are couched in adultomorphic terms and concepts. For example, to speak of an infant feeling omnipotent, as both Winnicott and Freud (1912) have postulated, is to attribute qualities to a child that has not yet achieved the cognitive capacities to feel or think in such terms. Nevertheless, as the mind matures, it eventually begins to regard itself with benign grandiosity and self-assurance. In some instances, those persons who have passed through a successful transitional phase become engaged in creative activity.

The lack of development or the maldevelopment of the transitional space leads to various types of borderline psychopathology. As discussed in Chapter 3, one of the outcomes of a successful transitional phase is the establishment of ego boundaries, which separate the internal world of the psyche from the external world of reality.

Reality is discovered as the child relinquishes the belief that he is the source of his own nurture. The mother is so in tune with her child's needs that her immediate response causes the child to believe that feeling a need, such as hunger, creates a gratifying response that is independent of the intervention of an external caregiver. Again, this is attributing qualities to the infant's mind that are beyond its cognitive capabilities. Still, the clinician can conceptualize a state of mind that maintains harmony and security because neediness is associated with anticipation and pleasure rather than feeling threatened and anxious. As children experience such internal harmony, they become willing to allow themselves to acknowledge that the source of nurture is external, and they can become comfortably dependent. This is the beginning of object relationships.

Patients who have had a traumatically constructed transitional space have difficulties in establishing ego boundaries and find it difficult to distinguish between the inner and outer worlds. They also feel threatened by the external milieu, which is perceived as dangerous and intrusive. These patients lack confidence and self-esteem, and, as is typical of the borderline patient, they feel confused and inadequate to deal with the demands and complexities of a poorly perceived reality.

Winnicott (1953) considered the transitional space to be the locus of illusion and fantasy. It is also a play area in which the internal world blends with external objects. These are transitional objects, and the process of creating them is called the transitional phenomenon. The connection to external objects consists of various feelings, many of them having a primary-process organization. Objects are played with, and their significance is not confined to concrete reality. They can be manipulated and anthropomorphized and acquire symbolic representation. Within the transitional space, objects are imbued with qualities that transcend the confines of reality. Thus illusions and fantasies are created.

The ability to indulge in such transitional phenomena leads to the capacity for psychological-mindness and relatedness. Such persons make ideal patients because they can be introspective and view others in terms of psychological processes. They are in tune with themselves and have sensitivity and intuitiveness about other persons and their feelings and behavior. As occurs with the transitional object, they make others part of the self, but later in life, not just for the sole purpose of viewing them as the source of a nurturing matrix or soothing. Rather, they can allow themselves to fuse with an external object or identify with a situation as a playful activity, which leads to empathic understanding. These are qualities that are desirable for both analytic patients and therapists.

The patients I am discussing, however, are almost totally lacking in any of these qualities because of problems in constructing the transitional space and having experienced transitional phenomenon. They lack the ability to produce illusions and even to have fantasies. When they seem to be experiencing something akin to flights of fancy, these are usually ominous, catastrophic, and border on delusion. These patients are not playful and do not have the flexibility to engage in "let's pretend" activity. To them everything is grimly real. These are the concretely oriented patients discussed in Chapter 6 who cannot get in touch with the inner recesses of their minds, and whose views and relationships with reality are markedly constricted.

The transitional space, as is true of the psyche in general, can in itself be viewed in terms of a hierarchical continuum. Not all patients can be expected to construct or reconstruct all aspects of this continuum. It depends on their inner resources that are based upon the structural integrity of the psychic apparatus as to how far they can progress in their further development. The rigidity of their maladaptations is also a factor that will impede the structuring of a well-functioning transitional space and determine what levels within this space can be attained.

As discussed, the formation of the transitional space leads to the differentiation between the inner and outer worlds and the establishment of beginning object relationships. This process is a basic quality of the transitional space and phenomenon, and it presumably occurs with most persons, with the possible exception of those suffering from the severest forms of psychopathology, such as some of the psychoses. Imagination, playful illusion, and benign fantasies belong to what might be considered higher levels of the developmental hierarchy within the transitional space. Many patients, especially the concretely oriented patients discussed, never reach these levels during the course of their development, and many never are able to achieve them in a therapeutic setting.

Clinicians may have to lower their sights as they review their goals with severely disturbed patients. There are narrow limits to what many of these patients can achieve. It may be enough that they form a transitional space that will strengthen ego boundaries, that is, so they can distinguish what does and does not belong to the self. They may be unable or unwilling to go any further. They achieve a better sense of self, but without any profundity and sensitivity to the intrapsychic determinants of their reactions and perceptions. They still behave and view the world according to a concrete perspective, never having developed the flexibility for illusion and playful activities. Therapy has helped them gain confidence and raise self-esteem, but they are still constricted because they have not been able to construct the higher echelons of the transitional space.

The construction of the transitional space in the treatment setting is associated with the formation of the holding environment. This is to be expected because, as repeatedly stressed, the holding environment is intended to be the antithesis of the traumatic and rejecting infantile milieu. The holding environment supplies a safe, protective external world that directs itself to the patient's needs. This, it is hoped, produces an interaction in which the patient has an opportunity to construct a nurturing matrix. He will not feel anything akin to being the source of his own nurture, but he may be able to recognize the possibility that some of his needs will be fulfilled in a trustworthy, nonthreatening world the therapist has created. This enables the patient to move tentatively into the external milieu as separation-individuation is gradually enhanced.

Separation-individuation is a term that Mahler (1968) introduced. As stated in Chapter 3, she viewed it as a hatching from a symbiotic fusion, a formulation that I have discussed and criticized. Here I wish to point out that the structuring of ego boundaries is a complex process that involves a movement toward external objects instead of a moving away as would occur in the separation from a fused state. The process I have just outlined is fundamentally different from what Mahler postulated. Furthermore, this is not the same as Masterson's (1976) and Rinsley's (1982) formulations that the borderline patient is fixated at the stage of separation-individuation. Within the context of the structural framework described, separation-individuation is not a developmental stage. Rather, it is the outcome of the successful construction of the transitional space. Most borderline patients have not yet reached in their developmental progression what I have called the lower echelons of the transitional space. They have poorly formed permeable ego boundaries, which place them in a more primitive structural state than that associated with a patient who is struggling with problems concerning separation-individuation.

These distinctions are not idle arguments about opposing theoretical positions. They are significant because they have important implications about therapeutic technique. Throughout this book and particularly in this chapter, I am stressing that the conceptual position determines how the analyst should react in terms of therapeutic strategy and technique. In psychoanalysis there are no rigid technical approaches and sequences the therapist can institute as a response to specific types of psychopathology; however, there are responses that may seem analytically correct but that are counter to therapeutic purposes. Certain formulations imply obvious courses of action. If they are incorrect or imprecise, the analyst's response could be disastrous to the construction of a therapeutic setting.

None of these defects and constrictions is absolute, as I have repeatedly emphasized. There is some movement in the external world, but it is limited. The manifestations of psychopathology are impaired relations with the outer world and inhibited functioning, but these are relative constrictions. They involve a lack of object relations and a relative inability to receive succor from the milieu.

More than with any other group of patients, the analyst has to make contact with this group. Of course, in all cases, contact has to be established, but it is particularly difficult and important for borderline patients. If they have not successfully passed through a transitional phase, a transition from the inner world to the outer world, then object relations are imperfectly established. This inability to make object contact will hamper the formation of a bond, a therapeutic alliance between patient and therapist.

With many borderline patients the chief therapeutic task is to construct such a bond, an especially important achievement because these patients have never bonded with their mothers, or if they have, it was a weak and tenuous bond.

In terms of the transitional space, these patients find themselves in an intolerable dilemma. The internal world is chaotic. They are overwhelmed with disruptive agitation, feelings of low self-esteem, vulnerability, and helplessness. There is little if any transitional space, and the external world is perceived in a distorted fashion based on the traumatic, assaultive qualities of the infantile milieu and the devastating rage that overwhelms all ego systems—executive, integrative, and particularly the perceptual system. Better integrated patients with a history of a modicum of gratifying relationships form such a bond relatively early in treatment, and it becomes the supporting matrix that makes analysis possible. With disturbed borderline patients this bond is the goal of treatment, because it enables the patient to move into the external world and to form other object contacts outside the therapeutic setting. It can establish some harmony with the external milieu rather than viewing reality as exploitive and adversarial.

These patients, as has been stressed, cannot benefit from potentially helpful experiences; in their eagerness to expel hurtful inner feelings and introjects and to protect themselves from what they perceive as dangerous and injurious, they erect protective barriers, shutting themselves off from the surrounding milieu. In rejecting the bad, they are also denying themselves what may be good. The treatment has to create a situation in which the patient will be able to internalize the helpful, constructive elements of the treatment process, what I have referred to as the formation of the *analytic introject* (Giovacchini 1965a, 1979a, 1986). In these instances, the construction of the holding environment has become the essence of the therapeutic process. Thus the holding environment blends with external reality, making the world relatively benign so that patients can avail themselves of opportunities and situations that can be gratifying.

One may ask the irksome question, Is this type of treatment analytic or simply supportive? Certainly, it takes profound analytic understanding to be in control of the treatment interaction. The analyst must know what is happening, which is never a simple task with confused patients who present us with chaos, misery, and terror. Still, some might argue that although patients and their therapeutic involvement can be formulated in a psychoanalytic context, the technical maneuvers that follow are not necessarily those that are characteristic of psychoanalytic treatment. Therapy might not be particularly directed toward the development of insight, as occurs with transference interpretations (see Chapter 12).

Creating an alternate reality to contrast with the patient's perception of the world as colored by the infantile milieu is a similar process to the construction of a holding environment that is oppositional to the traumatic childhood world. In this context I am emphasizing that the therapist is constructing a transitional space but that his approach is from the outside rather than the inside. Ordinarily the analyses of internal ego distortions and constrictions, that is, internal processes, are supposed to establish psychic equilibrium and activate a developmental potential. This is an insight-promoting process. The therapeutic setting I have described involves an opposite direction, that is, creating a benign outside world enabling the patient to meet it halfway via the transitional space. I believe that this external approach will cause many clinicians to label this type of treatment as nonanalytic.

To some degree, all treatment relationships are involved with external approaches. This may be another aspect of the holding environment that is not directed primarily toward the scrutiny of intrapsychic factors. The holding environment, as a metaphor, refers to an outside situation that holds the patient in the same way the environmental mother (Winnicott 1958a) holds her infant. Patients who have only a poorly constructed transitional space require what might be called a corrective environmental experience, which should in no way be compared to Alexander's (Alexander and French 1946) corrective emotional experience. The former is based on the analyst's true self rather than the contrived false-self role Alexander advocated.

Furthermore, there is still a good deal of focus on the patient's inner life, which is consonant with psychoanalytic technique. The more severely disturbed the patient is, the less influence interpretations will have (see Chapter 12). These patients, as discussed, are more concretely oriented than better integrated patients. Therefore they cannot comprehend, nor are they oriented toward, an intrapsychic focus. They are also more schizoid, which means that they withdraw from the outside world, especially if external objects (particularly the therapist) attempt to explore inner psychic processes. As emphasized in previous chapters, interventions are viewed as intrusive and assaultive.

With severely disturbed patients there is very little to interpret, at least at the beginning of treatment before a relationship has developed. Often these patients are very much aware of how external traumas have shaped and warped their personality. They know about their lack of cohesion of the self-representation, their fluid ego boundaries and maladaptive modes of relating to the external world. They are in touch with the primitive, painful parts of their psyches. They suspect that perhaps somewhere there are experiences and opportunities that will enhance them. This may furnish a ray of hope and motivate them to seek treatment, but for the most part they feel hopeless, believing that gratification is beyond their grasp. They know a good deal about themselves, and there is very little the therapist can add.

Later in treatment, analysts can point out connections the patients could not make or demonstrate to them how they propagate their self-defeating patterns. This occurs, however, only after the patient has made some significant inroads into the external world. The patient has to be able to internalize the analyst's interpretations, but this is preceded by the patient incorporating the analytic milieu and some of the therapist's personal values and viewpoints. Many complex interactions can be focused on that are within the purview of analysis.

Better integrated patients, those who are less isolated and withdrawn, are able to respond to interpretations as they simultaneously benefit from the internalization of the analyst and the analytic perspective. The latter is the analytic introject, which becomes integrated into the patient's ego and leads to an expansion of the perceptual system. Their transitional spaces are already somewhat functional and they are able to interact at the same time with both the external and internal worlds.

The formation of the analytic introject is a very difficult achievement for borderline patients. It involves more than just incorporating certain elements of the analytic interaction or expanding the perceptual system so that it can direct itself to the interior as well as toward reality, which means that the psyche has acquired a self-observing function. The therapeutic relationship, as it pursues its natural course, creates an environment that fills in gaps in the infantile milieu. Quite the reverse of the usual analytic treatment relationship in which the analyst views the world through his patient's eyes, these are therapeutic situations in which the patient views the world through the analyst's eyes. The analyst does not impose his viewpoint, but the patient gradually and often gladly adopts it. This leads to the creation of a weltan-schauung, which Freud often referred to.

Again, what follows may be considered quite removed from analysis. Although there is interpretative work, the treatment seems to be dominated by extra-analytic factors. The point is that in some instances seemingly hopeless patients improve and undergo significant character changes. They achieve a different view of the world and of themselves, and their consequent attitude may be analytic rather than rigid and concrete. Often they become proselytizers of analysis and good sources of referral. They have constructed an analytic introject.

I have treated several such patients whose behavior was hypomanic, or at least agitated, and disruptive to their family and friends. In some instances their actions could be labeled as sociopathic in that they were destructive, even physically violent, irresponsible, and delinquent. They were deeply involved with drugs, including alcohol, and frequently got in trouble with the law. They seemed to be poorly motivated for treatment, and the therapists some of them had seen were not particularly eager to become involved with them, an un-derstandable situation, inasmuch as their lives were chaotic and the therapists feared they would bring their chaos into the therapy.

THE INTRUSIVE AND POSSESSIVE EXTERNAL WORLD

The disruptive patients I have seen who belong to this latter group never made the initial contact. Their parents called me and insisted that I see them first. Such a demand would be expected if these patients were children, but they were not. They ranged between ages 28 to 45, and yet their parents were seeking therapy for them as if they were young children. Sometimes this was understandable because the parents were supporting them; materially, these patients were totally dependent.

The parents painted a dismal picture. They recited litanies of their childrens' delinquent and thoughtless behavior. Mother and father competed with each other to tell the therapist the largest number of misdemeanors and scrapes the patient had been involved in. They lamented and complained and created a tense, urgent atmosphere. At times, they cast me in the role of a savior who will rescue their child, but as might be anticipated, they did whatever they could to sabotage therapeutic efforts.

As is generally true for the treatment of children, the therapist has to contend with the external world of the family as well as the turbulent inner world of the patient. This is further complicated by the patient's acting out because of poor superego controls. Treatment becomes more difficult as these patients continue to create problems and chaos in their external lives, which often results in missed sessions and parents who intrude into the treatment because they are supposedly so upset by the manifestations of their child's psychopathology.

In the discussion of the therapeutic process, clinicians have to take into account external pressures and how they are often aimed at sabotaging the treatment. As a rule, when dealing with fairly motivated adult patients this is not much of a problem. A spouse may on occasion feel threatened by the possibility that the equilibrium of the marriage will be disturbed if one of the partners undergoes a character change (Giovacchini 1958, 1961), but if the patient is sufficiently motivated this does not impose a serious threat to the course of treatment. Often the spouse will also seek treatment if the marriage has a solid foundation. For these borderline patients with sociopathic tendencies, life has no organization or direction, and thus they are extremely vulnerable to both internal and external pressures. Their parents can become so enmeshed in their lives that it is difficult to have them maintain a therapeutic perspective. They are sucked into the whirlpool of familial chaos and lose their already tenuous ego boundaries as they are forced into a destructive merger with their parents and other significant persons in their lives.

In many respects these borderline patients are similar to children. Many of them have never achieved the capacity for self-sufficiency, and even though some of them may be aggressive and streetwise, they are unable to survive without caregivers. There is a tremendous need for both the parents and their adult child to maintain a psychopathological equilibrium, as is often the case with younger children.

I once witnessed a particularly poignant situation outside the consultation room. I had been invited to a rather large dinner party by a friend who was the host's attorney. I did not know the host, but he had asked his friend to bring several guests, so my wife and I were invited. We were warned not to be startled by the presence of the host's son, who was reputed to be severely mentally retarded. This 30-year-old son lived with the host and hostess, who did not want to put him in an institution or otherwise keep him in a closet, so to speak. They would seat him among their guests, but they were careful to alert them to his presence.

It happened that he was seated next to me, so I tried to casually engage him in a conversation. At first, he was fairly taciturn and volunteered very little beyond simply answering my questions. As time went on, however, probably because I was directing most of my attention to him rather than to the other guests, he began making spontaneous comments. He did not seem at all retarded to me. His memory was good, and he seemed capable of reasoning at fairly high abstract levels. What I noted was some evidence of a thought disorder in a very frightened, fragile, vulnerable person.

Primary process occasionally broke through a seemingly logical sequence. I was also aware that he had withdrawn into a shell, but because I directed my attention toward him, he was willing to come out of his seclusion and meet me halfway. He did, indeed, express how frightening the world was for him, and how he feared being devoured. This was the material of psychosis but not of irreversible mental retardation.

The father had been apparently watching us converse, because after dinner he clearly stated, so that his son could hear, "Well, Doctor, you are sharpening your psychiatric skills by practicing on my son. I guess you can't help yourself on this busman's holiday." The young man now seemed to go into a state of shock. He completely retreated and did not speak another word the entire evening.

Later I told my friend who had brought us to the party that I was fairly convinced the host's son was not mentally retarded. I had concluded that he was very disturbed, possibly schizophrenic, but that because he had initially reacted well toward my engaging him in a conversation, he might possibly be able to get involved in treatment. At least there was some hope, whereas if he were as severely mentally defective as had been thought, there was very little that could be done.

My friend was delighted. He felt that what I had told him was good news, and he was anxious to share it with his client. In view of the father's sarcastic remark about my engaging his son, I was skeptical as to how he would respond. My apprehension proved to be correct. After the father heard what his lawyer had to say about my opinion regarding his son, he angrily retorted that I was speaking nonsense. His son was hopelessly mentally retarded, and this was a closed issue. There was nothing to discuss further, and he even subtly threatened that if my friend persisted he would find himself another lawyer.

The father's strong response and denial suggest an intense need to have a "sick" member in the family. When the possibility was raised that perhaps something could be done to change the status of his son's illness, he became very angry. Apparently some type of psychopathological equilibrium was threatened when treatment was recommended. Whatever organizing force the son's mental incapacity had, had to be preserved. The family, or at least the father, needed a sick child. Perhaps the son's irremediable mental derangement served to contain whatever insanity was inherent in the parents' psyche. They had constructed a relationship with their son based on denial.

In a similar fashion, the families of patients who belong in the borderline spectrum cling to their childrens' illness. They need their sons and daughters to be crazy to contain their own craziness. Furthermore, they get vicarious gratification when the child acts out. In spite of their anger at their children's delinquency and their attempts to forbid and punish aberrant behavior, they are nevertheless encouraging them to act out in a sociopathic fashion. Szurek and Johnson (1954) formulated that these parents have superego lacunae; they use their children to gratify their own forbidden impulses, which they can enjoy vicariously as their children express them.

The parents I have seen will focus on the smallest details of their child's behavior. They are obsessional in that their lives seem to revolve exclusively around their child's illness. As stated, they indulge themselves in litanies of complaints. They seem to be desperately seeking solutions and improvement, but their tenacious concentration on negative factors disrupts attempts to seek positive adaptations. I was reminded of obsessional patients who are preoccupied with cleanliness. They always seem to be able to find dirt, as occurred with one of my patients who had to avoid dog excrement. He seemed to have a unique talent to find feces everywhere, whereas another person seldom encountered such dung. The mother who constantly keeps warning her daughter not to get pregnant is another example, for the effect is, often enough, to drive the daughter to become impregnated. These parents gleefully attack their children for being so wicked or recklessly irresponsible, and therapists can sense the pleasure they get from complaining about them.

During therapy this parental attitude can become a serious obstacle. The parents often have a voyeuristic interest in the treatment, which may cause them to torment the patient with innumerable questions as to what is happening. They may periodically call the therapist on the telephone or request an appointment to discuss their child's progress. Again the therapist is faced with a litany of complaints, which now includes their opinion that they have seen little or no progress.

Another factor involved is their need to sabotage treatment; in spite of their protestations that they want their children to get well, their obvious need is not to let them grow up. They cannot allow their children to be autonomous and to grow apart from them. They need to keep them as children and to merge with them.

They use their children as transitional objects but they cannot allow them to have their own transitional space, which would permit the children to move away from them.

These children live in a paradoxical and confusing world. Their parents preach morality and try to beat them into a submissive, conforming pattern of behavior. Often they literally beat them, and many of these patients are victims of physical abuse, their childhoods punctuated by violence. As a rule, however, they do not withdraw or otherwise become submissive. They rebel either covertly by displaying passive hostility, or overtly by being disruptive, antisocial, or even violent.

I surmise that they are not cowed by their parents' admonitions or punitive assaultive reactions, because they feel a push driving them to disruptive and sociopathic actions. They are, indeed, victims of the double bind, as described by Bateson (1951). These patients feel rage as a reaction to parental brutality, but at deeper, unconscious levels they are driven by the parents' impetus to overstep the bounds of conventional restraints and morality. As stated, this is confusing and causes internal disruption and agitation. They listen to the parents' unconscious rather than responding to their moralistic onslaughts.

A disruptive ego state presents special difficulties in treatment. The patient may not be against becoming involved in treatment, but an unusually significant symptom is unreliability and irresponsibility. The parent focuses on these traits to the extent that the therapist feels resentful. The parents' interference, under the guise of wanting to be helpful, becomes the main therapeutic obstacle and serves as a major resistance even though its source is external. As the treatment helps promote self-esteem, the parents belittle the patient at every available opportunity, which leads to developmental constrictions in the past and treatment impasses later.

THE THERAPEUTIC INTERACTION WITH THE MILDLY SOCIOPATHIC PATIENT AND INTROJECTIVE PROCESSES

The following is a good example of a patient whose parents are similar to those just discussed.

As is often the case, the parents made the initial call. They both insisted on seeing me and presented a dismal picture of their son's mental state. He was reported to be a heavy drinker and a heavy drug user, especially of cocaine. His drinking frequently got him into trouble such as barroom fights. He was also in more serious trouble with the law, having been caught several times driving under the influence of alcohol. He worked as a sales-man for an investment firm, but he seldom made any money. His father was suspicious as to the legitimacy of his transactions. Their focus, however, was on what they reported to be his almost daily use of cocaine.

They painted such a gloomy picture that I wondered whether treat-ment on an outpatient basis was possible. The parents emphasized that he did not want treatment, and they expected me to tell them how they could maneuver him into seeing me. They were willing to pay for his therapy, and they had some leverage in that they were, in essence, supporting him. He did not make enough money to be able to support himself. I told them that I had no specific recommendations. I suspected that their son was very angry and did not think very highly of them. I suggested that they concentrate on his strengths rather than his deficiencies and mention to him that I had seen them and would be interested in seeing him. I did not believe they heard me when I recommended taking a positive attitude toward their son, but I felt they would tell him about my wanting to see him.

I did not hear any more about the prospective patient for several months until I received a telephone call from the parents, who wanted to see me again. I discouraged them because I did not have anything further to contribute. The mother asked me whether they should threaten to cut off financial support if he did not see me. I replied that I could not advise them. I added that perhaps that might force him to make an appointment, but I wondered if this might not be the same as leading the proverbial horse to water but not being able to make him drink. They thanked me, and we did not set up another appointment.

I expected that was the end of it, but 2 weeks later the son called me for an appointment. I gave him one but was not surprised when he did not keep it. I was ready to write it off, but the next morning his father called me and almost begged me to give him another appointment; he promised to pay for the missed session.

At the time, I wondered why the family was so intent on their son receiving psychotherapy. If they had a need for his psychopathology, then therapy might be viewed as a detriment. Whatever equilibrium they had established with him would be threatened by the treatment interaction.

Later I learned that matters had reached uncontrollable proportions. It is in the nature of symptoms that they are needed to maintain psychic equilibrium, but they can cause disharmony in adapting to the external milieu. This is usually why patients seek therapy, apart from internal disruption and feelings of anxiety, depression and misery. In this case the family was afraid of being compromised by their son's behavior, by scandal and the denigration of their reputation. In their community, they were prominent and respected.

More was involved, however. They did not expect the treatment to succeed, and in actuality they did a good deal, by their intrusions, to see that it did not. Consequently, they could both console and justify themselves by saying they had done everything possible but that it did not change their son. He was simply a bad person who would not change, and they did not have to feel guilty. They had done everything that could be done.

As they revealed much later, their fundamental belief was that their son was suffering from an organic, genetic defect. His was a "bad seed," and although they had hoped he would improve with treatment, nothing could really be done, and they would have to reconcile themselves with their misfortune, with the cross they had to bear. The only other alternative was to cut off his support and to banish him from their lives. They had threatened to disown him on several occasions, but they had no intention of carrying it through. On one occasion, when they closed one of his charge accounts, the patient definitely told them he had no need for their money and that he would never ask them for anything again. The parents mollified him and insisted that they reopen the account for him. They had to argue with him to accept it.

The patient was 15 minutes late for his next appointment. He seemed eager to see me and was extremely friendly and polite. When asked why he was seeing me, he answered in general terms. He stated that everyone could be helped by analysis and felt that it was a good idea to "improve" himself. He did not, however, believe that he had any special problems.

I asked him why his parents were so eager that he seek treatment, a question that he was neither able nor willing to answer. He complained about their intrusiveness, and he was particularly critical of his father. I had wondered whether his father, having pushed treatment, might cause him to rebel against the therapy. This did not happen. He seemed genuinely pleased about seeing me.

Nevertheless, I was aware of certain resistances. He suppressed all material that would have revealed his antisocial behavior and his use of drugs, particularly cocaine. He also was frequently late or missed a session, usually because he had overslept after bingeing on alcohol or drugs. He did not tell me about these escapades, but I was kept well informed by his parents even though I had told them that I found the information they gave me burdensome and nonproductive (see Chapter 12). He missed many appointments, but he usually called me to apologize. His excuses were obviously contrived and related to his work as a salesman or being caught in traffic. He was, nevertheless, anxious to have a regular schedule.

During sessions, he concentrated his attention on the family. Just as they had indulged themselves in a long list of complaints about his drug use and irresponsibility, so he had a litany of his own about their brutality when he was a child and how they tried to infantilize him as an adult. He was resentful of their treating him as if he were still a child.

His father often nagged his son for being a spendthrift. The patient, according to him, spent too much money on clothes, sporting events, and expensive restaurants. He was especially chagrined about the amount of rent the patient was paying for his apartment, frequently urging that he move to a cheaper place. The patient was very angry at him and would present these encounters with vehemence and indignation. He was obviously seeking my support.

I noted that he constantly sought my affirmation. He would, for example, discuss his father's joyless and constricted viewpoint about pleasure-seeking activities, and then he would ask for my opinion. I found myself being drawn into the discussion and stating my opinions, which were opposed to those of the father and more in line with those of the patient. It was interesting that the patient was far from certain about his viewpoint but that it became more secure when I reinforced it. We were talking about general issues and a philosophy of life rather than the specific items his family had picked on.

Actually, the patient's view of life was just as constricted as his parents'. He had read practically nothing, knew very little about music except for some popular rock tunes, had no experience with fine dining, and he had never been to an art gallery or museum. Yet, as he reviewed various current issues he showed sensitivity, demonstrating he had a keen, agile mind. He was also interested in my tastes in art and music, and in my more liberal attitudes than those of his family. He frequently questioned me.

He was struggling to create a weltanschaaung that would expand his horizons. He was trying to cultivate interests and tastes that would belong to a world vastly different from the infantile milieu. His pursuits of pleasure had been confined to certain spectator sports or to antisocial behavior and drugs. I suspected that he was also promiscuous, but he said very little about women during the early days of his treatment.

During childhood, he was diagnosed as having an attention-deficit disorder, and he was put on Ritalin. It may have helped a little, but it was not particularly effective. He was still hyperactive, and his behavior as an adult had hypomanic qualities.

As a child he felt as if he did not belong to the mainstream. This was true of his family, a Jewish family living in a predominantly gentile neighborhood. At school, the patient was the only Jewish student in the classroom, and he had to put up with many ethnic slurs. He was constantly fighting with his classmates and was frequently beaten up. To make matters worse, his father also would beat him for fighting as well as for other misdemeanors. Furthermore, he did not do well at school because he was unable to concentrate and retain what he was taught.

Thus he was imbued with a harsh, grim view of the world. His father preached that life was hard, although he was very successful financially. Nevertheless, he was austere and penurious and tried to instill in his son his standards of thriftiness, which approached miserliness. His son rebelled in order to establish some semblance of autonomy, but his struggle was self-defeating inasmuch as he got into trouble with the law and was unable to be self-sufficient. He trapped himself by being materially dependent on the family. He was also exacting revenge by making them take care of him.

In treatment he had to deny his transgressions of conventional morality. At the onset he admitted, however, that he had problems in keeping appointments and being on time. He did not speak about his use of drugs, and perhaps that he was involved in drug trafficking. Regarding his parents' complaints, he emphasized that they were angry about his lifestyle and the fact that he had little or no income. He was always in debt, and his creditors were constantly hounding him.

Eventually he told me about his drug addiction. This occurred at the time he had resolved to break the habit. He was gradually expanding his horizons and becoming interested in a variety of activities that, in the past, he never knew existed.

As he expressed various viewpoints, he always asked my opinion, which usually agreed with his. He would decry his father's constricted and prohibitive attitudes, usually about spending money, and then ask me what I thought about the situation. This might be related to indulging in some recreational activity, such as going to a baseball game or a movie, which the father thought was frivolous and unnecessarily extravagant. I found myself impelled to respond, and I usually took the more liberal position—that having fun was essential and that money, for its own sake, was not that important. He was seeking support for his position, but he was sincerely interested in how I viewed the world. As stated in another context, he wanted to view the world through my eyes.

Although he lived in Chicago, a big city, he was relatively naive and provincial. He considered me to be different from his father and viewed me as well educated, cultured, and sophisticated. From the comments I had made about how I would react to various situations that involved pleasure and spending money, he concluded that I was liberal-minded and not a slave to the Puritan ethic. It was quite clear that he was making me the father he wished he had. He was attempting to create a world for himself that was modeled after mine.

For example, he once asked my opinion of a restaurant that a friend had recommended to him as an elegant place to celebrate his girlfriend's birthday. In part, this restaurant was recommended because it was reputed to be inexpensive. However, a colleague of mine had been to this restaurant and told me that it was quite expensive and that the food and service were both mediocre. He also added that the decor was rundown and seedy, and it was so noisy that conversation was almost impossible. I reported this to the patient and he asked me for another recommendation, which I gave him.

He went to the restaurant that I had recommended, and he and his girlfriend thoroughly enjoyed it. From then on he became interested in food, wine, and gourmet restaurants. I do not believe the patient knew it, but these are areas of particular interest to me. He accepted me as an expert and continued seeking my advice about fine wines and restaurants. He became actively interested in the sophisticated life, as he called it, and was pleased that he was availing himself of pleasures he never knew existed. He became chauvinistic about Chicago because it had so many good restaurants and cultural opportunities.

He also became involved with classical music, particularly Italian opera. This time, he suspected that I might be knowledgeable in the area because of my nationality. He attended a few isolated performances and would discuss them with me. If I had seen that particular opera, he was again eager for my opinion, which I gladly shared with him. These were lively and pleasant exchanges, and he always felt in an elevated mood after one of these sessions. He was especially pleased because I was tacitly approving of his ventures in cultural spheres, rather than questioning their value and expense as his father was prone to do.

He became a gourmet, a connoisseur of wines, and well acquainted with the restaurant scene, keeping current on new openings. Furthermore, he got a season's ticket for the opera but also kept the one he had for football games. He complained about his father's narrow vision and lamented that he did not have my orientation toward life.

We had found a mode of communicating with each other, something that he had never had with his family. He did not believe they could relate to him outside of their own needs. By contrast, I was introducing him into a world whose existence he had never suspected and he felt I was providing him with an education that helped develop new needs and methods of gratification. He recalled with bitterness how embarrassed he felt when out to dinner with his family, an infrequent occasion, when his father was rude, brusque, and stingy. He felt like cringing and crawling under the table when his father made a scene by questioning the size of the check. He saw his therapy as opening new vistas that led him into a world of "genteel sophistication."

I found his reactions extremely interesting in view of his chaotic, somewhat rough sociopathic behavior. He had cut down considerably in his drug use and had developed a sense of humor. Previously he had been compliant and polite, but his behavior was contrived and had a false-self quality. He was fairly concrete and his outlook was grim.

Although he was still financially dependent on his parents, he did some work for the family business. His father complained that he was not "pulling his weight," but he could not deny that his son was responsible for several very profitable transactions. He was able to manipulate customers as a confidence man might. This was in keeping with his sociopathic orientation, but now he was operating within the law, if only just inside the border. He viewed his work for his father's firm as a game, and he approached it with a playful outlook.

His father finally had to admit that he was an asset, but according to the patient, he continued to nag him about spending too much money and living a lifestyle beyond his means. Again the patient would turn to me for solace and approbation. I had become the approving father who made him feel "good." By this he meant that the therapeutic process served to bolster self-esteem. His father had constantly torn him down, but the treatment relationship counteracted the negative consequences—that is, the attacks on his self-esteem—of his father's admonishments. At the beginning of his employment in the family business they were constantly quarreling, the patient protesting that he was not being paid enough money to support himself, and his father retorting that he was not worth what he was being paid. They finally had a showdown when the patient threatened to quit. In addition to his salary he was put on a commission basis, which enabled him to make the money he required and demonstrated to his father that he was an asset to the business rather than a liability.

As stated, the therapy had created a new world for the patient, or, more accurately stated, permitted him to discover areas of reality that were not previously available to him. In contrast to the infantile milieu, this was a benign pleasurable world that gave him a good sense of well-being. I had become a surrogate father who created an external world that was in synchrony with pleasure-seeking impulses. This is a similar condition to that of the infant during the transitional period who feels a need and finds the external world in synchrony with that need. It responds and leads to a sense of well-being and, according to Winnicott (1953), creates the illusion that the infant is the source of his own nurture. This leads to the further structuring of the transitional space.

My patient did not have the omnipotent feeling that he was the source of his own nurture, but he gained increasing confidence that he could provide for himself. He was gradually constructing a transitional space, as evidenced by a relaxed, playful attitude toward life in general; and his feelings toward his father became more benign. His interest in elegant dining and music represented cultural achievements that, again, according to Winnicott (1953), belong in the transitional area. Through therapy he discovered facets of the external world that were not presented to him in the family environment. In a sense, treatment created a new reality or expanded the old one so that the inner and outer worlds could blend and then create a transitional space.

Clearly he identified with me, the benign father, but in so doing he also constructed an analytic perspective as he relaxed his rigid, concrete hold on reality. He became interested, for example, in understanding his father's motivations and how they might have developed from his hard and impoverished background. He acknowledged the existence of an inner world, which is an important determinant of how a person adapts to the external milieu. He looked inward, having acquired a self-observing function, which is the essential feature of the analytic introject.

The treatment of many borderline patients has features similar to those just discussed. These patients incorporate various aspects of their therapist's personality, perhaps his ideology and general philosophy of life. The analyst by no means imposes his values. On the contrary, patients are eager to find new ways of relating because they have been miserable owing to their lack of satisfactory adaptive techniques.

Their sociopathic behavior is based, in part, on this dissatisfaction and represents a rebellious attempt to liberate themselves from the constrictive, oppressive effects of the family's influence. As discussed, the parents are also forcing their sociopathic tendencies onto their children and get vicarious pleasure as the children act out for them.

The creation of the transitional space and the formation of the analytic introject represent advances in psychic development, and this is the goal of treatment for patients suffering from characterological disorders. This therapeutic activity is not analytic in a strict sense, because the therapist is not focused primarily on the interpretation of intrapsychic factors that will enhance autonomy and give the patient a wider choice of adaptive techniques. Still, by identifying with their analysts and incorporating their standards of value, these patients are in fact expanding their adaptive range. They are expanding the horizons of the perceptual system, the ego's executive system, and the external world. Their autonomy is enhanced, and their self-representation gains greater cohesion and fuller dimensions. Though the therapy is not exactly analytic, the goals are comparable.

Besides being a structural accretion and a developmental achievement, the formation of the transitional space is also tantamount to the construction of a holding environment. More precisely, the activity and interaction that lead to the construction of the transitional space constitutes the holding environment. As stated, this holding environment is the antithesis of the infantile milieu. Philip Giovacchini (1990) discusses a patient who was able to construct a transitional zone during treatment. He wrote: ". . . I think it was able to develop because the holding environment of the therapy was, indeed, different from the chaotic intrusion and pervasive solitude of the patient's infantile home" (p. 152). As occurs with the analytic treatment in general of borderline patients, this supportive background makes possible a more conventional psychoanalytic interaction based on transference interpretations (see Chapter 12). When my patient had constructed an analytic introject and became introspective, he naturally drifted into what might be called analytic discourse. He still talked about restaurants and music and he allocated the first 10 or 15 minutes of the session to them. We would have an exchange, keeping current and exchanging our experiences. Then he would lie down and free-associate. He spoke more and more of his feelings, and had less to say about his father's foibles and unfairness.

He seemed to need a preface to the analytic session to reinforce the holding-environment aspects of the transitional space. It was as if he required an introductory period of play before he could allow himself the perilous journey into the intrapsychic. Being able to get in touch with the unconscious, that is, his inner life, was an ability he gained from the construction of the transitional space and the analytic introject. It was a function of the transitional space that had to be, in a sense, energized at the beginning of the session. The analytic introject resides in the transitional space as it makes connections between the inner and outer worlds. He was then able to discuss his sociopathic behavior and his use of drugs in terms of inner needs rather than just as rebellious and defiant reactions against overt parental values. He was trying and is still trying hard to free himself of his addictions.

This apparent compartmentalizing of sessions is not an uncommon phenomenon in the treatment of severely ill patients. They need some type of reinforcement or affirmation before they can relax their defenses sufficiently to enable them to explore the inner recesses of their mind. They need support and protection to maintain a therapeutic perspective. This is especially true for patients with sociopathic tendencies and for other patients who have a tenuous hold on reality. To become engaged in the treatment relationship requires that, to some extent, patients allow themselves to partially release their rigid hold on the external world, as well as their defensively constricted perception of reality.

With some patients the therapeutic interaction develops the capacity to support reality testing. Some severely disturbed patients, perhaps closer to psychosis than most borderlines, have only a blurred and confused perception of the surrounding world. They have difficulties in orienting themselves to reality, and their sense of separateness is poorly developed. From a practical viewpoint there is no transitional space because there is little distinction between inside and outside. The transitional space enables the child to make such a distinction, but its absence is associated with blurred and weak ego boundaries. These patients tend to fuse with external objects rather than relating to them on the basis of two persons interacting with each other.

Some patients in treatment use the treatment to validate their actions, which eventually means their existence, as separate and apart from an external world they perceive as engulfing and destructive to individuation.

For example, a 19-year-old schizophrenic girl would catalogue all of her activities a week at a time. She kept a detailed diary of everything she did. She recorded only actions, never venturing any opinions, impressions, or thoughts about what she experienced or what happened to her.

She had only one session a week, having refused the offer of more frequent sessions. At the beginning of a session she would pull out her notebook and quietly and precisely read every word she had written during the week. If, by accident, she skipped over a sentence or paragraph, she had to start all over again. She would go back to the beginning, requiring that she read accurately and completely everything she had written, an endeavor that might take as long as 15 or 20 minutes. She required my undivided attention, but could not tolerate any interruptions or questions. If, as happened when she first started this practice, I asked a question or requested elaboration, she would not respond; instead she would react as she did to any omission or interruption by beginning again. This could be quite time-consuming.

During the course of treatment I realized that she needed me to hear about her experiences so as to confirm and acknowledge them. If I were not there as an audience to listen to her recitation, then she was not certain that anything had really happened in her life. Psychically speaking, I reflected back what she had written; I was functioning as a mirror in which she could more clearly view the reality of the past week. This enabled her to feel herself as a person, and then she could continue with the session on a two-person basis. She used treatment to validate her impressions and to make them real. Treatment served a useful purpose, providing her with a structure that she needed and that permitted her to function as a patient.

9

The Psychoanalytic Paradox and the Transitional Space

I have throughout this book repeatedly stressed the importance of the construction of an appropriate holding environment for the treatment of patients who fall within the borderline spectrum. There are, however, analytic situations that unwittingly replicate some of the noxious elements of the traumatic infantile milieu. The analytic setting may be essentially benign, but it can work at cross purposes to the treatment process. There can be certain intrinsic factors to the surface aspects of analysis that, for some patients, are antitherapeutic. The analytic setting may be phenomenologically similar to the childhood environment or it may frustrate some fundamental needs that are essential to a meaningful treatment experience. Rather than constructing a supportive holding environment, the analysis reinforces disruptive aspects of the patient's past or denies him some experiences that have to be worked through for analytic resolution.

As discussed, working through involves a reliving of conflictual situations as they emerge in treatment in the form of the repetition compulsion and in the context of the holding environment. The analytic setting, as manifested in the analyst's professional decorum, sometimes makes it difficult to bring fundamental conflicts into focus.

I have written elsewhere about a rather simple situation in which a patient has to experience a fundamental sense of loneliness (Giovacchini 1979a). The analyst's friendly presence prevents the patient from getting in touch with such a basic feeling. For example, a patient, a young single lady, had not achieved "the capacity to be alone in the presence of someone else" (Winnicott 1958b). The analytic setting interfered with the attainment of this goal. She had a structural defect similar to that of patients who cannot form and hold a mental representation without the actual presence of the external object, the failure of evocative memory Fraiberg (1969) described and the sense of aloneness Adler and Buie (1979) wrote about.

This patient demonstrated the converse of this situation in that she could not capture the sense of aloneness unless the external object were absent. The analysis impinged on her perceptual system, and she could not create the void she had to experience in order to face situations of frightening loneliness such as characterized her childhood. What in most instances would be propitious to analysis—that is, a benign understanding setting—in this clinical situation proved to be detrimental to analytic progress, an example of the psychoanalytic paradox. There was, however, a strong bond between patient and therapist, and the patient was eventually able to feel the sense of aloneness even in the presence of the analyst. The analyst had become the environmental mother Winnicott (1958a,b) described—that is, a background, holding, soothing mother—in addition to being the object mother who represents the foreground of the maternal interaction that supplies the nurturing substance.

Other clinical interactions are more complicated in that patients believe they require specific responses from their analyst rather than the just-discussed general presence or absence of the therapist.

A middle-aged businessman complained that I never fought with him. He informed me that some of his friends in analysis would have shouting matches with their analysts, but that I never responded to his attacks. He felt he was missing something vital. He was implying that he had to actively experience angry turmoil and that simply understanding what had happened was not enough or sufficiently helpful to make him feel better about himself. He suffered from low self-esteem and sought relationships that would lead to narcissistic enhancement. As expected, he was frequently disappointed, leaving him in a state of bitter resentment and self-recrimination. In this mood, he was combative and often went out looking for fights, verbal rather than physical encounters.

He was puzzled as to why he was so critical of himself. He was doing reasonably well in his business, and he had a fairly wide circle of friends, both men and women. He was well liked, but he was unable to sustain a close relationship. He was afraid of commitments and had problems with intimacy. On several occasions when he got close to a woman, the relationship usually broke up in the midst of turmoil and bitterness. His estranged girlfriends would bitterly attack and revile him as the relationship ended. He would also be angry, but his dominant feelings were humiliation and shame. He felt inadequate, lonely, and vulnerable after one of these unhappy affairs.

Often during his sessions, he would jokingly ask me to praise and admire him or to reassure him that he was a likeable person. He was humorous, but I could sense that he was desperate and needy underneath his facade of wit and charm. He also wanted me to admonish and attack him because of his neediness. He did not directly acknowledge that he felt vulnerable and wanted me to protect him, but he tried to manipulate me into discussing his strong points and virtues. At the same time, however, he wanted me to confront him with his childish needs and to be somewhat of a disciplinarian, a role that I did not assume. This is what he meant when he criticized me for not fighting with him.

We were both puzzled as to why he felt so vulnerable and inadequate and was basically an angry person. His anger pervaded many relationships and interfered with his finding an intimate relationship. One of his goals was to achieve the capacity to become involved in a heterosexual relationship. He wanted to make a commitment, but his relationships always ended on a sour note. He wondered whether he was perfectionistic and asking for too much. He asked whether he was hypercritical of others in the same way that he was critical of himself.

On the surface, there was nothing in his background that could account for his feelings of vulnerability and what appeared to be reactive rage. His father died before he was born and he was raised by his mother and an older sister. Both of them reportedly adored him. Although he was fond of his sister, he was very resentful of his mother. He depicted her as an intrusive, controlling woman who attempted to manipulate him by making him feel guilty. Still, in childhood she seemed to idolize her only son; he was a source of narcissistic pride. She constantly praised him for his agile mind and physical beauty.

He did well in school, but he did not believe there was anything outstanding about his scholastic performance. In fact, he was bitterly disappointed when he was unable to get into medical school. He was very angry at being rejected, and he decided, in the spirit of revenge, to make a lot of money. He did well, but he was by no means rich. He had built up some comfortable real estate holdings.

Regarding being a beautiful child, he had no recollection of himself as being physically attractive. Rather, he saw himself as an ungainly, clumsy, scrawny child who was frequently picked on by stronger, more robust peers. He was not afraid of them and fought back, but he invariably lost. Still, he was spunky, and he would become uncontrollably angry and fight with such fury that his antagonists would be cowed by the intensity of his feelings and would back off even though they could have subdued him.

There were marked discrepancies in the way his mother viewed him and how he perceived himself. There was also a vast difference between her behavior toward him as a child and how she treated him as an adult. He believed that he was being subjected to different facets of her personality. Through analytic exploration, we concluded that his mother was projecting hated and hateful parts of herself into her son. These consisted of what she perceived as damaged, and, as Melanie Klein (1935) would have formulated, by putting them into her son, she was trying to repair them. The mother lavished praise on him to enhance her narcissism, not his. In turn, he felt miserable and the mother felt relieved inasmuch as she was able to rid herself of inner misery and painful feelings of inadequacy.

As the patient was able to recall in treatment, he felt very uncomfortable with his mother's praise, which is understandable if our formulations about using him as a receptacle for hated parts of the self are correct. Not only did he feel that she had unrealistic expectations of him, but he felt guilty because even in ordinary relationships and accomplishments, he believed that he was falling below the mark. He was not living up to his ego ideal. His reaction to the dilemma of being idolized but feeling miserable and inadequate was global anger. Anger, as is often the case, had become a defensive adaptation that permitted him to construct a sense of autonomy and a modicum of self-esteem.

His rage toward the world was a generalization of his anger toward his mother. It was both a reaction to a conflict and an adaptation. The conflict involved feelings of inadequacy. He had to absorb his mother's vulnerabilities and then transcend them, which he was unable to do. He was caught in a bind and he was angry at being forced into such an untenable position. On the other hand, he could use his rage as an attempt to separate himself from his mother. Directing it toward his mother reassured him that he was not merged with her. He could place his anger between her and himself and, thereby, maintain a minimal sense of autonomy. Rather than just maintaining separation, anger had become a distancing mechanism that was generated in the interest of self-survival.

It served him well, but, as is true of any defensively constructed adaptive mechanism, it was the source of his greatest difficulty. He felt lonely and isolated, the main reason he sought therapy. He desperately sought an intimate relationship but his anger interfered with his being able to make a commitment.

In therapy, although he was able to relax and ask for narcissistic gratification, he still felt a need to create a setting that would support his chief adaptive modality. He wanted me to scold him so that he could fight back. The analytic setting, by restricting itself to the exploration of psychic processes rather than reenacting modes of relating that had helped him survive, was at variance with the patient's psychopathological needs. Still, inasmuch as there was an asynchrony between the patient's adaptive modes and the analytic setting, the treatment was facing a psychoanalytic paradox.

The qualities of the psychoanalytic paradox often determine specific characteristics of the holding environment. As discussed elsewhere (Giovacchini 1979a, 1986), if the infantile milieu was low-keyed and neglectful, the analyst provides a relatively high-decibel attentive atmosphere where there is considerable input and lively interchanges. As repeatedly stressed, analysts naturally fall into these behavioral modes, which are consistent with their professional self-representation.

The situation with my patient was different. We were facing a psychoanalytic paradox, but it was the outcome of a clash between the analytic setting and a mode of relating he had created in order to survive and to protect himself from a destructive merger with his mother. In fact, he was attempting to externalize aspects of his infantile environment and the defenses he had constructed in order to cope with it. I could not become involved with him at the level he was demanding. The role he wanted to assign to me was not consistent with my professional self-representation.

Furthermore, reinforcing his propensity to externalize would merely strengthen his defensive adaptations, that is, distancing mechanisms that would not lead to commitments and the achievement of intimacy, which were his stated goals of treatment.

This patient had sufficient ego strength that he could tolerate the frustration of his defensive needs. He understood that he was trying to manipulate me into participating in an interaction that would make him feel safe but which was basically self-defeating.

THE TRANSITIONAL SPACE AND THE THERAPEUTIC INTERACTION

This patient is typical in that the intrinsic holding qualities of the psychoanalytic process are not congruent with his defensive adaptations. With better integrated patients, the noncritical, nonjudgmental qualities of the analytic perspective alone can be sufficient to furnish the therapy with a supportive matrix. With most patients, however, as was true of my patient, there is an impetus to externalize their adaptive modes in the consultation room, and this may appear to be at variance with analytic decorum.

Patients may protest the low-keyed elements of the therapeutic atmosphere, but they are also able to eventually derive benefits from it. The conflict between the patient's externalizations and the analytic modus operandi often sets the therapeutic process in motion and stimulates the construction of a treatment transitional space. If the patient requires a particular conflict to vitalize treatment, this type of conflict may suffice to initiate an emotionally meaningful experience. For many patients, the clash between the analytic setting and the patient's defensive style is inevitable, but the therapeutic atmosphere has generated sufficient trust and security that the clash becomes productive rather than destructive to the course of treatment.

At best, the patient was able to recognize the interplay of various needs and was able to accept his dilemma with some degree of humor. Later in treatment, he began, with my help, to examine the various consequences that might ensue if I purposely tried to give him narcissistic gratification or allowed myself to be drawn into arguments. On occasion, I might let myself be engaged in a mock argument, but usually I supplied both sides of the dispute. It would frequently begin with my stating that he would complain to me that I was not being sufficiently supportive because I did not praise him enough or indicate he was my favorite patient. He would gleefully accept my statements and then, perhaps, amplify them. Since I was required to fight with him, I had to retort with some derogatory remark, which would take the form of an insulting interpretation. This might be a remark about his narcissism, arrogance, or haughty and standoffish behavior.

I must emphasize that I did not feel any anger or tendency to depreciate him when I participated in these mock arguments. The words I used were his words when he was being self-critical. As I play-acted the argument, most of the things I said were quotes of what he had said during previous sessions. He thoroughly enjoyed my presentations.

We had succeeded in creating a play space in which our treatment interactions took place. As we reviewed his needs and his production of defensive anger, he keenly felt his childhood vulnerabilities and lamented the absence of a father who might have protected him from an exploitive mother. Although the mood in my office was often jovial, there were, nevertheless, many moments when he was acutely suffering and he was able to show me how he felt as a miserable and frightened little boy.

I believe that, in general, the treatment of borderline patients takes place in the transitional space. As discussed, the therapy has to create such a transitional space, and with many patients, this is quite a developmental achievement. This patient probably was not as severely disturbed as most of the patients discussed in this book, although if he could have made comparisons he would have protested that he was, indeed, very severely ill.

In view of the playful character of our interaction, it would be easy to assume that his problems were not particularly serious. He emphasized how joyless and gloomy his household had been and lamented that he had never had a father who could play with him. In creating a transitional space we had also constructed a holding environment, in that our setting was diametrically different from the dark and sad household of his past. His mother sustained herself by merging with her son, but basically she was a very depressed woman. He carried her depression with him and felt incapacitated. For example, he had problems with his capacity to feel pleasure. Although this was a serious deficit, it was far from absolute. Besides providing a setting in which to conduct treatment, the transitional space also served as a holding environment, permitting the patient to feel some good feelings that helped him relate to the external world and reorganize his inner life without the burden of depression.

His material vacillated from describing experiences in the external world and his reactions to those experiences, and the playful reenactment with me of childhood relationships. I viewed this as moving back and forth from reality into the transitional space.

This back-and-forth movement eventually led to better relationships with both men and women, although at the time of writing he has not yet been able to commit himself to a relationship in which he could achieve emotional intimacy. He no longer became defensively angry to establish ego boundaries. He also understood that he was confused as a child. He became aware that his reactions had been paradoxical: although he was admired by his mother, his peers denigrated and made fun of him.

Narcissistic gratification did not ultimately lead to enhancement. If he was held in high esteem at home, he was made to feel very inadequate by friends and schoolmates. He was respected for his intellectual abilities, but he did poorly in areas that were valued, such as physical prowess and athletics. In therapy he wondered about this discrepancy between the way his family and the outside world treated him. As we played out various relationships, he gained understanding, which he carried into the outside world.

He recognized that he was reacting at two levels, a surface phenomenological level and a deeper unconscious level that was operating under the sway of introjective and projective mechanisms. He began viewing his current relationships in terms of these two levels. He noted that there were several women in his life who were very seductive toward him. He did not have much feeling toward them. He enjoyed their company but did not find them particularly attractive. He finally admitted that several of these women were, in fact, attractive, and he was puzzled by his reactions. He concluded that he was projecting the devalued parts of himself into them and using them as his mother used him when he was a child. He was accepting their praise, but he believed he was introjecting their devalued parts of the self. The difference between these current relationships and that of the past with his mother was that now he projected devalued parts of the self back, whereas in the past he had integrated them into the self-representation and had consequently suffered from low self-esteem, so that he would allow himself to be treated in a devalued fashion. During treatment, his feelings of inadequacy were no longer as intense as they had been, and he generally felt more comfortable in the outer world, whereas in the consultation room we were re-creating the early relationship with his mother.

As an adult, his relationship with his mother had changed markedly. She no longer idolized him; rather, she constantly criticized him for being selfish, ungrateful, and negligent. She attacked him on the grounds that he was not appreciative of all that she had done for him and that he was basically a bad person. Apparently, she was being much more overt in projecting the hated parts of herself into him and then tried to maintain control by making him feel guilty. Ordinarily, he would feel both angry and devastated by her attacks, but now he believed she was just a silly old woman.

I believe these interactions demonstrate a general principle of the therapeutic process. Aspects of reality as they enter the transitional space are converted into fantasies. Grim reality becomes converted into playful fantasy, which can then be used in the service of therapeutic resolution and expansion of the personality. Feinsilver (1980) has discussed a comparable process in the treatment of schizophrenic patients, but I believe there is a similar sequence in the treatment of all patients who undergo psychoanalytic or psychoanalytically oriented therapy. There is a movement into the transitional space, where phenomena are placed in an intrapsychic context. This means they can be viewed in terms of internal motives, indicating that, to some extent, the patient has some control. Ordinarily, these patients consider themselves to be the hapless victims of traumatic circumstances.

Knowing how they are involved with complex feelings that are the outcome of introjective–projective processes and that their orientations create and repeat relationships of early life gives patients a sense of direction and some assurance that they have something to say about their destiny. In the transitional space, they develop some degree of flexibility. Reality is rigid and constricted, whereas fantasy has fluidity and can be manipulated. When these patients leave the transitional space and return to the external world of reality, they often approach it with the flexibility they developed while they were working in the transitional space. The intrapsychic focus and fantasies are not subjected to the same rules that govern reality testing. A sequence of events in the external world may be immutable, but the course of a fantasy can be changed if a person has awareness of why he is being driven in certain directions. The inexorable and self-defeating sequence of various object relationships can be changed to a more favorable outcome, especially after they have passed in review in the transitional space.

THE TRANSITIONAL SPACE, LUCID DREAMS, AND WORKING THROUGH

The flexibility of the intrapsychic focus can be demonstrated by the structuring of dreams. Although dreams have not been extensively scrutinized in terms of their spatial position in the psychic apparatus, they are generally thought of as unconscious mental activity and as belonging to the lower depths of the personality. They have a hallucinatory vividness, however, as they are manifested in pictorial representations that are the products of visual imagery. The latter incorporate, albeit in distorted form, elements of reality, so to some extent dreams represent a blending of reality and intrapsychic processes. From this perspective it would be easy to conclude that dreams are transitional phenomena, but usually they are considered to belong to the internal world rather than to external reality. If, however, there is a continuum between fantasy and dreams, then it would be conceptually consistent to view dreams as extending upward into the transitional space, as they assume the more obvious wish-fulfilling characteristics of fantasy.

Lucid dreams, a particular type of dream in which the dreamer knows he is dreaming, certainly belong to the transitional space, in that higher integrative and perceptual centers are operating simultaneously with primary-process mental operations that ordinarily reside in the domain of the unconscious. Some dreams are unusually clear (this is often a characteristic of lucid dreams), which indicates that the perceptual system is still quite active even though the dreamer is asleep. Inasmuch as the dreamer is making evaluations about his dreams, something akin to conscious awareness is operating, which includes making judgments and evaluations.

There is a balance between primary- and secondary-process, secondary elaboration, as Freud (1900) initially stated. In lucid dreams there is more secondary process—which includes other qualities beside perceptual clarity—than primary process. As mentioned, judgments and evaluations are made, which sometimes culminate in reality testing, although much of the content of lucid dreams defies reality testing. Lucid dreams can demonstrate the flexibility of processes that reside, at least partially, in the transitional space, and this is relevant to our study of the therapeutic process.

The combination of two frames of reference, inner and outer reality, that occurs in the transitional space is also characteristic of lucid dreams.

A patient told a lucid dream he had had during adolescence. He was flying above the city, enjoying himself immensely. Then he started picking up skyscrapers, moving them around as if they were pawns in a chess game. He marveled at his superhuman strength, and he was ecstatic. Up to this part of the dream, he was not aware that he was dreaming. He was too immersed in what he was doing to be reflective. As he continued his Superman activities, he finally became aware of the astounding nature of his performance. He said to himself, "I must be dreaming." A voice replied, "Of course, you're dreaming, and this is the best part of the dream." While still asleep, he realized that he was dreaming, and within the context of the dream he felt terribly disappointed because he realized that he was not really Superman. He recognized that he was acting out unattainable wishes.

This was another example of what Freud (1900) wrote about, namely, the dreamer's defense that "this is just a dream." It was different, however, in that the patient was disappointed when he realized that he was not really Superman, that he was just dreaming, whereas Freud's subjects were relieved when they recognized they were dreaming because the dream content was unpleasant and often dangerous.

This dream, as is true of many lucid dreams, contained both primary- and secondary-process elements. Dreams, in general, are a blend of primary and secondary process, but in lucid dreams there is an additional self-observing function included in secondary-process operations. This places the dream closer to the reality-oriented surface than to the deeper recesses of the unconscious. The balance between primary- and secondary-process in this dream is characteristic of phenomena that occur in the transitional space.

On occasion, the dreamer may be able to dictate the course of the dream. This means that the subject has acquired control of what are essentially primary-process operations and is able to create a setting that is gratifying and pleasurable. These lucid dreams, as they unfold, reflect elements of the therapeutic process. Both in the dream and in therapy there are internal rearrangements that occur in the transitional space. There is a playful quality to the dream action as fantasies and illusions are realized. In treatment, the grimness of the reality the patient has, in part, created becomes transformed in playful fantasy, which can then be controlled. As discussed, this progression is the essence of the working-through process.

The flexibility of intrapsychic processes in the transitional space was remarkably demonstrated by a middle-aged housewife's production and use of lucid dreams. What began as an unpleasant dream was changed by the dreamer to render it innocuous. At the beginning of the dream she felt helpless and vulnerable, but then she took control and converted a grim and dangerous situation into one where she felt powerful and omnipotent. Her dreams changed as she was working through essential defenses and maladaptations. I believe these dreams were pictorial representations of the therapeutic process, but before discussing this I will first present something about her background and the course of treatment.

As a child, this patient had been sexually and physically abused. She recalled many beatings from both parents. Thus her view of the world was of a hostile, assaultive environment, and she was fearful and timid. She had a poorly developed sense of identity and was frightened of intimacy when she began treatment. She used splitting defenses or was overwhelmed with anxiety when facing situations that were symbolically reminiscent of infantile traumatic incidents.

She had been in treatment with another therapist for 10 years before she saw me. Her former therapist, a benign and gentle woman, retired from practice and moved to another city. The patient had, at first, been wary of her and did not know whether she could trust or rely on her. Throughout the years, however, she was able to allow herself to be dependent on her, a considerable achievement in view of her extremely traumatic background. The patient was bitterly disappointed about her therapist leaving her, but because the therapist had referred her to me, she was glad to see me.

She quickly formed a positive attachment to me, and she was able to focus on intrapsychic processes. In her previous therapy there was considerable discussion about her relationships in the outer world. She knew very little about the nature of her basic insecurities. She was aware that she did not see herself as a distinct person, separate and different from others. She viewed herself as blending with her surroundings, and this was a devastating experience.

She was also unaware of being involved and having been involved in many sadomasochistic relationships, in which her sexual partners, usually women, would physically and sexually abuse her. It was not apparent to her that she was being mistreated, because all she had known in childhood was harsh treatment, much harsher than what she was experiencing. By contrast, her current relationships were relatively gentle, although in actuality they were not.

I gradually learned, to my surprise, that her relationship with her former therapist also had sadomasochistic elements. Some of her therapist's remarks were tinged with sarcasm and depreciation, but the patient was not aware of their hostile significance. Over the course of several years, I formed the impression that this therapist was ambivalent about her patient and, at times, had hinted that she might do well to terminate treatment and see a different therapist. From some of the patient's quotes of her exchanges with her former therapist, it was quite clear to me that she was annoyed with the patient, but the patient was totally oblivious of any negative feelings toward her, either in the treatment relationship or on the part of some of her lovers.

Because she had been raised in a violent environment, it seemed strange, at first, that she was not sensitive to being attacked. Actually, she was extremely frightened of being assaulted, but she only responded to gross attacks. Subtle, covert hostility was below the threshold of her perception and sensitivity; her perceptual system lacked the capacity to make fine discriminations, thus making her an easy victim of exploitation. Besides her poorly structured perceptual system, she lacked cohesiveness and unity of the psychic apparatus and the self-representation. Her somewhat dissociated psyche led to a constricted view of various object relationships. Her attitudes seemed naive, and she found the process of living difficult. What seemed routine and pedestrian for most people, she experienced as burdensome. Just carrying out the tasks of daily life was painful. She found everything grim and gloomy.

During the first 3 years her of treatment with me, we examined how she let herself be masochistically exploited. As she became able to understand the destructive basis of her various relationships as well as how her previous therapist had sometimes reacted to her, she was able to get in touch with her inner rage. It was interesting that in the past she had never felt angry, which struck me as astonishing in view of how much she had been violated. It was now clear that she used splitting mechanisms to encapsulate her anger, which would have proven to be disruptive—as it did, to some extent, when it emerged during our sessions.

She was able to face rage in the context of a positive transference. She had idealized me as she did her previous therapist, but not to the same extent or with the same megalomanic fervor. I was not deified and she could be aware of my shortcomings, an awareness she did not have about her former therapist. I was not promoted to a godlike status, and on occasion she would direct her anger toward me.

When this occurred, it had a slight paranoid flavor. She would then view me as exploitive, which meant that I was treating her only for financial gain or that I wanted to make her over in my own image. She would accuse me of seeking personal aggrandizement by curing her, thoughts she never had toward her first therapist. Still, her attacks were short-lived and not particularly intense. She felt fairly comfortable and was somewhat pleased with her newfound anger; it gave her a sense of definition.

Her attitudes also changed, especially toward her husband. She was able, apparently for the first time, to recognize how condescending and insulting he was. He relentlessly criticized her for being a poor housekeeper and a terrible cook. She remembered many social situations when he had made disparaging remarks about her ineptness and lack of personal hygiene. Then she had had no reactions; she was not even aware of what was happening. Now she looked back on these experiences with shame and humiliation, and felt very angry toward her husband. Primarily, however, she was angry at herself for having been so insensitive and letting these intrinsically embarrassing situations develop.

She became more assertive in her marriage and began fighting back when her husband attacked her. Some of their arguments were fairly violent, and on several occasions she forced him to leave. He eventually realized that the relationship could not continue on its usual basis. He became extremely depressed, and although he was contemptuous of persons in psychotherapy, he sought treatment for himself.

The transference took an interesting turn. As stated, she began to view me as the attacking husband and as her exploitive, assaultive parents. This was a discovery that lessened, but did not destroy, her idealization of me. Her newfound anger toward me took a specific and unique form. She began to believe that I was responsible for the pain she was beginning to feel, but unlike another patient who had similar feelings (Giovacchini 1979a), she also had some positive feelings about what I had apparently done to her.

She both blamed and credited the analysis for "creating" feelings within her that did not previously exist. Now, she felt anger as well as humiliation and shame. She was aware of being attacked and vulnerable, whereas in the past she either split off these uncomfortable feeling states or had not yet acquired the ability to structure her percepts so that she could be aware of the demeaning circumstances she was facing. Her capacity for observation and self-observation was underdeveloped. Through my observations and my assessment of what she had been subjected to, she was able to expand the domain of her perceptual and integrative ego systems. This was an acquisition both gratifying and painful.

Her anger toward me lasted only a few months, and her grim and depressed demeanor lightened considerably. From a Svengali who controlled his Trilby, I was changed into Pygmalion. She used many colorful metaphors and found numerous examples in both classical and modern literature that gave poetic descriptions of her previous lack of self, and how she had been transformed from a puppet, Pinocchio, to a human being. She cried when she saw the cartoon movie of Pinocchio, having feelings she never suspected she had. I felt that we were relating to each other in a somewhat playful manner as she was feeling some excitement about the observations she was making about herself.

She was making discoveries, and I was acknowledging and confirming them. I was also making connections between her need to conceive of herself as a creative, secure person and strivings in the external world directed toward achieving that aim. There was still a strong tendency to consider herself a failure, and she viewed some of her behavior as stemming from the inadequate, insensitive, nonexistent parts of the self. More frequently than not, she was asserting herself and seeking acknowledgment as a productive and competent person. I would stress the adaptive potential of her behavior, and she usually accepted my explanations as correctly pointing to creative endeavors.

In the past, she had dreamed of being pursued by monsters or other frightening situations and catastrophes. The manifest content seemed to be very primitive; she dreamed of rotting cadavers, mutilation, or drowning in vats of feces.

Like the literary allusions mentioned above, her dreams can be considered transitional-space activities, which were the focus of the therapeutic process. She was beginning to feel more and more that she was gaining control over her destiny, and this was reflected in her dreams.

Her dreams changed markedly in that some of them were pleasant. She believed she could control and change the course of some of her dreams as she was dreaming. For example, she dreamed of driving her car, a middle-price-range model, in the neighborhood she had lived in as a child. She was feeling good about herself and felt peaceful and tranquil as she approached the family home. She believed that at this point in the dream she might have been aware that she was dreaming. In a whimsical mood she decided that she wanted a Rolls-Royce, so she simply changed her useful but unpretentious automobile into a splendid Rolls-Royce convertible. This was a magical accomplishment of a lucid dream.

The dream scene suddenly shifted. She was in the midst of the turbulent activity of a circus. She was watching wild animals perform while being controlled by trainers. She was in awe of the feats the animals were capable of without losing control and attacking their trainers, as one might expect of lions and tigers. She then decided she wanted to join the melee and, as she again recognized she was dreaming, she decided that she wanted to fly as a trapeze artist. She flew toward the top of the tent, looking down at the wild animals and enjoying herself immensely. She was aware of being able to do whatever she pleased regarding locomotion, a pleasurable, omnipotent feeling. She finally returned to earth, at which moment a huge gorilla escaped from his cage and chased after her. At first she was afraid that the gorilla would kill her, and then she reminded herself that she was in control of her dream, so she simply stopped and faced the beast, who became frightened and slunk away.

In the final scene of the dream, she was standing on a sidewalk with a fairly large group of people. They were waiting for their parked cars to be returned to them. The woman in charge of the parking lot was an ugly witch or hag. The patient knew that she would be one of the last persons to get her automobile. As the other cars were being delivered, she became increasingly angry. She also gradually developed the conviction that she was never going to get her car. She knew it was no longer a Rolls-Royce, and she was still aware that she was dreaming. She reminded herself that her automobile was safe and sound in her garage, but she was still dissatisfied and angry. She wanted to fight with the witch about the car, although she knew it really did not matter whether it was delivered to her. She lamented that many of her dreams were frustrating because she never achieved what she was striving to do. She persisted and continued to want to fight with the old lady and to retrieve her car. She was also angry about her failure to get what she wanted in her dreams, although this was not strictly true, as evidenced by her omnipotently manipulating in other segments of lucid dreams. She nevertheless wanted to vent her anger on this witch and to make her deliver the auto, even though she knew it was only a dream. She finally grabbed the old woman by the neck, and they both fell screaming to the ground. Obviously, her feelings were out of control, and she awakened from the dream.

It is not certain whether she was totally awake, but she claimed that she was in touch with her surroundings and could even hear the electric hum of the clock. The dream was still on her mind, and she continued to feel angry at the whole situation of not being able to get her car, although she was fully cognizant that there was no issue. She was able to differentiate the dream from reality, but she wanted to remain concerned and involved with the dream material. She thought she was being foolish, and she was somewhat amused that she not only wanted the car back but wanted it once again converted into a Rolls-Royce, although in reality she did not particularly like Rolls-Royces. She also wanted to punish the elderly manager of the parking lot.

Her anger was not modulated by waking up. She focused on how she had been mistreated and ignored, and her rage for the injustice and rudeness she had experienced. She was well aware of the fact that the dream was entirely her creation, and that from one viewpoint every character in the dream was part of herself. In spite of her insight and her recognition that there were humorous elements in this situation, she wanted to go back to sleep so she could get back into the dream and fight for her rights.

She "forced" herself to go back to sleep, and she managed to put herself back into the parking lot. She grabbed the old woman by the hair and cruelly threw her to the ground. Then she stepped on her chest and screamed that she must bring her a Rolls-Royce immediately. The woman became frightened and submissive and fled to bring her the automobile. She returned with a Rolls-Royce convertible, and the patient felt euphoric and triumphant. She said to herself in the dream that this was the first time she had been able to bring a dream to a happy and satisfactory conclusion, although in the final analysis it really did not matter. She also reminded herself she did not like Rolls-Royces, but then humorously added that maybe she could sell it and be rich.

The patient associated the first part of the dream to the analysis. She is returning to her childhood neighborhood, an allusion to the psychoanalytic exploration of her infantile milieu. As is so often true in dreams, driving an automobile refers to the therapeutic process or journey. Converting it into a Rolls-Royce is an expression of her idealization of the therapist, as occurred during the first phases of the treatment. Her later remarks, that she did not particularly care for Rolls-Royces, were the outcome of her recognition that idealization does not lead to anything particularly useful. She had remarked that you cannot park a Rolls-Royce in a parking lot of a supermarket and, as occurred in treatment, her idealization of me diminished considerably. She no longer stood in magical awe of me, although much of the magic had become internalized and expressed in the dream.

In the next sequence, she accomplished magical feats by defying gravity. She was involved in playful, megalomanic activities that are characteristic of the transitional space. Again, there is a blend of a primary-process orientation and self-observing reality, which defines both the transitional space and the lucid dream. She felt free and could fly beyond the usual boundaries. When she returned to earth, however, she was confronted with the beast from her childhood, the devouring gorilla-father. For a moment, she was seized with her primordial internalized terror, but knowing that she was creating and in control of her dream, she subdued her would-be attacker.

Magical manipulation was involved throughout the dream, but it was therapeutically effective in that it dealt with the frightening and frustrating elements of the infantile environment. In the dream, she has regressed to a primary-process mode. I am not proposing that the work of therapy occurred in the dream space. As stated, I believe the therapeutic interaction occurs in the transitional space, and this patient's dream is a sleeping pictorial representation of the therapeutic transitional space. Within the dream context, psychic activity is closer to unconscious mental processes. Mastery and control appear as megalomanic activity, but the patient still had at least one foot in a reality-oriented world. Her handling of the gorilla-father and of the witch-mother was omnipotent and powerful, but dreams, as Freud (1900) taught us, express ordinary events in melodramatic, magical terms. Perceptions and actions are intensified, and what may appear as trite in the external world may acquire heroic proportions in a dream.

To some extent, this type of intensification also occurs in the transitional space. In fantasy and play ordinary feelings are magnified, but this occurs in the context of safety and security, as is typical of lucid dreams.

The gorilla, the representation of the assaultive, traumatic infantile milieu, no longer overwhelmed her, and this was reflected in increased security in her daily life.

In the last part of the dream, she demonstrated a need to solve her problem in the transitional space and to remain in that space until the problem was solved. From one viewpoint, there was no problem in that she recognized her car was lost only in the dream state; she knew that, in reality, the automobile was safe and snug in her garage.

The car was a symbol of her treatment, but it also represented how she viewed herself as she was involved in the therapeutic process. It was a dream element that expressed our being fused in a constructive fashion. Not having it returned meant that her mother was trying to prevent her from achieving self-esteem, autonomy, and freedom from anxiety and misery. Inasmuch as her mother had hostilely rejected her and had done everything to intensify her vulnerability rather than protect her from the gorilla-father, the patient, while in treatment, was able to get in touch with her rage, and she felt a compelling need to express it in her dream.

We both wondered whether her rage had been previously repressed or split off. In view of her never having experienced anger prior to treatment and the rather undeveloped state of all her feelings, it seemed likely that anger was an analytic creation, perhaps not entirely, but at least to some degree.

In any case, she wanted to experience her anger and use it to change or alter her past. She did not want to completely return to the current reality without having cleared up a problem that dominated the infantile milieu. She had to return to the dream to rewrite history. In a sense, she wanted analysis to provide her a new past, just as it had been able to produce feelings such as anger. I believe that in the treatment of many patients who belong in the borderline spectrum, more is involved than the resolution of infantile traumas. The treatment process deals with the creation of pleasurable affects as well as the recovery of painfully repressed or split-off terrifying experiences. The former becomes a foundation that supports a psychic apparatus without clearly recognizable feelings of self and security in relating to a nonthreatening external world. The patient needs to develop a sense of continuity between the current and infantile milieu. Thus a hierarchy can be established between earlier, primary-process levels of organization and later, secondary-process oriented structures. This leads to unity and cohesion between various parts of the self in patients whose psychopathology caused them to be fragmented.

Another patient stressed that he wanted to reclaim his childhood rather than mourn it. He needed to get in touch with his childhood, but not as it actually was. At least in fantasy, he had to change what had happened, and in the transference to take advantage of what had been the lost opportunities of childhood. Within the transitional space, the past is re-created in play. This forms an illusion that is incorporated into the psyche and fills in the space that was occupied by the early environment. The patient, of course, remembers many elements of the actual past; but as a functional entity contributing to the achievement of gratifying and creative experiences, the past begins with the holding-environment and transitional-space activities for many patients.

COMPENSATORY STRENGTHS AND TRANSITIONAL SPACE INTERACTIONS

I repeat that I do not wish to give the impression that the treatment relationship is lighthearted and playful. The patients I am discussing are suffering from severe psychopathology, and their lives are hard and grim. Many of them are depressed and have very little capacity to experience pleasure. Their outlook, in general, is joyless and humorless.

In spite of feeling oppressed and often terrified, most patients have at least a spark of humor, that is, a microscopic tendency to view themselves and their experiences in a lighter fashion. It is this vestige or tendency toward playfulness that has to be teased out to help establish a treatment relationship.

I recall a consultation with a middle-aged woman who had begun treatment with a new therapist shortly after having been hospitalized. She had been hospitalized several times a year for the past decade and had seen innumerable psychiatrists. None had been able to stand her.

She was a volcano constantly exploding as rage consumed all of her therapeutic encounters. She was a bottomless pit of demands and complaints. She hated all her therapists because they were vicious, stupid, and incompetent. Nevertheless, she called them at all hours of the day and night and would become violent if they failed to respond or tried to set limits. She physically attacked one psychiatrist and trashed the waiting room of another, who was forced to physically subdue her. In every sense, she was an impossible patient. I received this information from the attending psychiatrist during her last hospitalization and a former therapist whom I had supervised.

I was astonished when she called to set up an appointment. She spoke in a quiet, charming, well-bred fashion. When I saw her she was well-dressed, fairly attractive, and mild-mannered. She in no way resembled the monster she was described as being. She spoke calmly about herself and her experiences in treatment, and hoped that I would be able to help her current therapist so that she would be able to continue in treatment with him. I could not reconcile what I saw to what I had heard about her.

She did not deny that she was a difficult patient and was able to speak about her assaultive, disruptive behavior, but her manner of expressing herself could have indicated that she was describing another person. She lamented that she was such a troublesome patient, but she also described some of her reactions with a degree of humor. She was able to see something funny in the turmoil she had created and could not understand why her therapists were so upset. She emphasized that her actions were the manifestations of her psychopathology that she could not or should not suppress. Therapists should know that she was simply revealing herself and should react to her in a professional manner rather than being personally disturbed.

I smiled and agreed with her but then added that her behavior would require a therapist with infinite patience and wisdom, and so far no one with those qualifications has entered our earthly domain. The patient laughed and replied that she doubted that celestial analysts would want to treat her, so she would have to settle for what was available. She demonstrated that, as severely disturbed as she was and however sordid and grim the circumstances of her past, she still had considerable capacity for wit and humor. It was seldom manifested during treatment, but it was nevertheless there and could be used for therapeutic purposes.

I discussed my interview with her with the current therapist and he was thereafter on the lookout for the sanguine attitudes that she had revealed to me. Occasionally he detected flashes of wit and humor and he responded to them playfully. By so doing he was able to create openings that brought her self-observing function into service. This was similar to what had happened in our consultation room. When she was feeling some amusement about her irrational demands and behavior, she was commenting about her actions and parts of the self. She was in a self-observational frame and her therapist was able to use these interactions for therapeutic purposes.

Clinicians are faced with another paradox, besides the psychoanalytic paradox, when treating severely disturbed patients. I have postulated that the psychoanalytic interaction takes place in the transitional space, but many borderline patients either have not reached the developmental level in which they can create a transitional space, or else they have constructed a defective space. As has been repeatedly discussed, patients have traversed all developmental stages, but there are varying degrees of coherent organization and defective organization in the spectrum of emotional development. Furthermore, in many patients suffering from character disorders there is uneven development, and certain areas of the mind may function very well while others may be practically paralyzed. In therapy this unevenness may create special problems if defective, nonfunctional psychic structures include the transitional space. But within the transitional space itself there is some unevenness, and those elements that are viable and functional may be sufficient to permit a therapeutic interaction, as seems to be the case with the patient just discussed.

In Chapter 3, I discussed the wide range of character disorders that are found in the borderline spectrum. The varying degrees of structural psychopathology are reflected in the construction and functioning of the transitional space, and this will determine whether psychoanalytic psychotherapy is possible.

The concrete attitudes that make patients difficult to treat are also manifestations of a defective transitional space. The inner and outer worlds are not firmly differentiated. This blurred distinction leads to confusion as to the causes of frustration and disruption that were experienced as external assaults. Later, there is a tendency to view everything as coming from the outer world, and insofar as it is not particularly separated from the inside as occurs when the transitional space is consolidated, the acknowledgment of internal sources seldom occurs.

Still, therapists have to be alert to the strengths and positive qualities of various aspects of psychic structure so they can be brought into the therapeutic interaction; these may exist side by side with the most extreme forms of psychopathology. The combination of strengths and severe defects may be characteristic of patients who reside in the borderline spectrum and may account for the extreme swings of behavior ranging from efficient adaptive behavior to psychotic delusional activity. The distinction between these two extremes can also be blurred, as the following case illustrates.

My purpose in presenting this patient is to demonstrate the diversity of the transitional space in that it could function at the highest levels or regressively deteriorate to ego states in which there is an almost total loss of reality testing. The simultaneous structure and lack of structure of the transitional space is especially relevant to the study of the therapeutic process, and inasmuch as there are highly developed elements in that space, there is also a resiliency that is therapeutically useful. This resiliency in my patient succeeded in saving a treatment relationship that was on the brink of destruction.

The patient, a bright scientist in his twenties, played a musical instrument as a hobby, but he was reputed to have nearly professional musical skills. He revealed that when he played his instrument he would hear voices that would benignly instruct him how to play. They would make comments about various aspects of his technique, which were invariably helpful.

Did he actually hear voices? He stated that he did. What he heard was absolutely clear as if another person were talking to him. In spite of their quality of externality he knew that they came from within his head. The sensory quality of what he was experiencing was hallucinatory, but his belief about their origins was not delusional. He thought of himself as possessing an unusual perceptual talent, that of being able to hear himself think.

This was a playful, pleasant activity, which can be conceptualized as taking place in the transitional space. He had the *illusion* that he had a helpful mentor who was playfully teaching him how to play a musical instrument. He was delighted and amused by this arrangement as well as proud, because he felt he had an edge on fellow musicians. Long hours of practice were fun, rather than tiresome and tedious.

It seemed as if this patient had developed an extraordinary capacity for fantasy and play, and this was also evident in the social and professional areas of his life. Such a capacity would be indicative of a well-constructed transitional space. His psychopathology, however, could destroy all elements of transitional activity and reduce him to a psychotic, delusional state.

This patient sought treatment because he was unhappy. He had several friends he believed were fond of him, but he had no close relationships. His work concerned him the most because he did not believe he was sufficiently appreciated and that his superiors were jealous of his capacities. There was some data to confirm both these assertions. Still, there was a paranoid element to his demeanor, which he interspersed with humor. He could understand that the more conservative scientists would shy away from a maverick such as himself, who had unconventional ideas, but he felt their attitudes were comical. Regarding stealing his ideas, he felt a certain generosity and consoled himself by noting that his teachers had little talent, especially if they needed to plagiarize his work. He had so much to contribute that it did not matter if they took a little from him. It made them feel good and it did not particularly hurt him. This magnanimous mood, however, did not persist.

He began treatment in a grandiloquent fashion, praising both of us. He wanted to establish a megalomanic alliance. He was quite playful and would talk with glee about some of the pranks he had concocted. He acted as if he were a mischievous little boy.

Gradually his mood changed. It became grim. The change began when the helpful voices changed their tone. They became harsher, and their critical remarks were no longer benign. They also strayed away from their original interest to help him play a musical instrument. They started criticizing his appearance, intelligence, and other personal traits. He felt that they were moving further away spatially as they finally attacked him for being a homosexual.

He was demonstrating a regressive degradation of perceptual hypersensitivity. What could be considered an expansion of the auditory mode of his perceptual system was dragged into the service of paranoid projective mechanisms. Hearing himself think was transformed into an auditory hallucination where he believed someone outside the self was persecuting him. The transitional space, characterized by the fluidity of the inner and outer world, was torn down as the patient made pathological distinctions between inside and outside. What had been partially internal and external, the benign instructor voice, was no longer a transitional phenomenon. It had been placed in the external world and represented a psychotic distortion of reality. The compartmentalization of an inner percept into the external world was a typical paranoid sequence. The patient became very upset and blamed me because I could not protect him from what had become a persecutor. He had also become suspicious of my motives and wondered whether I wanted to exploit him. I was also being cast out of the transitional space and thrown into the external world as a potential persecutor. He became increasingly disturbed and suspicious in my office, and his behavior in his daily life was disruptive.

For example, his anxiety mounted to an intolerable level as he convinced himself that his fellow scientists, the CIA, and I wanted to steal his ideas and then either lock him up or kill him. Suffering from intense tension, he frantically requested to be seen by the chancellor of the university where he worked. He told the chancellor about the CIA and my involvement, which also included a communist conspiracy. The chancellor asked to be excused and walked into another room to telephone the security guards. The patient heard his conversation and rushed out of the house, running down an esplanade in front of the chancellor's mansion. The police had no trouble in finding him, because as he ran toward the lake he shed his clothes until he was completely naked. He was taken to a psychiatric hospital.

These experiences occurred during a weekend. Apparently he was able to convince the staff that they should let him attend his Monday morning session. When he arrived, he was still quite paranoid and delusional. He looked frightened and cowed as an animal might be. As I moved toward him, he shouted at me to back up. He wanted to keep a 15-foot distance between us. I understood that he wanted to be absolutely certain that there would be no blending of our spaces. This would create a transitional space where the boundaries between the two of us would be blurred. He had to keep our spaces absolutely separate and intact.

I could not accede to his request that we maintain a space of 15 feet between us inasmuch as my office was not large enough to maintain such a distance. To reassure him, I told him he need not worry. I was not at all concerned that he would hurt me. I assumed he was afraid his destructive feelings would get out of control. He screamed that he was not at all concerned about hurting me; rather, he was terrified that I would kill him. Nevertheless, he lay down on the couch.

He was very angry at me. He explained that I had been hired by the Mafia and paid an enormous sum of money to pick his brains. He literally meant pick his brains, that is, ramming an ice pick through his skull and macerating his cerebral cortex. I chuckled and he suddenly sat up and looked at me with a look of shocked surprise. I explained that I did not understand why the Mafia had to pay such a large sum of money to do something that was already in my job description. I did not need additional money to do something that was intrinsic to my professional orientation. It was included in my job description.

The patient was, at first, astonished as he held me with a fixed gaze. Then he burst out laughing and said: "You enjoy picking my brains?" I replied that of course I did, and that I had learned many good and useful things from him. His demeanor and voice changed from those of an angry, frightened person to those of an impish child. He understood "picking his brains" as a metaphor. What had been a cruel, sadistic act was now transformed into a metaphor that both amused and narcissistically enhanced him.

We had moved from the harsh, concrete world of reality into the playful, poetic transitional space. He discussed all of his actions that afternoon when he was psychotic, but he was pleased with everything that he had done and with what had happened to him. He accepted that his accusations were ridiculous, but he applauded them as the products of a rich imagination. He saw his behavior as the manifestation of various parts of the self, much in the same way clinicians would view a dream. During the session, he was removed from his paranoid, tainted reality and was correlating his fantasies, and he recognized them as fantasies, of people wanting to steal his ideas concerning theoretical issues in which chaotic unpredictable phenomena can be understood and regulated. Chaotic and unpredictable phenomena and being persecuted were equivalent. He moved easily from personal issues to scientific problems.

Our interaction did not prevent future episodes of paranoid acting out and accusations directed at myself from occurring. We were able, however, to understand his reactions as stemming from traumatic incidents in the past when he was, in fact, exploited.

10

Kernberg's Expressive

Therapy

Many psychoanalysts have shifted from a drive-dominated theoretical perspective to an object relations viewpoint. This is, of course, a gross oversimplification, but changes in our conceptual orientation have led to modifications in therapeutic approaches, as I have been discussing throughout this book. Many articles and books have been written that are extremely useful to clinicians. Other writings have purported to introduce innovations, but often they are restatements or cliches.

There are many major contributors to the literature discussing the borderline patient. It would be impossible to list all of them, so I will choose two psychoanalysts who, in my opinion, have received the most attention by mental health workers, namely, Kernberg and Kohut. This of course does not mean that others have not made as significant contributions.

One might argue that some authors have been unfairly neglected because so much attention has been focused on Kernberg and Kohut. Until recently Winnicott had received very little attention, and during my training at the Chicago Institute for Psychoanalysis, Melanie Klein's work was unknown. They are being rediscovered, and many of the ideas that have been attributed to Kernberg and Kohut can be found in their writings as well as those of other authors. Kernberg, as a rule, has been careful to document the history of his concepts, but Kohut has virtually ignored most of his predecessors.

Both Kernberg and Kohut began writing and formulating their theories and techniques when clinicians were becoming aware that the patients they were treating could not be understood in conventional psychodynamic terms or treated in a standard psychoanalytic fashion. Out of clinical necessity, therapists were eager to receive guidance and looked up to these authors to help them understand and treat patients. As so often occurs in psychoanalysis, polarization quickly sets in, and Kernberg and Kohut have been cast in oppositional roles. There have been considerable discussions and arguments as to which viewpoint is preferable, polemics that often go beyond the subject matter.

I will begin with Kernberg's recommendations regarding treatment, which are derived from his concepts about borderline psychopathology. The latter are fairly traditional within the context of ego psychology and object relations theory. Still, he does not leave the classical frame entirely in that he believes that borderline patients also have to be understood in terms of instinctual vicissitudes (Kernberg 1975).

He emphasizes that borderline personality disorders are pathologically fixated at lower levels of ego organization. The weakness of the ego is characterized by a lack of tolerance for anxiety, poor impulse control, and "a lack of developed sublimatory channels" (p. 70). These remarks, especially his mention of sublimation, point to his retention of some principles of drive theory, but he also emphasizes distortions in ego functioning brought about by the use of pathological defenses such as splitting, primitive idealization, projective identification, denial, and omnipotence.

Regarding structural psychopathology, Kernberg stresses the pathology of internalized object relationships. He follows Hartmann (1939, 1950), who considers the ego to be an overall structure that integrates substructures and functions. The specific structural derivatives of internalized object relationships contribute to the form of psychopathology, and here he is following Melanie Klein (1946).

Kernberg discusses early ego levels that are primitively organized. In borderline personality disorders an excess of oral aggression causes pregenital fixation, which may lead to a premature development of oedipal impulses. Sexual and aggressive feelings become fused, and this may cause problems in the treatment relationship. Particularly difficult is the patient's demanding dependence, which may be based on oral-cannibalistic strivings. These primitive strivings cause a weakness of the ego so that it cannot tolerate transference regression, making it susceptible to the development of a transference psychosis.

Kernberg does not advocate supportive therapy for the treatment of borderline personality disorders. A supportive approach interferes with the establishment of a working alliance and bypasses the development of negative transference, which he believes has to be experienced by these patients if they are going to relinquish pathological defenses. Instead, he recommends for most borderline patients a form of modified psychoanalysis.

Kernberg postulates an overall treatment strategy. He believes these patients have to experience a systemic elaboration of the negative transference without attempting to make full genetic reconstructions. He advocates emphasizing the here and now aspects of the patient's material by interpreting it in the context of the negative transference. To make such interpretations meaningful and effective, he strongly recommends limit setting in order to prevent the acting out of transference impulses. This may require considerable structuring of the patient's outside life, according to Kernberg.

He does not recommend that the analyst interpret the less primitive manifestations of the positive transference, because he wants to promote the development of the therapeutic alliance. Interpretations generally should be directed to the patient's primitive distortions of the analyst and the analytic interaction, which Kernberg believes will strengthen the patient's ego and cause structural changes that will lead to further development beyond the fixation of the borderline organization.

These are general pronouncements about the therapeutic approach to borderline patients. His most striking statement concerns the recommendation *against* supportive therapy in favor of a modified psychoanalytic procedure or psychoanalytically oriented psychotherapy. Kernberg acknowledges his agreement with Boyer and Giovacchini (1967), who advocated the psychoanalytic treatment with minimal parameters of severely disturbed patients, which includes the borderline patient, many years ago. His further suggestions, especially those involving interpretations are quite similar to what Boyer has recommended. His concepts about the role of the negative transference differ markedly from Kohut's (1971) but are in agreement with Searles (1975, 1986), who has written extensively about clinical interactions with severely emotionally disturbed patients for many years.

I am implying that Kernberg's formulations are not original in substance. Still, he has pulled many loose ends together, and by organizing and systematizing a large volume of data and assigning them to various levels of abstraction, he has made major contributions. If anything, he has probably gone too far in his systematic approach, especially within the therapeutic realm, because when dealing with patients there is seldom an orderly sequence that can be dealt with by formulaic responses.

Kernberg and his associates (1987) have very definite ideas about the treatment of borderline patients. They begin by forming a contract with their prospective patients. Inasmuch as borderline patients have a propensity for destructive and self-destructive acting out, the authors wish to construct a manageable therapeutic setting. They demand that patients stay alive and come to sessions in a relatively stable and sober condition. Patients must maintain a certain decorum in that they behave in a sufficiently constrained, nonviolent fashion.

They are also instructed to free-associate, but in a modified fashion in that they can present experiences and events that have been troubling them or that are dwelling in their minds. If they have nothing in particular to present, they can let their minds wander and verbalize whatever occurs to them. They are also instructed not to suppress their thoughts and feelings and to be honest. If they continue to lie for 6 months, treatment is discontinued.

Kernberg has always advocated the use of psychoanalytic techniques for seriously ill patients. He is attempting to create a setting in which the psychoanalytic method can be used, and he calls this type of treatment *expressive psychotherapy*. Because of the severity of psychopathology, he and his colleagues give considerable weight to management.

It is understandable that there has to be a certain amount of structuring in order to safeguard the therapy. On many occasions, however, management seems to dominate, and attempts at getting in touch with the primitive parts of the patient's mind recede into the background. True, Kernberg's focus stresses that the purpose of treatment is to enhance the borderline patient's ability to experience the self and others as coherent, integrated persons. This involves getting in touch with dissociated components of the internal milieu, which are "revealed in rapidly emerging transferences to the therapist" (Kernberg et al. 1987, p. 9).

Kernberg's view of the therapeutic process strikes me as concrete and somewhat simplistic. He states that by continuously clarifying and interpreting the split-off parts of the self, they will gradually become integrated and incorporated into a core self-representation, or what he calls the *total self-representation*. This will lead to basic unity and a more realistic relationship with both the inner and outer worlds.

Basically, Kernberg is stating the same thing Freud said about the therapeutic process; that is, its aim is to make the unconscious conscious and then the patient will get well. Later Freud (1914b) added that the patient has to become involved in working through the conflict that has been made conscious through transference interpretations.

Kernberg does not discuss how the integration of split-off parts takes place beyond their reaching the sphere of consciousness. He postulates that split-off psychic elements, by being outside the general psychic organization, acquire primitive qualities as impulses are thrust outside the ego sphere into the realm of the id. The only differences that Kernberg offers in the formulation of the curative process is that instead of instinctual conflicts, he writes about psychic structures. The latter, in essence, undergo the same vicissitudes as instinctual impulses. By being cast out of the system perceptual-consciousness, they create psychopathological configurations. Emerging once again because of therapeutically effective interpretations, they become incorporated into the higher levels of the psychic apparatus.

As I have repeatedly stressed throughout this book, the treatment process is considerably more complicated than described here. Kernberg emphasizes the difficulties in treating these severely disturbed patients, but he attributes them to the patient's erratic behavior not permitting the establishment of a therapeutic relationship, and of course, he is quite correct. The problems he discussed have to be overcome, or at least controlled. But there are covert interactions in the transference–countertransference constellation that are subtle and complex and go way beyond the clarification and interpretation of split-off parts and their subsequent reintegration into the psychic mainstream, as Freud (1938) stated. These interactions, in turn, are also related to management, and certain conditions that may have been imposed to preserve the treatment may actually make it impossible to achieve the resolution of psychopathology.

As discussed in Chapter 5, there are regressions in which patients get in touch with the infantile parts of the self. They are operating at primitive levels that cannot be understood in the context of interpretations aimed at revealing and identifying split-off parts of the self. *The patient is more concerned with experiencing than observing*, and this is an essential and vital feature of the therapeutic process.

Patients are struggling to achieve what Kernberg advocates, that is, to integrate fragmented parts of the psyche into a cohesive whole. They are, however, not able to accomplish this task through interpretation during regressed states, because the primary-process character of such early orientations precludes the operation of the self-observing function and other sophisticated cognitive capacities. As stressed in Chapter 5, trying to explain the patient's feelings with words is fruitless because words belong to a higher psychic level than what the patient is feeling. To put the experience into words, if they are heard, moves the patient away from a crucial therapeutic event. As emphasized, the patient is trying to reintegrate split-off parts of the self, but the analyst's attempts at interpretation call a halt to what is a painful but nevertheless healing process, a striving for cohesion and unification.

I have stated that the analyst has to react to the "baby" parts as if they are real. Interpreting them introduces another level of discourse, and in most instances the patient is well aware of what he is feeling and his transference expectations. When my patient cried "I want my mommy," he wanted to be nurtured and loved, not a discussion of the maternal transference.

To repeat, there are different types of regression. In most regressions there are some elements of the self-observing ego that participate in the analytic process. Many borderline patients have to get in complete touch with the primitive and fragmented parts of the self that have to be exclusively focused on. They can only deal with one segment of the personality at a time. As stated in the treatment of many borderline patients, analysts are relating to part objects rather than whole objects.

What Kernberg discusses as the curative process refers to an achievement of therapy rather than its modus operandi. I grant this may cause difficulties in the maintenance of our analytic identities, because our professional self-representations have many operational elements; that is, they are based on our technical orientation and methodology. Patients may demand that we assume roles that go beyond our boundaries as therapists, usually to become directly involved in caregiving activities.

Borderline patients are frequently rigid and constricted in that their defensive dissociative adaptations rob them of a multifaceted orientation, which would be a reflection of a flexible, dynamic character structure. For the analyst to insist on a particular approach represents a similar rigidity and a unidimensional orientation. Many of these patients are asking us to be sufficiently free to join them at their infantile level, but we have to know how to behave when we meet them there. This means we do not use a mode of discourse that is much too structured and sophisticated for the setting they have created, and which threatens to destroy that setting.

These patients are attempting to gain accretions to their split-off unidimensional psychic organization. In a comparable fashion, therapists have to also reach other aspects of their character and integrate them into their therapeutic approach. In the situations I have described, this means being with the patient during painful but potentially constructive regressions. I have discussed how a therapist may comment on the subjective nature of the patient's feelings without structuring them to the degree that they lose meaning (Chapter 5).

Kernberg's approach is systematic and orderly, perhaps a helpful contrast to the patient's life, which in many instances has been unstructured and chaotic. By introducing order he hopes to create a manageable setting in which the patient will develop trust and security. Still, a clinician can question how this can be achieved if the therapist issues directives and is confrontational when the patient deviates or resists some of the basic elements of the therapeutic contract.

Many borderline patients have had traumatic, assaultive childhoods in which most relationships were based on a sadomasochistic interaction. These patients have felt controlled and exploited. Any attempts to control their behavior may be considered an attack on their integrity and a rejection of their needs.

For other patients a world of rules and regulations is incomprehensible. There are no internal structures to resonate with it. Consequently, they may be confused, and inasmuch as they view such a milieu as a series of impingements, feelings of inadequacy and insecurity are intensified. This would seem to be working at cross purposes with the establishment of a holding environment.

Again, I have to admit that even if the patient cannot understand it, there has to be at least a modicum of order if treatment is to proceed; and that Kernberg is correct when he considers certain recommendations as being favorable for treatment. I surmise that setting conditions for treatment is a matter of attitude and personal style. Rather than being confrontational, the therapist can stress that the interest of the treatment is what requires particular standards of conduct. Confrontation usually conveys blame and criticism of the reactions of a patient who feels vulnerable and helpless. Treatment issues revolve around the question of how much order a patient can tolerate and still be able to maintain sufficient stability so that a treatment relationship can be established.

Often the therapist can make pointed recommendations in a fashion that is nonthreatening, but the reverse is more frequently true. Analysts may unwittingly issue directives to their patients. They may not be particularly aware that they are being managerial or that their statements have moral overtones. As I read some of the patient–therapist dialogues in Kernberg and colleagues' (1987) handbook of treatment, I had the impression that at least one of the therapists was being confrontational and directive and that he was confronting his patient with a series of "don'ts or shoulds."

A patient missed a session because he had been hospitalized for having made a suicidal attempt by taking an overdose of an over-the-counter drug. The therapist is notified of the suicide attempt by the patient's brother. He confronts the patient by stating "You didn't call me. You didn't explain anything" (1987, pp. 41–42). He adds, "You called after thinking that I might be annoyed. . . . You didn't call before that" (p. 42). Later the therapist admonishes the patient for not having called to inform him that he was not going to keep his appointment because he was going to take drugs. The therapist is, of course, concerned whether he can conduct outpatient treatment with a suicidal patient. He believes it can be possible and feels the situation could have been worse, as he indicates by the following remark: "I appreciate your honesty. It certainly would have been much worse if you were not telling me the truth."

In this sample case, the therapist gives his reasons for his interventions. He explains that he was focusing on the patient's behavior as it impinged on his ability to participate in therapy. He believes that his comments were nonjudgmental in that he was restricting himself to remarks addressed only to actions that were incompatible with keeping appointments. He stresses that he was not exploring motivations, which he feels would have been detrimental at this point in treatment.

I wonder, however, if emphasizing behavior and remaining exclusively in that frame of reference can ever be totally nonjudgmental. On the other hand, dealing with motivations, that is, introducing an intrapsychic focus, can be reassuring in that the patient may be able to gain some control over what he had felt was beyond his grasp. To some patients the therapist's discovery of intrapsychic elements indicates that he understands them better than they understand themselves. In this context patients may develop a need to keep their appointments.

Clinicians have to appreciate the therapist's efforts to construct a treatment setting and to have a live patient. Still, although his remarks were undoubtedly stated in a benevolent fashion, there are moral overtones that he is conveying, which may be felt as intrusive to many vulnerable and hypersensitive patients. The patient is expected to be honest, reliable, and responsible, certainly desirable qualities for any form of treatment but beyond the capacity of many borderline patients.

Kernberg's recommendations about technical procedures, as mentioned, are also orderly and follow a linear sequence. His concepts about interpretation are similar to Fenichel's (1945, 1953) in that he postulated a progression from the surface to depth and a movement from the present, the "here and now" as I have noted, to the past in the form of genetic reconstructions. I believe that in general, he is recommending principles that have been found effective in psychoanalytic treatment. Again, with borderline patients they may be effective if they are not rigidly applied. As will be discussed in Chapter 12, the study of borderline patients causes us to expand our concepts about all aspects of psychoanalytic treatment, and this includes the interpretative process. The modern clinician can no longer rely on a collection of shibboleths that for some years has been taken for granted as being the foundation of psychoanalytic technique. That is why, as I have stressed in the preface and the introductory chapter of this book, the borderline patient has become the central hub around which concepts of psychopathology and technique revolve. They are truly the essence of psychoanalysis.

I wish to make one final comment about Kernberg's approach, which is in keeping with the tone of this book. I find thinking of the patient–therapist relationship as a contract inappropriate. I know what Kernberg means when he writes of contracts, and that his personal orientation is one of strict probity and creative endeavor. Still, the term *contract* has a commercial quality that I believe is not consistent with a clinical, nonjudgmental orientation. The sanctity of the therapist–patient relationship has in recent times suffered many assaults from third-party payers and the commercialization of outpatient clinics and hospitals.

I have been discussing the thinking of a major contributor to our understanding of the clinical interaction with a group of patients who represent the majority of the patient population. Theoretical innovations in psychoanalysis tend to be far ahead of treatment advances. I believe Kernberg has made contributions in both areas, but his therapeutic orientation does not keep pace with the subtleties and enigmas that borderline patients present to clinicians. This is understandably a difficult and ever-evolving task, which many clinicians, including myself, continue to pursue.

11

Kohut's

Self Psychology

Kohut, in contrast to Kernberg, strays from a strictly psychoanalytic frame of reference. He purports to emphasize structural rather than instinctual factors, but his developmental continuum is sufficiently unique that it is difficult to work out a consistent therapeutic approach that would be compatible with his theories. Kohut attempts to formulate the treatment process, but many of his formulations are far removed from standard analytic doxology. This is not necessarily detrimental for the treatment of borderline patients, but clinicians have to judge his ideas on the basis of their merit and applicability. As repeatedly stated, our insights about structural pathology may require a therapeutic procedure that differs considerably from the maxims of classical analysis. On the other hand, without acknowledging it, he retains many elements of standard, classical analytic technique.

Kohut, like Kernberg, has established himself as a new wave on the horizon of psychoanalysis. Therefore, his orientation has to be examined to determine whether he accomplishes the task of taking us out of the realm of Newtonian physics into the domain of a world understood according to relativity and quantum theory, as has been claimed by some Self psychologists. This could be translated as meaning that we are moving from instinctual to structural factors, as has been stressed in this book and by countless other authors. The therapeutic model evolved from treatment efforts directed at structural psychopathology are comparable to the laws that have superseded Newtonian mechanics.

Kohut's system has been called Self psychology because it gives the self-representation and its vicissitudes central prominence and importance. Although Kohut and his followers believe this is a unique formulation, it is inherent in any conceptual system that stresses psychic structure rather than instinctual clashes. In fact, even the classical orientation places the self, which in the expanded structural hypothesis is referred to as the self-representation, in the center of psychic activity.

Freud (1923) examined psychopathology in terms of activities that revolved around the ego. It had to serve three masters, the id, superego, and reality, but its stability determined the integrity of the psychic apparatus. It was referred to as that part of the mind that contained the subjective experience of being. This resided in the system perceptual-consciousness. Today, as an extension of these formulations, clinicians place the awareness of being and the sense of aliveness and identity in the self-representation, a distinctive part of the ego that also dips into the id.

I will not extensively discuss Kohut's theories, since I have done so elsewhere (Giovacchini 1977, 1979a). I will merely refer to those concepts that are specifically and directly related to his treatment approach. Again, I wish to examine and determine whether he supplies us with new paradigms, as Ornstein (1979), in particular, claims. It is important that therapists recognize whether they are being introduced to new clinical vistas and treatment orientations. Are clinicians being given insights about therapeutic settings that are the outcome of significant innovations, or is it simply a matter of a new language, of old wine in new bottles when it refers to Kohut's doctrines?

Kohut, as is generally true of psychoanalysts, gives the transference a pivotal role in the treatment interaction. He (Kohut 1971), focuses on two types of transference, the mirror transference and the idealizing transference.

These transferences supposedly are the characteristic manifestations of an early developmental phase, that of primary narcissism. As I have discussed (Giovacchini 1979a), this is a conceptual inconsistency in that both mirror and idealizing transferences involve external objects, albeit part objects, whereas primary narcissism, according to accepted theory, is a preobject phase. All transferences require some contact with and recognition of the outer world. Patients may regress to preobject phases and still retain some later acquired characteristics, but this does not mean that transference manifestations are intrinsic to the regressed state.

It is somewhat surprising that mirror and idealizing transferences have received such wide publicity in the psychoanalytic literature. Kohut defines the mirror transference as a transference in which the patient wants to be admired by the external object; in therapy this is, of course, the analyst. This is exactly the same ego state that is characteristic of any narcissistic transference. In fact, being admired is the essence of narcissism, and the original myth of Narcissus is that of a youth admiring his reflection in the mirror of a pond. The idealizing transference is also a common phenomenon described by many analysts, especially Melanie Klein, who discussed idealization from various perspectives ranging from the need to elevate the denigrated self by fusing with an idealized object to projection of positive part objects in order to keep them separated from bad and destructive internal objects. I have discussed patients who idealize their analysts when they project good parts of the self into them in order to protect these good parts. The analyst assumes the function of a safety deposit box (Giovacchini 1975b).

Although these transferences have been familiar since long before Kohut, he makes some noteworthy comments about their fate in analytic treatment (Kohut 1971). He stated that the working through of the mirror transference releases constrictive aggressive drives, whereas the resolution of the idealizing transference leads to internal regulation and what might be considered to be a consolidation of the ego ideal (Ornstein 1979). In the former instance, he is discussing internal changes that are concerned with the readjustment of instinctual equilibrium. By contrast, the successful outcome of an analyzed idealizing transference leads to structural rearrangements and expansions. It is interesting that Kohut still views analytic progression from a broad perspective based in both camps, those of classical instinct theory and of the structural revisionists. This might be the direction the treatment of borderline patients is headed toward, although Kohut was primarily interested in narcissistic personality disorders.

As discussed in Chapter 3, the borderline spectrum is broad, and most of the psychopathology Kohut has discussed fits into the category of structural or characterological psychopathology. He has concluded that when the patient's distortions of the perceptions of the analyst are corrected, there will be specific internal responses involving both instincts and psychic structure. He views the impact of analysis as far-reaching and profound, again not an original thought but one clinicians can identify with as they struggle in their treatment of difficult patients.

The reader may wonder why I seem to stress that much of Kohut's writings are not based on his own creations but are often familiar concepts garbed in new terms. I have extensively discussed this question elsewhere (Giovacchini 1979a) and do not wish to review specific "Kohutian" expressions in this context. I continue, however, to point out the lack of originality of many of his concepts because he presents them as if they were truly his own. His bibliography is noteworthy because of the many authors that are not included in it. I have also commented on how some of Kernberg's theses were derived from elsewhere, but he makes no pretense of being the original discoverer and he is meticulous in reviewing his predecessors. As far as I can ascertain, Kohut's selfobject, as he has changed the rules of syntax to graphically represent a merger, really belongs to Modell (1963, p. 285), who used the expression several years before Kohut, an acknowledgment Kohut or his followers have never made.

I have made some general statements about Kohut's conclusions regarding the treatment of patients when their mirroring and idealizing transferences are analyzed. Now I wish to review his conclusions in a more detailed fashion. The resolution of the mirror transference must mean that the patient's narcissistic needs and adaptations have diminished and that what might be considered unhealthy narcissism has been transformed into productive, assertive behavior, that is, into healthy narcissism. Apparently the constrictions of adaptations created by pathological narcissism are relaxed, and the psyche can get in touch with repressed or split-off aggressive impulses, which can be used in the service of creative adaptations. This would naturally lead to increased self-esteem, most likely manifested as the self-confidence and security characteristic of healthy narcissism.

As is self-evident, this sequence of events is an involved and complex process, and the question has to be raised as to how it occurs. For the moment, I just wanted to describe what happens when the narcissistic transference is successfully analyzed. I will discuss the events and interventions required for successful resolution later when dealing with Kohut's specific technical recommendations.

Regarding the idealizing transference, it would be expected that its resolution would lead to internal changes concerning idealization. There are many reasons why a patient may need an external object to idealize, as I have already discussed. The nature of the need being served by idealizing is what will determine the internal changes that occur once that need is overcome. It seems reasonable to conclude that whatever the initial motivations were, changes will involve idealization and perhaps affect the ego ideal, as Kohut implied. Still, the effects on the self-representation will vary depending on the patient's character structure and the qualities and extent of psychopathology. In dealing with the complexities of the human psyche it is not possible or feasible to postulate rigid and concrete cause-effect sequences.

I wish to maintain some sense of balance when discussing Kohut's contributions to the treatment of patients in general and severely ill patients in particular. In the past I have introduced some negative notes because of the substance of his writings and his claims to originality, which at times are as grandiose as some of the clinical situations he describes. More significantly, I wish to counterbalance many of the extravagant claims of his followers, some of whom have elevated him to sainthood. I have much evidence to support these statements, derived from attending meetings of the Chicago Psychoanalytic Society before Kohut's death over a decade ago. This is another instance in psychoanalysis where personal factors have invaded the conceptual and technical domains, and which requires a rational evaluation of the significance of clinical contributions. The ad hominem factor has to be, if not eliminated, at least put in its proper perspective.

At one time, I knew Heinz Kohut well and recognized that he was a person with rare intellectual and clinical gifts. I sat with him through many clinical conferences and was impressed by the quickness and depth of his comprehension and his skilled and tactful therapeutic responses. He was a charismatic teacher, and it is easy to understand why some of his students and analysands idealized him. To place these positive personal attributes into a theoretical system underlying therapy does not necessarily mean that the conceptual product is valid. It behooves the clinician to determine whether such qualities as empathy, intuition, and sensitivity—certainly relevant talents—can be prescribed and become the conceptual basis of a treatment orientation. Similarly, the idealization of a system of thought does not make idealization a fundamental interaction around which the treatment relationship revolves. Furthermore, what might have been second nature to Kohut cannot be legislated and become part of the technical armamentarium.

Kohut (1979) explicitly claims that he has discovered a new analytic approach to patients based on his theoretical formulations. To illustrate and prove this assertion he presents a patient who had two analyses with him, one in which he used the old classical approach and another that was conducted on the basis of his new insights. I believe the examination of these treatment relationships will be extremely helpful in clarifying the questions that I raised at the beginning of this critique, regarding the significance of his alleged innovations.

In any conceptual system about the psychoanalytic process, the transference assumes a core position. Whatever our orientation, classical, Kleinian, or an object relations focus, working within a transference context is an essential feature of the therapeutic process, although, as will be discussed in the next chapter, other factors are also involved. Kohut (1971, 1977, 1978, 1979) gave the transference top priority in his Self psychology and what he believed would be the logical extensions of these formulations into the treatment interaction. Now, more specifically in both a developmental and treatment frame, I wish to discuss the mirror and idealizing transference further; in Kohut's system they are phenomena that reflect the essence of psychopathology and define the path that leads to therapeutic progress.

I do not know whether Kohut initially coined the terms *mirror* and *idealizing* transference, because I have not delved into the literature to determine whether he had predecessors, as was the situation with the expression *selfobject*. Certainly mirror and idealization are familiar words attached to familiar concepts, but it may be true that Kohut first used them as adjectives to modify the noun transference.

Transferences are reflections and replications of childhood relationships that occur later in life and are then relived. Children have transferences, but they are also repeating past experiences. These interactions are characteristic of specific developmental stages, so transference manifestations can refer to early development stages. In fact, as Kohut believes, a developmental phase can be described in terms of the qualities of the transference, and he postulates what he considers to be two important developmental stages: a phase where the child requires mirroring, that is, the infant needs to be admired; and a subsequent phase in which the child needs to idealize an external object, which Kohut refers to as the idealized parental imago.

The infant, during the early months of life, has no capacity to experience idealizing feelings or feel the need for narcissistic enhancement, which is what mirroring means. These are adultomorphic constructs, which are acquired later in the course of development and then attached to these early infantile stages. The question can be raised, however, as to whether they intrinsically belong to these phases as an aspect of an orderly, sequential developmental progression. As later acquired qualities and needs they would not have been included in a particular developmental level, but there may have been precursors that could later be elaborated into narcissistic gratification and idealizing processes.

I believe that the sequence from infantile precursors to ego qualities that are reflected in the mirror and idealizing transferences involve both qualitative and quantitative factors.

Babies obviously have needs. They become upset when needy and require nurture and comforting. Once they are again comfortable, they experience what to the adult seems to be pleasure and satisfaction. This could mean a rudimentary sense of security, which later may become elaborated into self-esteem. As the infant has been taken care of, he moves into and explores the outer world. The mother, as part of that world, engages herself with her child. She invests herself intensely in the interaction with the infant, which evokes delight in both and which sometimes approaches the heights of ecstasy. This playful relationship is mutually enhancing, leading to the attainment of higher levels of emotional development.

This playful interaction between mother and infant is the antecedent of what later is manifested as narcissistic gratification and becomes the foundation of self-esteem-promoting experiences. Kohut has referred to the need for such an interaction within the therapeutic relationship as the mirror transference. There is nothing special about the mirror transference as an innovative concept. It is the manifestation of the first positive emotional interaction of infancy, and it becomes modulated in adulthood in self-esteeming and intimate relationships that maintain a healthy narcissistic balance.

When narcissistic needs become the mainstay of the transference during psychoanalytic treatment, the patient is usually expressing psychopathological needs. As mentioned, there are quantitative differences in the needs themselves. They are more intense and urgent than the ordinary needs for love and companionship. These distinctions have important treatment implications, which I will soon discuss.

Like the mirror transference, the idealizing transference can be viewed as a manifestation and intensification of ordinary childhood events that lead to developmental progression. Its psychopathological and defensive features have been mentioned and discussed by many authors. Its diluted form as an expression of developmentally enhancing events has not been stressed and is not frequently encountered within the treatment setting. Healthy idealizations do occur, however, especially during childhood and adolescence, and persist in a milder form in adulthood.

As infants mature, they begin to recognize that the source of pleasure and gratification resides outside the self. If their caregivers have given them nurture and love, children gain the security that they will be well taken care of. They view their parents as strong and reliable and capable of facing any vicissitudes. They attribute powers to them that appear to make them omnipotent, but this is a child's view of omnipotence, which is restricted to the parents' capability to relate to their needs. Their parents are viewed as strong and invulnerable. In view of the child's dependence, helplessness, vulnerability, and relative size, the parents are truly giants who will nurture and protect them. My father can beat up your father, or My mother is more beautiful than your mother is the credo of many secure children. From such crass thoughts spread the seeds of later idealizations, which can lead to creative accomplishments (Giovacchini 1965b, 1981).

I have dwelled this extensively on the mirror and idealizing transferences because many of the conclusions reached in their discussion are pertinent to our understanding of the therapeutic approach that supposedly springs from the conceptual bastions of Self psychology. Following in the tradition of classical analysis, for Kohut the analysis of the transference is the essence of the therapeutic process, the difference being his exclusive concentration on what he prefers to call the mirror (and its subgroups) and the idealizing transference.

Kohut believes that he discovered a new method of treatment, which can still be considered as belonging in the psychoanalytic domain. He believes that the best way to illustrate and prove his point is to present a course of treatment of a patient who has been treated by the classical method and another course of treatment that has been determined by the canons of Self psychology. His position is strengthened when these two courses of treatment involve the same patient.

He (Kohut 1979) presents the case of Mr. Z., an only child. According to Kohut, Mr. Z.'s analysis took place in two installments, the first having lasted 4 years when the treatment was terminated, supposedly successfully but with some apprehension that perhaps all was not well. After 5½ years the patient returned to treatment, which lasted another 4 years.

I wish to stress at the outset that I do not have any quarrel with Kohut's therapeutic maneuvers and skills as he reports them. He is again impressive as the astute clinician. It is the significance and meaning of his interventions that I choose to discuss, with an emphases on certain subtle interactions and attitudes that are misleading in that the reader may be led to believe that certain orientations are intrinsic to classical analysis and rejected by the "new" therapeutic method.

The patient, a graduate student in his mid-twenties, complained of vague symptoms and mild somatic difficulties. He felt socially isolated and had difficulties with interpersonal relationships. He was unable to become involved with girls. In essence, he sought treatment because he felt alienated and unhappy in his everyday life, reactions that are common in patients suffering from characterological problems and who have problems in maintaining narcissistic supplies and self-esteem.

Mr. Z. was, as stated above, an only child; he lived with his widowed mother. He was extremely lonely and tried to relieve his loneliness by reading, going to movies and concerts alone or with an unmarried friend. Sometimes his mother would accompany them. Apparently, his friend became interested in an older woman, and this caused a breaking up of the triumvirate. It was at this time that he sought treatment.

To drastically summarize, Kohut formulated that the mother and child were involved in a narcissistic fusion. She fed him immense amounts of narcissistic supplies, but at the expense of not being able to move away and establish his autonomy. Developmentally this was a destructive fusion, but the patient received exclusive attention and satisfaction related to an emergent grandiosity.

Kohut (1979) reports that in the first analysis, he dealt with the patient's material as if it were a defense against a basically oedipal configuration. He reports that the main theme during the first year of analysis was a regressive mother transference. The patient's narcissism was expressed by

> unrealistic, deluded grandiosity and his demands that the psychoanalytic situation should reinstate the position of exclusive control, of being admired and catered to by a doting mother who . . . had, in the absence of siblings who would have constituted pre-oedipal rivals and, during a crucial period of his childhood, in the absence of his father who would have been the oedipal rival, devoted her total attention to the patient. [p. 5]

His overt arrogance and grandiosity were the outcome of an imagined oedipal victory.

Kohut focused on what he then believed was the defensive nature of the patient's grandiosity, which would have been instrumental in maintaining the repression of oedipal strivings. In a sense, he was struggling with the patient to give up his defenses so that the underlying oedipal material could be dealt with. Kohut admitted that, at times, he wished the patient would work through his narcissistic demandingness and defenses and an arrogant sense of entitlement.

In discussing this first analysis, Kohut continued to elaborate the oedipal theme. He discusses the fear of the father and castration anxiety, but he particularly emphasizes the libidinal tie to the mother. He had understood the idealization of the mother as a conscious manifestation of his incestuous wishes toward her. Kohut was not particularly aware at that time that the mother's actions and attitudes emotionally enslaved the patient and stifled his strivings for independence and autonomy. Instead, he concentrated on narcissistic defenses against oedipal issues, and the patient occasionally became angry and upset at such interpretations. It could be assumed that the patient felt frustrated because he was not getting narcissistic gratification. From a classical viewpoint this anger would be considered as a resistance.

Mr. Z. felt calmed and soothed when Kohut's attitude, at least momentarily, softened, as evidenced by a different response to the patient's narcissistic demands. He made a sympathetic rather than a challenging or confronting statement. He empathically told the patient that it must hurt when one is not given what is felt as being one's due.

Kohut later concluded that the patient had changed because his narcissistic demands had been heard and validated. Initially, he had felt that the patient's positive response was due to the effectiveness of his interpretations. It was with this thought in mind that the first analysis was terminated, but apparently Kohut had some reservations about its outcome. He felt the termination was unexciting, and this could be a sign that something was wrong.

I suppose he meant that there must be some good feelings on the part of both analyst and patient when an analysis has been successfully concluded. There is often a certain amount of sadness, a bittersweet reaction as patient and therapist say good-bye. The intensity of feelings that characterize most well-conducted analyses brings about a closeness that is enhancing to both patient and analyst. To have gained something in this instance also means that something has been lost.

Kohut states that he was using classical technique in Mr. Z.'s first analysis. He was interpreting the patient's surface material as defensive and resistance, inasmuch as the patient refused to accept his interpretations. He does not tell us if the patient ever indicated that he had integrated insights that might have been derived from his interpretations. The reader knows what Kohut believed, but it is far from clear what the patient understood.

Nevertheless, the patient and therapist decided that the treatment had been sufficiently successful that it could be concluded. Kohut believed that he had been engaged in a standard analytic interaction. Within the transference context, he had analyzed the patient's defenses and had finally reached the oedipal core. If he had been correct, this would mean that he had used the classical method to analyze a classical patient, that is, a psychoneurotic patient whose psychopathology was based on the Oedipus complex. Kohut later recognized that his patient's psychopathology went beyond oedipal problems and included disturbances originating in earlier developmental stages.

The analyses of patients whose psychopathology is based on pregenital fixations rather than on an oedipal neurosis would be quite different from the orderly sequence many analysts assume to be characteristic of the typical neurotic patient. Whether the type of analysis Kohut was attempting in the first analysis of Mr. Z. occurs or is possible is an arguable question. In psychoanalytic institutes candidates are taught that there is an analytic sequence beginning with the analysis of defenses to finally reach the oedipal core, but seldom do clinicians find patients whose material unfolds in such an orderly manner. In most analyses patients relive early phases of development in the transference context. It is not surprising that Kohut would have had problems with Mr. Z. in the first analysis, in view of his discovery that he was treating a patient with pregenital fixations as if the problem were that of a classical oedipal neurosis.

Kohut himself questioned the validity of the therapeutic success of the first 4 years of Mr. Z.'s analysis. He conjectured that whatever improvement the patient experienced was due to a transference cure. I am reminded of the control case I discussed in Chapter 3 who seemed on the surface to manifest a classical oedipal neurosis but who could be better understood in terms of pregenital fixations and characterological problems. In both cases, mine and Kohut's, we were misled and tried to make the patient conform to a standard treatment approach, which we had been taught was the essence of psychoanalytic technique. To change our therapeutic strategy so that it is tailored to the patient's needs does not mean we have introduced innovations or new treatment paradigms. It may be that analysts are simply applying analytic principles to deal with particular types of psychopathology, as has been discussed in all the chapters of this book.

Kohut's attitude shifted during the second analysis. At first he believed that sexual problems had not been resolved. He concluded that sexual fantasies had been suppressed but that there had been no structural changes. The patient, however, formed an idealizing transference, which was then followed by narcissistic demands. Kohut then decided that the reason the patient returned to treatment was to get narcissistic gratification through the mirror transference.

Apparently his therapeutic stance changed. Instead of trying to analyze away the patient's narcissistic needs, he now viewed them as an analytically valuable replica of a childhood condition rather than expecting the patient to grow up. Ornstein (1979) commented that Kohut avoided the "burdensome iatrogenic artifact, namely, the unproductive rage reactions and clashing with the analyst could now be avoided" (p. 368). Ornstein further commented that the patient's rages and childish demands represented feeble attempts to disentangle the self from noxious self-objects. I assume he meant that the patient was trying to free himself from a destructive and self-destructive fusion state with the mother, that he was struggling to separate himself and to become independent and autonomous as he was seeking cohesion of the self-representation.

Both Ornstein and Kohut agree that in analytic treatment it is valuable to relive traumatic childhood experiences in the transference context. They both seem to believe that this is a valuable insight and represents a new treatment approach.

For years, many clinicians, too numerous to list here, have stressed that behavior and symptoms have to be viewed in terms of their positive adaptive aspects. From the very beginning of psychoanalysis, both Breuer and Freud

(1895) recognized that traumatic experiences had to emerge during the course of treatment. They were discussing particular traumas which, on the surface, seem different from what Mr. Z. was demonstrating through his narcissistic demands. Still, if these demands were the outcome of a feeble attempt to free himself from a noxious self-object, as stated by both Kohut and Ornstein, then the patient was reacting to a traumatic situation rather than an incident that characterized his childhood and that persisted throughout his life.

Freud (1920) wrote extensively about the repetition compulsion as an attempt to master a state of passive vulnerability. Mr. Z.'s mirror transference represents a transference manifestation of the repetition compulsion. This does not mean it is not a defensive manifestation, since behavior and feelings are multidetermined. To stress its positive adaptive value can be therapeutically beneficial, but Freud and many other analysts were quite aware of and familiar with such interactions long before Kohut wrote about them.

Ornstein's description of the first analysis as an "iatrogenic artifact" and "clashes with the analyst" strikes me as strange in that he accepts such an interaction as noncritically typical. There may be such clashes, and in some instances they may be unavoidable, but they are not characteristic of analysis, either classical or nonclassical. Nor do analysts have expectations of patients to grow up. Freud (1912) explicitly stated that analysts should not have expectations or therapeutic ambition; rather, they should follow the patient's material without preconceived notions and allow themselves to be surprised at every turn.

In discussing the second analysis of Mr. Z., Kohut repeats a therapeutic approach he discussed in his first book (Kohut 1971). He had recommended that the therapist supply the patient with narcissistic gratification, which means to stress accomplishments and even to praise the patient. After a sufficient time, which is not defined, the therapist stops supplying narcissistic needs so that the patient will progress along the developmental pathway.

This strikes me as manipulation rather than analysis and seems similar to Alexander's "corrective emotional experience," which has been maligned throughout the years (Alexander and French 1946). It is dubious how a deliberate maneuver to give the patient narcissistic gratification will serve as an impetus for emotional development. As discussed, the patient's grandiosity has some defensive significance and is out of tune with reality. To play into it would intensify a defensive adaptation and remove the patient further from reality. Though the patient may be making narcissistic demands to free himself from a "noxious self-object," this does not mean that they are an appropriate solution to the patient's problems and that they will help overcome the traumatic elements of the past so that he can achieve independence and autonomy. The gratification of infantile needs as an adult is vastly different from the gratification of needs that are appropriate to an infantile developmental stage that is not dominated by stress, trauma, and an engulfing mother. To some extent, the patient is deluding himself when he believes that being grandiose will give him power and freedom. The therapist would be colluding with unrealistic expectations, and in patients with severe psychopathology, he would be supporting and fostering a delusion.

Furthermore, to change tactics, as would occur when the therapist decides not to keep on giving narcissistic supplies, would create a dilemma in that the patient would feel betrayed. The holding environment turns out to be inconstant and untrustworthy. Kohut (1979) states, ". . . and I can still remember the slightly ironical tone of my voice meant to assist him in overcoming his childish grandiosity" (p. 14).

Kohut gives the impression that his second analysis of Mr. Z. was successful. It is hard to understand the dynamics of therapeutic resolutions based on the technical maneuvers he describes. Although Kohut might have been ironical, the patient may have built up sufficient trust and respect toward the treatment setting that he could gain self-esteem. By identifying with and idealizing Kohut – and Kohut was easy to idealize – he may have introjected some of his security and self-confidence. He could have identified with Kohut and lived comfortably with the prestige of his association with him.

The patient and his wife are identified by Kohut as professionals. Perhaps they are in some branch of mental health, and, like the Wolf Man, the patient may have profited, at least emotionally, from his treatment with a famous psychoanalyst. Unlike the Wolf Man, this patient, who had many features in his background that are remarkably similar to Kohut's past life, has, as far as I know, never revealed himself. This is also hard to understand because it would be expected that such a narcissistic person would want to exhibitionistically step forward and claim his contribution to the realm of Self psychology, which, in a sense, is justifiable.

While discussing Mr. Z., during a workshop I recently conducted, the question arose as to what specifically are the new therapeutic techniques that are the essence of Self-Psychology. The participants stated that responses to the mirror transference were examples of empathic attunement, that is, supplying the patient with what he was not able to experience as a child because of the weakness of the mother–infant bond. These responses are deliberate, consciously conceived interactions initiated by the therapist.

In general, analysts stress the adaptive qualities and motivations behind the patient's feelings and behavior. The treatment interaction through empathic responses creates a setting in which the patient feels understood and self-esteem is enhanced. The Self psychologists believe that they are using a specific technique to handle a particular phase of therapy.

As has been discussed repeatedly throughout this book, the construction of the holding environment is designed to achieve such objectives. We are not dealing with just a phase of treatment; self-esteeming, empathic responses are the essence of the psychoanalytic interaction from the very beginning to the termination of treatment. They are not unique to any particular school of thought; they are fundamental for the treatment of all patients and especially patients who belong in the borderline spectrum.

12

The Unsettled Issue

of Interpretation

In psychoanalytic treatment, interpretation has been considered to be the chief technical tool. Freud first discussed the therapeutic interaction as a struggle to overcome resistance, specifically a resistance to making the unconscious conscious. He emphasized the battle between patient and therapist as the patient refused to follow the fundamental rule of free association. In the *Studies on Hysteria* (Breuer and Freud 1895), where he first discussed these issues, he did not stress the role of transference as a factor in the patient's resistance. Rather, patients did not want to reveal themselves because they were frightened or ashamed. They were reacting to an internal conflict, which invariably involved the superego.

As has been repeatedly stated, the goal of treatment was to make the unconscious conscious; to achieve this, the analyst conveyed his discoveries to the patient. As patients reveal themselves by free association, the analyst gains understanding about feelings and impulses that the patient does not consciously know. Analysts share their insights with their patients, a communication that is referred to as *interpretation*. Patients may or may not accept these interpretations depending on the strength of their resistance.

Thus the classical psychoanalytic treatment interaction involves two levels of resistance. First, patients resist free association in that they may consciously suppress whatever thoughts or feelings occur to them. This is followed by a resistance to accepting an interpretation. Freud stressed that the analyses of these resistances was one of the most important features of the analytic relationship.

Analyses should be orderly and follow a recognizable sequence. Although the analyst should not have preconceived notions as to what will happen and how the material will unfold (Freud 1913), the course of analysis supposedly will follow a path and maintain a direction. The analyst, through interpretations, will occasionally inform the patient of where he is going. Verbal insights maintain a role of central importance, but Freud did not go into any particular detail about their transference content. He was aware of the immense power of transference, but he did not systematically include his clinical observations of transference into his concepts about the therapeutic efficacy of interpretation.

Since Freud, many writers have insisted that effective interpretations are interpretations of the transference. Kernberg, as mentioned, prefers to limit (at the beginning of treatment especially) interpretations directed to the present aspects of transference rather than to antecedents in the past, which are genetic interpretations and reconstructions. Gill (1979) has also been a strong proponent of the transference interpretation as the essential element of the analytic process.

These ideas about interpretation have been generally accepted by both classical analysts and the more recent group who have organized their ideas around object relationships. There has been relatively little controversy regarding the importance of transference interpretations, but with the exception of Gill, not much has been written about it in terms of its conceptual underpinnings and the psychic processes involved in the patient–therapist relationship.

Although Freud did not draw such a sharp focus on transference interpretations, his ideas served as the groundwork for the recognition of how transference occurs and becomes involved in the therapeutic process. I am referring to his formulation of the repetition compulsion and its role in the traumatic neuroses. He also emphasized the susceptibility to trauma based on experiences of the infantile past and how some of these experiences led to the formation of the repetition compulsion.

In treatment, the infantile repetition compulsion is revived, and as has been discussed in previous chapters, the therapist is assigned a role within the scenario the patient creates. The analyst, in turn, makes the patient aware of how he is repeating the past and trying to implicate the therapist. This occurs through transference interpretations. Viewing the present relationship in terms of the past is the essence of transference, and if the therapist focuses on the current relationship his interpretations are based on the "here and now" transference interaction. Our recent ideas about transference can be directly traced back to Freud's concepts about treatment and the repetition compulsion.

Concepts about transference interpretations have not been challenged by either classical analysts or those who work with patients suffering from primitive mental states. There may be an area of disagreement about genetic and "here and now" interpretations, but it has not been a strong controversy. Some clinicians value both types of interpretations as long as they are kept within the transference context. They usually advocate the use of genetic reconstructions later in treatment.

Our concepts about interpretations once again illustrate that although there have been major revisions concerning concepts about psychopathology, there has been little change in our attitudes about treatment and psychoanalytic technique. I have discussed some of Kernberg's and Kohut's ideas concerning treatment, but these do not provide us with any significant differences in, or accretions to, our understanding of the functions and operations of interpretations. This is odd, for if clinicians accept different perspectives concerning psychopathology, then it would be expected that treatment issues and technique would also be further scrutinized. Inasmuch as interpretations are so fundamental to psychoanalytic treatment procedures, they should be explored in the context of our orientations toward borderline patients. Can we accept the dicta regarding transference interpretations when we are dealing with psychopathology that predominantly involves psychic structure?

As has been repeatedly emphasized throughout this book, more is involved in the treatment of borderline patients than the conveyance of insight. Structure-promoting treatment involves different techniques and further understanding of the therapeutic interaction than is required in the therapy of patients who are seeking resolution of intrapsychic conflict. Consequently, our vistas about our chief therapeutic modality have to be expanded.

There are different types of interpretations that are functionally distinct and belong to separate facets of the therapeutic interaction. The role of the nontransference interpretation has to be explored as well as the psychic processes that are set in motion when a transference interpretation is assimilated (Haesler 1991). The insight-promoting qualities of interpretations have to be explored alongside their intrinsic supportive potential. Furthermore, the definition of an interpretation, that is, what constitutes an interpretation, has to be examined. There has been a tendency to take some of these issues for granted.

The concept of interpretation is much broader than simply verbal communication. An interpretation is a far more inclusive process than one manifested by a disembodied stream of words. There are many subtle nuances in the patient–therapist relationship that have communicative value and structure-promoting qualities. The construction of the holding environment also has to be understood in terms of interpretationlike qualities, that is, as an interaction between two psyches, each in turn gaining accretions to its psychic organization. Interpretations can be viewed as contributing to a reciprocal interaction that becomes the basis of the treatment process. Our concepts about the transference–countertransference axis also have to be expanded to include, in greater depth, communicative modes, which, as they are constructed, expand the ego's adaptive capacities.

As clinicians become further aware of different types of communicative patterns, both conscious and unconscious, some previous distinctions are no longer seen as valid. Perhaps it will not be possible to postulate absolute categories such as transference and nontransference interpretations as we come to understand more about communicative processes. Furthermore, the facilitating qualities of these interactions as they lead to both discovery and integration have to be illuminated.

INTERPRETATIONS AND THE ANALYTIC SETTING

Many patients suffering from primitive mental states require treatment to be a stabilizing experience. Insight, per se, seems to play a minor role. Still, patients may learn from the therapeutic interaction, a form of learning that leads to psychic integration but is not necessarily cognitive. The overt communication may not resemble an interpretation at the surface level, but its effects may be similar to a conventional insight-promoting exchange.

I will draw on no less a personage than Winnicott to provide a clinical example (see Winnicott 1972).

Winnicott's patient, a young doctor, was generally depressed and felt bad because most of his ventures were unsuccessful. He lamented about his unhappy life and his numerous failures.

It happened that he eventually achieved a modicum of success. He was quite elated about it and was eager to share it with his analyst. He went into considerable detail as he enthusiastically told Dr. Winnicott what had occurred. His analyst was pleased at this turn of events.

The patient, however, was not satisfied with Winnicott's response. He had wanted and expected a more intense reaction. He was disappointed in what he considered to be the tepidness of his analyst's reaction.

He revealed his feelings to his analyst and bitterly complained about his lack of reciprocal feeling. Winnicott calmly replied that he did not get as elated as the patient did, but then, neither did he get as depressed as him. It is interesting that Winnicott prefaced these remarks by stating, "I made an interpretation." He was not directing himself to the patient's feelings or reactions. He was simply telling the patient about the limits of his feelings, but he nevertheless must have believed he was making an interpretation.

What had Winnicott said about the patient's psyche, and inasmuch as the patient felt better, where is the transference?

I believe that when Winnicott was discussing the limits of his reactions, he was, in a sense, defining the analytic setting. He was describing the width of the spectrum of his feelings. Any reactions beyond the intensity he permitted himself belonged to the patient's expectations. Feelings outside the spectrum, either depressed or elated, were rooted in the patient's projections. They were aspects of infantile wishes for nurture and narcissistic gratification. Though he was not cognitively explicit, Winnicott was pointing out that any response or feeling outside the spectrum he outlined was a manifestations of transference. The patient wanted his analyst to react with a particular level of intensity, which contrasted with what Winnicott actually felt. The accretion the patient desired was a transference expectation and the outcome of projection.

To repeat, although Winnicott's statements did not appear to be interpretations, they had similar effects in that the patient learned that what he wanted from his analyst was not a realistic expectation; rather, it was the outcome of frustrated infantile wishes that had been projected onto the analyst. The patient might have initially felt that Winnicott was also one of a long line of ungiving caretakers. He might, at a deeper level, have anticipated that he would not get the response he had hoped for.

In any case, this interaction was based on complex transference interactions, which were not explicitly discussed. Nevertheless, by discussing his own feelings Winnicott was defining the limits of the analytic setting. In some instances, this type of interpretation is more suitable than interpretations aimed at revealing repressed feelings or split-off parts of the self. Patients suffering from structural defects need a reliable and secure setting to promote stability and integration. The therapist, by stressing the constancy and boundaries of his analytic identity, helps the patient to distinguish past expectations from what can be expected from the current milieu.

I again turn to Winnicott for further data. Somewhere I heard that Winnicott made interpretations for two reasons: first, to let the patient know he was still alive, and second, that he was not omniscient, that he was capable of making mistakes. I once asked him if he had ever made such a remark, and he believed he had. This rather witty retort is another example of the definition of the analytic setting and helps reveal to patients some important aspects of infantile feelings and expectations.

Being alive means that the analyst is still there, that he has not abandoned the patient as many borderline patients feel they were, or actually were, abandoned in childhood. The analyst is demonstrating to the patient that the current treatment setting is different (even antithetical) from the infantile environment. As repeatedly discussed, the differences between the two settings represent the essence of the holding environment. They also demonstrate to the patient that the fear of being abandoned, a transference expectation, clashes with the analytic setting, which makes it easier for patients to view their feelings as stemming from past rather than present relationships.

The same can be said about the analyst not being omniscient, that he is capable of making mistakes. Winnicott could have been subtly interpreting the patient's idealization and his need to be omnipotently rescued by his analyst. By casting himself as a fallible human being, he might have been correcting what in essence are transference distortions. He presents to the patient a view of himself that is in sharp contrast to the way the patient needed to see him based on transference projections and infantile needs.

I have not been describing interpretations in the traditional sense, in which analysts reveal to patients through words what is chiefly unconscious, but rather in the sense that because of the analysis of resistances, repressive barriers have been weakened and unconscious material proceeds toward the surface in ego realms. Interpretations facilitate that process.

The emerging unconscious material, whether it be feelings, parts of the self, or traumatic infantile constellations, is painful. It is difficult to integrate it into the main psychic current as discussed in Chapter 5. Patients do not want to face these painful elements of their psyche and their hidden vulnerabilities.

Patients suffering from primitive mental states need more than interpretation in the traditional sense. If they are to expose the innermost destructive and self-destructive elements of their psyche, they can only take this risk in a safe and secure setting, one in which they can feel protected and esteemed. The unconscious can be made conscious only if the world of conscious awareness, as it is created by the analytic interaction, is a safe and accepting world. Again, I am stressing the importance of the holding environment, but I am indicating its importance in the context of interpretative activity. The holding environment makes it possible for patients to acknowledge what is going on within themselves, that is, to accept interpretations. Thus the analytic setting has a dual function: it detoxifies the destructive elements inherent in unconscious or split-off material, and it, itself, constitutes an interpretation in that it places the patient's expectations, whether traumatic or overcompensatory, in a transference context.

Although psychoanalytic treatment is primarily concerned with intrapsychic processes, there is nevertheless a balance between inner and outer reality during the course of therapy. There has to be some degree of harmony between the inner world of the psyche and the outer world of the treatment setting if psychic shifts and integrations are to occur. Freud (1925) had discussed how such interactions between the inner and outer world operate in the act of perception, which involves synthesis and integration.

In the topographic hypothesis, memory traces are allocated to the preconscious (Freud 1915b). It is that part of the psychic apparatus that is used for storage of both inner and outer experiences. They remain there in a somewhat dormant fashion but they can be made conscious relatively easily.

External percepts do not fall on a tabula rasa. Freud (1925) stated that the preconscious sends out feelers from memory traces to meet incoming percepts "halfway." He called this process the "notational function of attention." Thus a conscious perception is the outcome of a conjunction of inner percepts and external stimuli. This is a smooth and synthesized operation rather than conflictful; and the internal percept, that is, the memory trace, has to be associatively and perceptually linked to the stimulus in order to reinforce it so that it can be perceived.

Something similar occurs with interpretation and insight information, the acquisition of insight being analogous to a percept that is momentarily registered in the system perceptual-consciousness, and then permanently stored as a memory trace in the preconscious. The marked difference is that, unlike the perceptual process, there are no memory traces in the preconscious of what will later be the substance of the interpretation. These elements are either split off or buried in the unconscious, and not available to consciousness or the preconscious. Thus the interpretative process initially involves a movement toward the preconscious.

If this is to occur with borderline patients, they have to have developed a certain degree of trust in the therapeutic relationship. For them to expose themselves to dangerous internal processes requires the constant presence of a protective analyst. As mentioned, this establishes an interpretative context, and a distinction between transference expectations and anxieties and the current setting. Once a patient has been able to get in touch with the primitive, traumatic parts of the self and partially integrate them and bring them to preconscious levels, the analyst has to communicate to him in a way that is in synchrony with the patient's preconscious balance. As the memory trace's feelers helped guide the incoming stimulus into sensory levels, so the analyst's interpretations have to help take the edge off the disruptive qualities of traumatic forces, thereby serving as an adaptation.

In a sense, what has just been described is a reversal of what ordinarily occurs during psychic maturation. In the course of emotional development, the child has to acquire adaptations to an ever-expanding external world. The internalized infantile environment can facilitate or impede the acquisition of these adaptations, depending, to some extent, on how compatible the early milieu is with current reality. The early world can lead to self-confidence and trust in the capacity to meet the exigencies children have to confront at an age-appropriate time, that is, when they have integrated helpful experiences and their psychomotor apparatus has achieved sufficient maturation. Children acquire adaptive mechanisms most successfully when there is a smooth continuum between the infantile milieu and the external world the child is exposed to in graded doses.

In establishing and defining the analytic setting in an interpretative context, the therapist is able to present his interpretation in a fashion that will help the patient deal with internal traumatic forces and elements. Analysts help patients put primitive material in an adaptive context, but this occurs because the external world of the analytic setting has been modified to be in tune with the patient's psychic orientation. What had formerly been disruptive becomes adaptive because of a shift of balance, but this shift begins outside the psyche. Unlike the perceptual process, the incoming stimulus helps guide internal elements so that they can reach conscious and preconscious levels.

Consequently, these patients have become able to understand themselves in a noncritical, accepting fashion as the analytic setting has been tailored to furnish them with a modicum of confidence and self-esteem. Being accepted in the treatment setting while primitive traumatic forces have been exposed further enables these patients to expand their reality beyond the analytic context. The patient incorporates the analyst's nonjudgmental, approving attitude and directs it toward psychic elements that had threatened internal stability. The creation and definition of the analytic setting lead to internal rearrangements that strive for higher levels of ego organization and synthesis.

THE INTERPRETATIVE PROCESS AND ITS DEVELOPMENT

As the preceding discussion indicates, interpretations cannot be simply defined. They involve complex mental processes and shifts in which various parts of the ego are able to accept feelings and parts of the self that had been previously barred from higher levels of psychic functioning. Perhaps the only definition of an interpretation that is possible for the present is an operational one, but in a broader sense than the standard operational approach, which focuses on how various phenomena are measured. I am referring to the impact of interpretations and how they become involved in psychic interactions.

Interpretations belong in an object relationship context. Something occurs between two people in which one of them is ultimately enhanced, presumably without the exchange of any material substance except words. Unquestionably both participants benefit from successful interpretations.

The prototype for mutually beneficial exchanges is the nursing relationship. The mother supplies her baby with food and other ministrations that cause psychic stability and emotional and physical growth. If we accept the existence of an innate developmental drive, the caregiver protects the child from the vicissitudes that might interfere with and threaten the unfolding of the developmental drive.

As I have discussed elsewhere (Giovacchini 1979a, 1986), the nurturing interaction can be conceptualized as having two components: a foreground nutriment and a background soothing activity. The mother feeds her infant and provides a calm, soothing, protective environment in which the child can comfortably assimilate nutriment. To retain the feeding metaphor for a moment longer, the soothing environment permits the child to effectively metabolize what he has been fed so that he can grow properly. The developmental drive is unimpeded in its forward progression.

The nurturing relationship, as is true for any phenomenon associated with emotional development, can be viewed in terms of a structural hierarchy. First the infant is fed and made comfortable. Then the child moves into the outer world and gains pleasure in exploring and playing. Finally, verbal exchanges become dominant as satisfactory object relations continue to flourish.

Parallel with this developmental progression that focuses on exploring the surrounding world is the striving for self-exploration. First the body is explored, then external objects are investigated. Within the context of emotional development and maturation, there is an innate need to learn about both the self and the external world. Later this need becomes involved with the formation of adaptive techniques, since the more that is known about the complexities and subtleties of the external world, the greater the propensity to construct adaptive techniques to deal with them and to obtain satisfaction.

Having appropriate adaptations to gain gratification leads to increased self-esteem. As the outer world continues to be explored and the ego acquires knowledge and further adaptations, there is a corresponding delving into the inner world. Optimal development is associated with an active engagement in external activities, which includes participation of increasing levels of psychic structure. The psyche has reached higher and more expansive degrees of functioning and adaptive activities.

Thus, within the context of nurturing there is a continuum between being fed and soothed and a knowledge of the external world as it interacts with the psyche. When the analyst gives the patient an interpretation, he is conveying information related to this latter interaction and describing further how the positive outcome that might ordinarily be expected has, for specific reasons, not occurred. This communication constitutes an interpretation and is aimed at creating internal changes that will have a liberating effect, enabling the patient to experience reality constructively.

A successful nurturing experience as it extends from infancy to childhood and finally in a modified and reciprocal fashion in adulthood is accompanied by the healthy unfolding of the developmental drive. Good nurture is the interactional manifestation of satisfactory emotional development. The upper end of the nurturing spectrum is characterized by experiences with the outer world that lead in a positive feedback sequence to higher levels of psychic integration. The act of interpreting in an analytic relationship is part of the positive feedback sequence, but the substance of the interpretation is usually aimed at understanding what has gone wrong, what has interfered with developmental progression. Interpretations, especially during the treatment of borderline patients, are directed toward the manifestations of psychopathology rather than toward describing mutually enhancing higher level exchanges, which represent the more structured hierarchy of a gratifying nurturing interaction.

In a sense, I am distinguishing between learning and interpretation. Learning experiences accompany and lead to psychic growth. The ego incorporates knowledge of the external world, integrates it, and then is able to acquire adaptive techniques to deal with reality, based on the knowledge it has internalized. This is a smooth, synthesized process that proceeds without interference or conflict.

With psychopathology, however, the outer world is not benignly internalized, because experiences with reality for patients suffering from borderline disorders have been painful and dangerous. These patients have considerable learning difficulties. They cannot internalize potentially helpful experiences, and, as emphasized in Chapter 3, they have a paucity of adaptive techniques designed to deal with the vicissitudes and exigencies of the surrounding milieu.

As in learning, interpretations teach the patient inasmuch as they give him knowledge he does not have available to himself. This learning, however, is not an accretion to his fund of knowledge. What analysts impart to their patients is already somewhere in their psyche. What they receive is not entirely new, but it has been hidden and unavailable. Nevertheless, patients feel they have acquired something of value after a well-timed, revealing interpretation. Some analysts compare such interpretations to a good feed.

THE SELF-REPRESENTATION AND PHENOMENOLOGICAL INTERPRETATIONS

The ultimate goal of therapy for patients suffering from characterological defects is the acquisition of further psychic structure, which culminates in the consolidation of the self-representation. These patients always have problems with their sense of identity, and the reemergence of a stifled developmental drive is geared at patients developing a cohesive, differentiated, and relatively autonomous self-image. Most interpretations are directed toward teaching patients about themselves, who they are and how they can stand apart from others, as they also gain the ability to form close relationships.

The traumatic childhood of patients in the borderline spectrum has been rejecting and abandoning. As children, these patients were abused and their needs have in many instances been ignored. The analytic interpretative attitude is the direct antithesis of an infantile environment that does not acknowledge the existence of the patient. In the treatment situation, everything focuses on the patient. Not only is the patient's existence acknowledged, it is emphasized, and interpretations are formulated that stress the sense of being. The patient learns about and discovers different aspects of the self, and by so doing actually develops a better synthesized, coherent self-representation. Interpretations bring together disparate, split-off fragments of the self, forming a cohesive unity that becomes the fundamental basis of the identity sense.

Some borderline patients find it difficult to "digest" interpretations because they have had little or no experience of being understood. They may lack trust, feel confused, or be defensively hostile to any understanding environment. Their behavior has often been referred to as a resistance toward analysis, or more specifically, a resistance toward interpretations. This so-called resistance is reinforced by a concrete mental orientation, as has been discussed in previous chapters.

Still, in some instances, the analyst can direct his understanding and interpretations to the surface aspects of the self-representation and how it relates to the outer world. This may not be too painful, and although many borderline patients want to place the source of their difficulties in the external world, they may be able to tolerate some delving into internal processes if, initially, interpretations refer to what might be called the external qualities of the self: appearance, mannerisms, and attitudes.

This approach is similar to our dicta about interpreting from the surface downward, which means beginning at the level of manifest defenses and then proceeding to deeper id levels. In the treatment of borderline patients the analyst is concentrating on different facets of the self, rather than on ego and id. Whatever resistances the patient may have, there is always some gratification at being in the center of the stage with the spotlight on, rather than being cast into the shadows of oblivion and abandonment.

I recall a highly concrete patient who was eventually able to assimilate insights and emotionally grow because of the interpretative interaction.

He was 26 years old, short and thin, and his face was disfigured with acne scars. He complained that he simply did not get along with people; he had no girlfriends and he was socially isolated, although he had some male friends with whom he drank and went to the movies.

As might be expected, during the first years of treatment he complained incessantly about how unfairly he was treated. People were inconsiderate, insensitive, and rude, and he related innumerable instances when he felt he was unjustifiably attacked. If he was on a highway where everyone was speeding, he would be invariably pulled over by a policeman and given a ticket although other motorists were driving much faster than he. His neighbors would complain that he played his hi-fi system too loudly, whereas he could hardly hear it, and they, in turn, were the real offenders. It seemed that he was being constantly and unfairly blamed.

It was hard to understand why all these indignities were heaped on him. He described his experiences in a detailed, logical fashion, and it seemed that the patient was being abused by many people who were behaving irrationally toward him. As he reported, it seemed as if the world were against him. It did not make sense that he should always be victimized.

I, of course, kept looking for signs of unconscious provocation, how he could have somehow manipulated others into attacking him. I was not able to unearth any evidence to indicate that he was in any way responsible for what happened to him. He was unable to acknowledge that he had anything to do with these unpleasant experiences.

The fact that he encountered such situations frequently and repeatedly was striking and noteworthy, and I often brought it to his attention that there must be some reason, beyond coincidence, for this series of painful encounters. He agreed that it was strange, but he was not able to think in terms of intrapsychic sources and unconscious motivation.

He also concentrated on his feelings of inadequacy, and after several months of treatment he expanded his negative self-appraisal to include an assessment of his capacities as a person who had absolutely no talents. In fact, he had very little concept of himself as a person. His work was routine and mechanistic, and he compared it with being in the belt line of an automobile factory. He described himself as colorless and he viewed himself as a vacuum. People would pay no attention to him except to abuse him.

His background shed light on his current orientation. He was the middle of five children, with one younger and two older sisters, the youngest sibling being a brother. Apparently he was the ugly duckling of the family, his siblings being tall and attractive. The family joke referred to his being either adopted or conceived out of wedlock, a slur on the mother's taste in choosing a lover. He was chided by the family with these insensitive and cruel insinuations.

Still, being taunted was, according to him, the only attention he received. He reported that most of the time he was totally ignored, and if he had some small success, usually scholastic, his parents or siblings paid no attention to it. This was in sharp contrast to how the parents responded to his siblings' accomplishments.

Even though the similarities were striking, the patient saw no significance in that the world of childhood and the present reality were similar in many respects. On occasion, I pointed out that he felt he was being treated currently in the same insensitive fashion as he had been in the past. He acknowledged that this was true, but he wondered why; he was still not able to assume any responsibility for perhaps re-creating the infantile milieu. If he were able to simply consider the possibility of unconscious involvement, he would attribute it to his worthlessness, emptiness, unattractiveness, and lack of redeeming virtues.

My first remarks—I hesitate to call them interpretations—were, as mentioned, directed toward emphasizing that the patient had some responsibility for the unfortunate events that befell him and also for his being rejected and isolated. I was stressing that he had some control of his destiny if he could face the inner forces that were contributing to his painful relations with the outer world. He did not seem to understand or even hear me. He still had no concept of unconscious motivation.

I turned next to the exploration of his negative, poorly structured self-representation. I questioned why he had such little sense of himself as a person and why he felt so worthless and inadequate. He quickly responded to the latter by stating that this was a true evaluation of his capacities. He would then point out his lack of accomplishments. I asked if he could find anything of value within himself.

At first, he could not recall anything. He then referred to his capacity to guess who the murderer is in murder mysteries, but he did not see this as having any particular merit. I conjectured that this could mean he had some special reasoning ability and a proclivity for logic, and that these attributes must have manifested themselves in other areas. I wondered further why he was not aware of what could be a talent, and why others and he had not recognized it. He became quiet and pensive as if he were reviewing various incidents in his life.

He recalled his experiences during his senior year in high school, when apparently he had antagonized a mathematics teacher. Although his high school performance ranged from mediocre to average, he had managed to achieve A's and B's in mathematics, which gained him admission to a prestigious mathematics honor society.

The teacher of this exclusive group was known as a charismatic eccentric. She took an immediate dislike to the patient. In fact, she assumed he was not qualified to be in her class and in an exasperated fashion explained to him what grades he must have to join this club, indicating that she had assumed he could not meet such requirements. When he told her his grades in mathematics during his first three years of high school, she said nothing and walked away. He was, as might be expected, very hurt by this incident.

During club meetings she ignored him. He remembered, in particular, a contest in which the participants were given problems to solve on the blackboard. The teacher was very enthusiastic as she verbally gave her students various equations to solve. She would from time to time praise several students for their ingenuity, but she made no comment about him even though he had correctly solved every problem she gave the contestants. She was very much involved in this contest, which she stated would bring out the best in the best student of this honor society.

When a student failed to solve a problem, he was eliminated from the contest and would have to sit down. Finally there were only two students left, the patient and another young man who was very much favored by the teacher. She read the last problem to them, an especially difficult one. The patient solved it correctly, but the other student did not. The teacher stated that the contest was over and said nothing more. She did not even acknowledge that the patient was the winner. His fellow students were kinder than the teacher; afterwards they congratulated him and commented on the teacher's rude and brusque manner.

After this incident, he was more depressed than usual. He withdrew further from all social contacts, but he felt sufficient emotional pain that he consulted one of the school's social workers, a blunt, aggressive man. When he heard about the mathematics contest, the social worker became furious. I learned about his reactions because I occasionally supervised him. He knew I had been treating his former client, now an adult, and he still felt sufficiently angry about the whole incident that he was eager to fill me in as to what happened.

After he saw the student, he requested an interview with the mathematics teacher. He was ready to rebuke her severely. He began by telling her of the student's report of the mathematics contest, and, for a moment, she did not even remember it. When she did, she was not aware of anything unusual and could hardly remember who won it. The social worker reminded her of the exact details and sequence of events. He was quite angry and must have shouted at her.

When the mathematics teacher finally understood what had happened, she started to cry. She felt remorseful and guilty about what she had done. She could not tell why she disliked the patient, because she was hardly aware of his existence. All the other mathematical wizards had distinct and colorful personalities. They stood out in a crowd, whereas the patient was enveloped in a shroud of anonymity.

The teacher felt terrible and wanted to make amends. She was able to recognize how she had constantly denigrated him, and to make up for it she wanted to do something that would enhance him rather than make him feel inadequate. She decided to have him demonstrate the solution to the problem whereby he had overcome his competition and won the contest. No one else had been able to solve it.

She called him in to her office and apologized for her behavior toward him. She praised him for his mathematical talents and told him of her wish that he demonstrate on the blackboard the solution of the difficult problem he had previously solved. The proposal did not at all appeal to him. He refused to even consider doing what she had suggested. He wanted nothing to do with it, and, now, years later, he revealed for the first time why he had refused to participate in an endeavor that was aimed at elevating his self-esteem and consolidating his identity as a mathematician. He felt that since the teacher knew he could solve the problem, his performance would have no effect on her, and the same applied to the class. They would not value what he would show them. They might even consider him foolish and he would be further humiliated.

I told him I could not follow his reasoning except that I could understand that he would be distrustful. He would not accept anything positive at face value, because he did not have much in the way of self-esteeming support in childhood. Moreover, I felt that this teacher was sincere in emphasizing his identity as a mathematician. Although he had been highly successful in his mathematical studies, he never considered himself to be a mathematician. He did not consider himself to be anything.

I asked him if he remembered the equation he had solved in that memorable classroom. He wrote it down and showed it to me. I recognized that it was a very difficult problem indeed, and was able to tell him what class of equation it was. He was surprised that I was able to place it in a special category, and I confessed that I also had a special interest in mathematics. I added that anyone who could solve such a complex equation could certainly consider himself a mathematician. He was obviously pleased and went on to confirm my opinion by telling me about a calculus problem he had solved, one I had also worked on in college. We animatedly discussed this problem, which involved finding the diameter of a sphere that displaces the largest amount of wine in a wineglass. For the first time since I had started seeing him, he seemed to come to life during this discussion.

In later sessions, he wryly commented that I knew him better than he knew himself. I had discovered that he was a mathematician, something that he himself did not know and he had tried to resist knowing. I replied that I was certain that there were many other things we would discover about him, facets to his personality that he did not suspect existed. He wondered whether we would discover them or create them.

I was struck by this interchange because it was in sharp contrast to his usual concrete outlook. He was looking inside himself for the first time, and he was very much interested in our discussions.

They did, however, create some conflict, which could be placed in a transference context. He felt that I knew more about him than he did. To some extent this was gratifying, but he was also frightened because it made him feel vulnerable. I was viewed as strong and omniscient. If for some reason he incurred my anger, then he would be in my power. He was reassured because I had "made him a mathematician." On the other hand, if I felt hostile, I could transform him into a weakling or a monster. He believed I was helping him create a self but he was at the mercy of my whims.

Several noteworthy events had occurred in the treatment. As stated, by "discovering" an aspect of his identity sense, the therapeutic process was helping the patient structure an identity in a more general sense. He was beginning to feel himself as a person distinct from others, or, better stated, as a person who would be recognized and acknowledged by the surrounding milieu. This was still a rudimentary self-representation, but his bitterness about the rejecting or indifferent external world had considerably subsided. As long as I was pointing out individual characteristics, which he experienced as interpretations because I was revealing to him elements of the self that had not reached conscious awareness, I was at the same time helping structure what had been an amorphous self-representation. These were mutative interpretations (Strachey 1934) but ostensibly not of the transference variety. Simply knowing about the self creates a vista for the patient that enables him to view himself as the analyst does. Of course, there had to be confirmatory data based on the patient's experiences and accomplishments of which he was not consciously aware. The analyst's viewpoint also helps strengthen reality testing.

He rejected the mathematics teacher's offer to make his accomplishments known and, therefore, to make himself known. He could not accept it

as a potentially self-esteeming experience because he had no internal constructs that would enable him to incorporate and integrate it. That is why
both Kohut's mirroring and Alexander's corrective emotional experience are
of limited value to many patients in the borderline spectrum. There was
nothing in his background that could lead him to believe that there was
something of value inside of him. Consequently, he looked at the world as if
it could not really acknowledge any positive qualities, which is how he
reacted to the mathematics teacher.

When the analyst started exploring different aspects of the self-
representation and this was not restricted to just positive attributes, the
patient began to feel that maybe there was something of interest in him, and
he wanted to know as much as possible about himself as a person; it meant
that the whole world was not rejecting or abusing him. He began to entertain
the possibility that others might also want to know him, a total antithesis of
how he had viewed the world.

By blocking out the potentially helpful experiences that he might
encounter, he had had to preserve a constricted view of the external world.
Revealing both positive and negative elements of his personality expanded
his horizons and enabled him also to have an expanded view of himself.

Ostensibly, interpretations directed toward the self have no transference
elements. The patient is not projecting infantile feelings and assigning the
analyst various roles that correspond to the significant persons of his past.
The analyst is merely making observations about the patient that could be
considered phenomenological. He is not talking about the patient's deep
inner feelings. He is referring instead to different ways the patient might view
himself and contrasting these viewpoints to the constricted and negative
covert attitudes that have dominated the patient's perspective. Even these
covert attitudes have been outside the conscious sphere and have also been
"discovered" by the analyst.

For a concrete patient these surface phenomenological observations can
be understood. The analyst is not yet looking at inner sources and unconscious motivation. He is simply concentrating on how the patient might view
himself as he relates to the external world, not on how internal forces cause
him to suffer and feel miserable and rejected.

As discussed, especially in Chapter 5, there are patients who have been
so traumatized that they view any interpretation as a dangerous assault.
Their psyches have the qualities of festering wounds, and any impingement is
felt as dangerous and painful. It is hard, if not impossible, to engage in
interpretative discourse, because the analyst becomes blended with the
abusive, assaultive, traumatic past.

I have found, on occasion, that confining remarks to external factors
such as the patient's mood, demeanor, or appearance is less likely to incur

what at times has been violent opposition. This also applies to remarks about changes in the patient's orientation during the session. I call these *phenomenological interpretations*, and observations about the self-representation, as just discussed, belong in this category.

The self-representation is on the surface of the psyche. Other facets of the self-representation may be at unconscious or preconscious levels, but it is always, to some extent, at an interface with the outer world. This viewpoint is compatible with Hartmann's (1950) formulation of the self-representation as a supraordinate structure that has incorporated various levels of the ego apparatus.

Past traumatic experiences are encapsulated at deeper psychic levels. Patients who have split them off from general psychic functioning are concretely oriented, and because they are not in touch with these deeper levels, interpretations concerning them cannot be understood or are viewed as threatening and dangerous because the ego is extremely vulnerable to any external impingement. The self-representation, on the other hand, can to some extent be dealt with, because it is unconnected from the split-off traumatic layers. It may be vulnerable to the outer world, but interpretations concerning its structure and modus operandi are not associated with the traumatic past. As stated, the type of interest inherent in such observations is a far cry from what these traumatized patients have known. They may not, at first, recognize that kind of concern, as in the case of the patient just discussed, but eventually they may be able to use it and to allow themselves and their analysts to enter the inner world.

A middle-aged clerical worker felt that because of the treatment, he was beginning to find himself. He had at the beginning of treatment viewed himself as an amorphous mass, which he described as hard. He actually felt a hard mass within himself.

I asked him many questions about this mass. At first I was concerned that it might have been a tumor, but his reactions and poetical descriptions reassured me that he was being metaphorical. As I understood more about him I realized that his view of himself and that of the outer world was the same—a hard, harsh, unfeeling place where people behaved like robots with him, as machines and not persons. He had not participated in human relationships and he felt there was nothing human within himself.

He was the oldest child and only son, and his childhood was both harsh and violent. His father, an alcoholic, frequently beat him up. Throughout childhood he tried to be inconspicuous because to attract attention toward himself made him vulnerable to attack.

We discussed the reasons for his feeling a hard mass inside of himself. I kept addressing him in terms of his metaphor and related it to how he perceived the world. We both wondered about how the mass could be softened and made less amorphous.

In this context he began telling me about an older woman who had become interested in him. She looked upon him as a son. Her son had been killed in the Vietnam War, and clearly the patient was a substitute for him. She visited his apartment frequently, cleaning it, cooking for him, and taking care of his laundry.

Now, the metaphor changed, but I also participated in its transformation. We reconstructed it together. First the mass became softer, and instead of being totally amorphous, it became an amoeba. The amoeba was especially interesting because it could structure arms (pseudopodia) that could reach beyond itself, although it could quickly retract them and revert to its previously unstructured state if it encountered anything noxious in the external world.

In addition to helping construct the metaphor, I also interpreted its significance. I told him he was beginning to view himself as a better structured organism who was making attempts to make contact with the world around him. He was still tentative and quick to withdraw to an amorphous state if he encountered situations he perceived as dangerous or potentially dangerous.

I added that he was becoming more receptive not only to what I suggested to him but also to the motherly woman who wanted to look after him. Apparently she had found something in him that she could value, and he was developing the capacity to let others minister to his needs and to accept the fact that he was a worthwhile person.

The metaphor again changed. Apparently he knew a great deal about diamonds, and he viewed himself as a crude piece of carbon that was beginning to crystallize. He had been buried in a mine but he had been excavated. He was now in the hands of the diamond cutter. He was not too concerned about the diamond cutter, who could produce a valuable gem or, if unskilled, could destroy the multifaceted crystal.

A multifaceted crystal is an excellent metaphor for the self-representation. Different facets of the self-representation present themselves to the outer world at appropriate moments. The identity sense contains various levels of the psychic apparatus, which are called into action by specific settings, as I have discussed elsewhere (Giovacchini 1979a, 1986). What I found most impressive was that the patient was viewing the construction of a self-representation that could be valued in the context of an object relationship. He was relating to the diamond cutter/analyst who, through his communications, that is, phenomenological interpretations, helped unearth the initially crude diamond. What had been at one time a hard mass was in the process of becoming a multifaceted gem. The analyst had not only participated in this continuum but now had become clearly recognized as a person who could help achieve an optimal structural configuration. This is another example in which focusing on the self helped create a self.

The diamond cutter/analyst can be viewed as a transference figure, not that he corresponded to any person in the patient's past but he personified the father the patient wished he had. It was a transference expectation that had been realized.

TRANSFERENCE AND NONTRANSFERENCE INTERPRETATIONS

Once the patient was able to accept a phenomenological interpretation or at least consider the possibility that it might be valid, he had altered his perception of reality. Before treatment the mathematician patient, too, related to the outer world much in the same way he reacted to the traumatic infantile milieu. Inasmuch as his contemporary world was different from his past, as was evident from the mathematics teacher's offer to make amends, his views of reality were based on transference distortions. The analytic interaction moved in the direction of correcting transference distortions insofar as the patient was finally able to acknowledge that he was not being totally rejected or abandoned, as he had been in childhood. The patient could contrast the present with the past, as happens when the treatment interaction is dealing with the resolution of the transference.

Ordinarily this resolution is the outcome of transference interpretations. This is another instance, as discussed in the definition of the setting, in which the communication between analyst and patient does not contain any overt transference elements. The analyst is not referring to displaced and projected infantile feelings, but his remarks nevertheless lead to a correction of the transference distortion of current reality. This could be thought of as a process that consists of nontransference interpretations, where an ostensibly nontransference interpretation leads to a revision of the perceptual system, which is no longer dominated by a view of reality based on the infantile milieu, an outlook determined by transference mechanisms.

To return to the mathematician patient, in a sense these phenomenological interpretations created a transference focus. The patient felt the analyst knew more about him than he himself did. This was somewhat gratifying, but it was also frightening. The analyst, from the patient's viewpoint, was assuming considerable power because he was perceived as being omniscient. This caused the patient to feel vulnerable and, therefore, in a precarious position because the analyst might arbitrarily decide to abandon him. Since he believed himself to be such an inadequate and reprehensible person, this could easily happen. These thoughts and feelings were almost exact replicas of what he experienced in childhood, and when brought into the therapeutic relationship, they were the outcome of transference and had many elements of the repetition compulsion.

Definition of the analytic setting, as discussed in a previous section, and phenomenological interpretations serve to achieve the same goals as transference interpretations. Consequently, the question can be raised as to whether there are fundamental distinctions between transference and nontransference interpretations. Furthermore, could these so-called nontransference interpretations have a transference element?

As discussed, interpretations that involve the definition of the analytic setting indirectly refer to the transference in that the analyst's behavior and revelations conflict with the patient's transference expectations, which emphasizes their infantile sources. Something similar happens with phenomenological interpretations, but rather than the analyst's revelations being involved, it is the exploratory mode and the subject of explorations that are placed in a transference context. As discussed, the analyst is behaving differently from the significant persons of the infantile milieu, and when the patient perceives these differences he recognizes the transference element, although it may not be explicitly acknowledged.

Perhaps all interpretations have a transference element, although it may not be overtly apparent; and that may be the difference between a transference and nontransference interpretation. In some instances nontransference interpretations may be characterized by indirectly referring to the transference and the transference interaction becomes recognized later, whereas a transference interpretation immediately and directly relates to the transference.

Clinicians have noted that some patients apparently do not form transferences, thereby making it impossible to formulate transference interpretations. Still, the same question can be raised about the transference as has been asked about interpretations. Is transference a universal phenomenon in the treatment relationship? The transference may not be immediately recognizable, but as therapists become familiar with the subtle nuances of patients' psychic processes, they will eventually be able to unearth the transference connection.

In some instances the overt lack of transference is in itself a transference manifestation. Often these are schizoid patients who have found the world oppressive and burdensome. They have retreated from it into a cave of social isolation. Their chief mode of adaptation is withdrawal. In treatment they relate to the analyst as they do to everything in general. They are using infantile adaptations, which can be considered to be in the realm of transference because they are characteristic of the early environment and inappropriate in the current setting. The patient has transferred a schizoid adaptation into the treatment relationship.

Transference, in this instance, refers more to generalized defensive responses than to displacement. Nevertheless, the infantile nature of the adaptation qualifies its inclusion in the transference domain, although, as stated, for these patients there are no other modes of relating to contrast to their responses. They are unaware that there are other possible adaptations besides schizoid withdrawal.

Their transferences may be extremely difficult to resolve, for several reasons. First, it is difficult to conceive of their behavior as transference, because these patients do not bring material that has reference to either the analyst or the treatment situation. They have difficulties in understanding that nontransference is a form of transference. Furthermore, being oblivious of other and more efficient modes of relating—that is, that nonwithdrawing, active types of involvements have been strictly avoided because they are terrifying—does not provide them with a backdrop against which they can compare and highlight their orientation toward the world and the treatment relationship. The recognition of alternative forms of relating is implicit in any engagement aimed at discovery and at resolving the transference.

The psychoanalytic treatment of schizoid patients is often impossible, but there are occasions when the analyst may create a holding environment secure enough to lead to the establishment of a dependent transference. Again, the use of the word *transference* can be debated, because the patient never had a comfortable dependent relationship, so these patients are not repeating the past in the treatment setting. Nevertheless, the holding environment helps these patients develop a modicum of trust and confidence in the therapeutic process. This may cause them to relax their schizoid defenses and to begin relating to the therapist in a tentative fashion. As they bring their anxieties into the relationship with their therapists, they are also displaying some degree of transference. They are demonstrating their fears of making object contact because of childhood traumas, which are repeated in a modulated fashion with their therapists. The therapeutic process and the holding environment create a transference relationship, which can be gradually interpreted.

There are other patients who resemble schizoid patients superficially in that they seem to have little capacity for involvement and commitment. Their lack of relatedness also manifests itself as a lack of transference. It is different, however, from schizoid withdrawal. Although it is a withdrawal, it is not a general adaptive pattern; rather, it is a defensive maneuver designed to maintain a heightened narcissistic level.

These patients have often been diagnosed as having narcissistic personality disorders. Basically, they feel inadequate and have conflicts regarding intimacy. They do not allow themselves to form close relationships for various reasons, a prominent one being the fear of destructive fusion. As children, they have often been used as transitional objects by their mothers; the maternal interaction does not lead to a self-esteeming sense of aliveness and a healthy narcissistic balance. They withdraw from emotional attachments to enhance themselves, and that is how they differ from schizoid patients. The latter do not derive any narcissistic gratification from pulling away from potentially emotionally significant persons; they are simply protecting themselves from their incapacity to deal with the exigencies of the external world. There is no replenishment of narcissistic supplies, although, as is generally true, clear-cut clinical distinctions cannot be made and often there is a blending of schizoid and narcissistic features.

Many narcissistic patients are self-contained and preoccupied with themselves to the extent that they do not seem to form transferences. In these instances, however, the apparent lack of transference is, as with the schizoid patients, a form of transference. Some clinicians prefer to call this type of transference a defense transference, but even though it might be a defense against transference feelings, it is nonetheless still a transference, which would permit the formulation of transference interpretations.

Transference interpretations directed to narcissistic patients often have a paradoxical negative effect, whereas interpretations that do not seem to involve transference may be favorably received. Because some of these patients are basically vulnerable and their psychic balance is precarious, they cannot allow anyone to enter their mental sphere. A transference interpretation is dyadic and the introduction of the analyst into the ego as an external object representation is threatening. It is analogous to the destructive fusion with the mother who uses her child for her own narcissistic enhancement. From a psychic viewpoint, these patients cannot acknowledge the existence of anyone as separate from themselves and outside the sphere of their creation.

I recall, many years ago, being a guest on a television talk show. Among the guests was a celebrity. Before we went on the air, the rest of the group were chatting amiably among ourselves. This personage, however, was sitting slumped and isolated in a corner. He looked deflated. His head drooped, his arms hung loosely, and his whole body was in a hypotonic state. He had the appearance of a puppet who had been set down by the puppeteer.

Once the lights and cameras were turned on, he underwent a remarkable transformation. It seemed as if energy were being pumped into him and he came to life. He sat up straight in his chair and became alert. He dominated the discussion in an animated, witty fashion, whereas hitherto he seemed to be totally oblivious of his surroundings. When the cameras were turned off, he again sank into his previous oblivion.

A transference interpretation, for some of these patients, gives equal billing to the analyst, so to speak, and this takes something away from their narcissism. A nontransference interpretation, on the other hand, may focus exclusively on the patient, rather like turning on the lights and cameras on the talk show and putting the celebrity in the spotlight. (On that occasion it was interesting that the celebrity paid no attention to anyone else's contributions.)

I have been emphasizing that the question of transference versus non-transference interpretations is more complex than has been assumed. I believe that clinicians are recognizing these complexities as they continue to deal in depth with patients suffering from structural defects, especially patients who demonstrate discontinuities in psychic structure.

To repeat, discontinuity of psychic structure is a manifestation of faulty psychic development. Instead of a continuous and integrated structural hierarchy progressing from primary-process to secondary-process operations, these patients have lacunae in the developmental continuum. Early ego states do not smoothly blend into higher integrated psychic levels. Since various parts of the psyche are, so to speak, loosely held together, there may be very little connection and communication between early and later developmental levels.

As discussed, these patients are very concretely oriented and have little appreciation of unconscious mental processes. Part of the therapeutic task is to help these patients look within their psyche and to appreciate the influence of unconscious factors on feelings and behavior. This can sometimes be accomplished with the help of what appear to be nontransference interpretations.

These patients' concrete outlook causes them to look for the sources of their difficulties in the outer world. They tend to blame persons and situations. To interpret intrapsychic process at the early stages of treatment is meaningless because these patients have little or no contact with the deeper recesses of the mind. Their focus is on the outside world, and this frequently has a paranoid tinge.

There is very little if any evidence of transference with these patients. At the most, they might expect their therapists to be on their side, to join them in their paranoid orientation, which is often supported by reality. Analysts, in general, do not support their patient's paranoia, although they can be sympathetic about the indignities they might experience. The analyst does not blame the patient or the supposed persecutor. However, he does not immediately explore the patient's participation in creating whatever unfortunate turn of events he is facing. These patients might be sufficiently alienated and feel blamed that they might stop treatment if their analysts make interpretations dealing with unconscious motivation. The unconscious can be introduced to patients by exploring the outer world, and this can occur through the use of nontransference interpretations.

At clinical seminars I have frequently heard analysts make varieties of nontransference interpretations. They may refer to patients' unconscious feelings toward a father, mother, sibling, or any other emotionally significant person in their lives. They sometimes begin with an event that is the outcome of defensive displacements. Concretely minded patients may find it easier to learn that they are angry and wanted to kick their dog rather than their wife or mother.

The analyst's main and most arduous task is to introduce the domain of the unconscious to these concretely minded patients. Reference to the unconscious, initially, must avoid sensitive areas. For example, the patient may experience considerable guilt and anxiety about unconscious destructive impulses. He may fear retaliation or abandonment. He might, however, accept the existence of inner hostility if it is directed at a nonthreatening target, a product of displacement. This refers to a patient whose concreteness is, to some measure, defensive. In these patients, structural defects contribute considerably to their concrete orientations. Because of psychic discontinuity, they are unable to make contact with the unconscious.

They may begin, however, to gain some glimmer of the concept of psychic determinism by investigating the motives of external objects, some who have been cast in the role of persecutor. Some of these patients may not, for example, be able to acknowledge their murderous feelings toward their parents, but are capable of recognizing that others, usually displacements from parental imagoes, might harbor *unconscious* destructive feelings toward them. This recognition often enables them to accept that there is an unconscious mind and that they can have similar feelings toward various people who are not necessarily emotionally significant. Later, they may be able to direct these feelings toward aspects of, and various persons in, the infantile milieu.

This usually occurs in the context of an effective holding environment, which is difficult, and perhaps unnecessary, to distinguish from a positive transference. These patients often maintain this positive attitude, which can have both dependent and affectionate feelings, throughout the treatment, working out their destructive feelings toward their parents and the traumatic experiences of childhood. Their anger is so intense and self-destructive that they cannot direct it toward their analyst without destroying the therapeutic setting. At the most, they can achieve insights regarding transference as they project their feelings onto parental substitutes, but they cannot permit themselves to direct them toward their analysts because they need to keep their benign and supportive presence. These patients also tend to act out their anger.

Kernberg (1984) has stressed that the essence of the analysis of borderline patients is the analysis of the negative transference. In general, I agree that the analysis of the negative transference is extremely important for the analysis of most patients. With these particular concretely oriented patients, however, I do not believe that this type of analysis is possible.

Still, there are successful outcomes in which such patients have learned a good deal about themselves and changed their views about their parents and what they considered to be the hostile, rejecting aspects of the current milieu. They have become more expansive and tolerant as they continue to relate to their analysts with admiration and some degree of dependence. There are also many concretely oriented patients who cannot become engaged in an analytic relationship.

The following vignette illustrates some of the above ideas.

The patient, a man in his middle forties, came to see me because his employer had threatened to fire him if he did not seek therapy. Naturally, I asked what he felt about his need for treatment, and he replied that he did not mind. He did not acknowledge a need for analysis. It seemed that being motivated for treatment was an alien and incomprehensible feeling, but he had no objections to seeing a psychoanalyst.

At first, he claimed that his life was running smoothly. He was divorced but now had a girlfriend with whom he felt he had a satisfactory relationship. He liked to hunt and fish and had compatible companions. He believed that he had sufficient talent at work and that he was doing a good job. I wondered to myself why he wanted to see me.

Nevertheless, I did not challenge his reasons for seeking treatment. I referred, however, to his employer's threat to fire him if he did not seek help and wondered how he could reconcile that threat with what he reported as his more than competent performance at work. My question caused a sudden rush of material, much of it aimed at his employer. Apparently he had taken a fatherly interest in the patient, and since he had no sons of his own, he had envisioned the patient taking over the company some day. He also had a secret desire that the patient marry his daughter; the patient believed this to be true because his employer was very critical of his former wife and now he was constantly criticizing his girlfriend.

In the first year of treatment he concentrated on how his employer mistreated him. He never praised the patient for good work; he only criticized him and stressed his faults. He was also ungenerous with his other employees, but not with the same fervor as he was with the patient. The patient's anger throughout our sessions seemed to intensify as he became increasingly dissatisfied with the constant criticisms he had to face and what he considered to be an insufficient income. Both the patient's complaints, as he voiced them during his sessions, and his employer's constrictions and subsequent verbal attacks were incessant. I again quietly wondered why the patient continued working at the company if he could make more money elsewhere and be appreciated instead of being constantly depreciated. In our sessions he threatened to quit his job, but he never mentioned it to his employer. On the other hand, the employer on several occasions threatened to fire him, but neither he nor the patient ever took action.

The patient's material continued to focus on the employer, but he gradually included others in the sphere of unsatisfactory object relationships. He spoke of a childhood friend who was taking advantage of their long-standing friendship and good will. He would borrow records from him and never return them. He would ask the patient to purchase some hi-fi equipment for him and then never repay him. When his friend purchased something for the patient, he demanded the money in advance. The patient continued with a litany of complaints.

He felt that his former wife's lawyer was also treating him unfairly. In fact, he was angry at both of them because their demands were excessive, but the judge had ruled in their favor. He was in court several times because he defaulted on payments. He was also angry at the judge because he always upheld his former wife's claims.

Regarding his past, I will simply mention that his father was quite similar to his employer and much of the infantile scenario was being repeated at work. I do not want to go into further details because I wish to stress how interpretations helped him appreciate the extent and power of the unconscious.

I began by wondering why his employer needed to attack him. He was somewhat surprised by my assumption that his employer had a need to be dissatisfied with him. He had believed that he was the victim of misperceptions and narrow vision. I questioned further the reasons for such attitudes, indicating that more was involved than just constrictions and defects of character. The latter required explanation. The patient was quick to see that he had been similarly treated in childhood, but as yet he saw no connection between his behavior and how others reacted to him.

He became curious, however, as to why his employer behaved as he did. He reported what he knew about his background, his early days of poverty and frugality. He told of how hard his employer had had to work to achieve financial success and how he denied himself any pleasure or recreation. For him, life was hard work, and anything else was considered frivolous. He was still angry at his employer, but he was beginning to develop some compassion.

We conjectured that his employer perhaps envied the patient because of his freedom to enjoy himself. He could have felt threatened by the patient, who was younger, healthier, and more vigorous than himself. I speculated further that his employer was vicariously gratifying some of his needs through the patient, but because he felt guilty about them, he attacked the patient instead of himself. Following this interpretation about the employer's unconscious attitudes, the patient stressed that he was certain he was being manipulated into marrying his daughter. I replied that this meant that the employer, at some level, held him in high esteem, but that he might also be identifying with him insofar as he had some incestuous feelings toward his daughter. I was using the patient's remarks about marrying the boss's daughter as a confirmation of the interpretation about vicarious pleasures and identification. Now I had gone further and specifically addressed the nature of some of the employer's unconscious wishes. I felt I had gone pretty far—perhaps far afield by mentioning incest, but the patient did not reject my idea as preposterous or ridiculous. On the contrary, he believed it was an interesting thought.

Clearly the patient was becoming interested in the unconscious motivations of others. He derived narcissistic gratification from our discussions because the focus was on himself, that is, why people reacted to him as they did. It was striking, however, that he had relaxed his concrete outlook and was intrigued by the operations of the unconscious mind. He spoke of friends and their reactions to various situations in terms of hidden motives and impulses. He also noted many similarities in the way people related to him and how he had been treated by his family during child-hood.

He had been in treatment 2 years when he first began considering that many relationships were dyadic and that there were always two interacting participants. Though he was still resentful at the way he was being treated, he was willing to acknowledge that he had some responsibility for deter-mining what occurred to him. He admitted that he was an irritating and provocative driver and that he had a propensity to cause other drivers to get extremely angry at him. He also granted that he could understand how his hedonistic and extravagant lifestyle might aggravate his employer.

Now he is more than willing to examine his inner life and juxtapose it with traumatic childhood experiences, especially with his father's. None of his destructive feelings, however, have been directed toward me. He relates to me as a benign father who is especially in tune with his viewpoint on how to live. As has happened with some other patients in the borderline spectrum, this patient has sought my advice on various issues, social, political, and recreational. He knows of some of my interests and has, on occasion, pursued them. I have become the father he wanted, and he keeps identifying with various aspects of me. Nevertheless, he is very much focused on his inner life and is trying to control his provocative and exhibitionistic behavior.

It is difficult to determine the role of transference in this relationship. There is undoubtedly a well-established positive transference and holding environment, but the patient is not working out his conflictful feelings and his traumatic past by directing them toward me. My interpretations do not refer to projections of infantile elements into me, but they are focusing on the influence of the past on the present and how unconscious feelings determine his behavior.

There are other types of interpretations that do not appear to have transference elements and yet have been useful in dealing with severely disturbed patients. I am referring to what I have called *linking interpretations*, which are similar to dream interpretations (Giovacchini 1965a). When analyzing a dream, clinicians often seek the event that precipitated the dream, the day residue that was the impetus for its formation. Feelings and behavior can also have day residues, and unconscious processes can be linked to them.

Linking interpretations are especially important for patients suffering from primitive mental states. These patients have blurred ego boundaries, and the distinction between the inside and outside is not firmly established. Linking interpretations, by connecting an outside event with internal processes, emphasizes that two frames of reference, reality and the unconscious mind, are involved in feelings and behavior. These interpretations help the patient distinguish between the inner and outer world.

An anxious middle-aged woman was chronically upset because she had difficulties in distinguishing actions from fantasies. She was especially disturbed when she had the fantasy that she had drowned her baby while bathing him. She would often panic because she thought that she might have actually killed him. On one occasion, she called her therapist in a state of intense agitation and told him she had drowned her infant. He asked where the child was and she looked in the bedroom, noting that he was sleeping in his crib. She had simply panicked without investigating her child's whereabouts.

The therapist was able to discover events in her daily life that were symbolically attached to destructive feelings. For example, one day at a large shopping center, she saw a display of Die Hard automobile batteries. She mentioned this in association to feelings about wanting to strangle a younger sibling. As she was describing these feelings, she seemed to enter a trancelike state. Her therapist interpreted that her perception of the batteries, their name, had stimulated her rage at her sibling. She snapped out of the trance and felt relieved that she was dealing only in fantasy. Finding that the stimulus for her fantasy was in the outer world helped her strengthen reality testing. Again, this is a situation where there is no overt transference factor.

Whatever transference was present was not directly related to her destructive feelings. When upset and terrified, she turned to her analyst for help, and he was able somehow to prevent her from becoming overwhelmed with murderous impulses and anxiety. What was threatening to reach uncontrollable proportions was held in check by relating it to an external symbolic stimulus. The therapist constructed a link between a symbol and what the patient felt was an intense destructive impulse, which demanded expression in concrete action.

It was as if this linkage created a perspective in which fantasy and reality could be distinguished, thereby enabling the patient to gain control. She converted inner rage into external symbolic destructiveness, and the analyst played a crucial role in helping her achieve control. Inasmuch as she was able to turn to her therapist, she may have been acting in a transference context.

In some instances a transference factor can be uncovered. The very act of discovering it can be viewed as a transference interpretation. Here again, however, the patient's material may seldom include feelings about the analyst. These patients may be primarily concerned with themselves or their relationships to other persons, such as employers, spouses, or friends.

A middle-aged housewife reported what she considered to be a peculiar dream. She was sitting in her living room when her husband entered with a full bottle of champagne. Instead of offering her a glass, he emptied the bottle on her lap. This dream was highly multidetermined and depicted in a picturesque fashion her ambivalent feelings toward her husband.

He was described as a penurious man who was constantly depreciating her. She often felt humiliated by his refusal to spend money on even the basic essentials. The patient felt devalued and viewed herself as an inadequate person, although as she progressed in treatment she was becoming less tolerant of her husband's depreciating stance and his avarice. Nevertheless, she initially interpreted the dream as a depiction of her depreciated position and her inadequacy as a self-respecting person. In the dream, her husband was maltreating her. At first, she attributed no other significance to the dream than that of simply depicting the marital relationship.

She saw no transference elements. She felt that I overvalued her, that I refused to see the flaws her husband constantly complained about. This was another example of where she was being humiliated, and she reviled herself for being so spineless as to let herself be treated in such a shameful manner. The only reference to me that she could initially acknowledge was that she disagreed with my positive evaluations of her as a person. She indicated that I had always thought of her as better than she was. Still, the intent of the dream was not to point out that I was wrong. It was simply a statement about her status.

I remarked that her husband's reactions in the dream were bizarre. I then added that he would never behave in such a fashion, and again she agreed. I finally stated that although he seemed to be making a fool of her, she was in fact humiliating him. This penurious man would never waste an expensive wine such as champagne by literally throwing it away. He was not prone to waste anything, often refusing to replace worn-out items until they were totally useless. As for champagne, he would never even buy it, let alone spill it all over his wife.

She had created a clever caricature in the dream by making her husband the diametric opposite of himself. If he really did act in this wanton fashion, he would have had to be out of his mind, a person who had lost his wits rather than a well-integrated person who had a need to have an inadequate person to oppress. The patient was exacting revenge on him by having put him in a role of ridiculous extravagance.

I stressed that basically she did not want to be put in a depreciated position, and that she really wanted to think of herself as worthwhile. These remarks are examples of a phenomenological interpretation. I was commenting about her self-representation and pointing out something she had not recognized, that is, that she wanted to value herself and by understanding that she had such a wish, she really valued herself.

Still, more was involved than a phenomenological interpretation and an apparent lack of transference. She was incorrect when she stated that the purpose of the dream was to prove me wrong. On the contrary, its purpose was to prove me right. She was telling me, through her dream, "Even though I seem to be letting my husband humiliate me, I am reducing him to a state he would find intolerable." In terms of his standards, to be so flamboyantly wasteful was equivalent to having gone berserk, having lost both his wits and capacity for control.

She was showing me that fundamentally she agreed with me, but she was ambivalent about acknowledging or displaying the positive and assertive qualities of her character. I need not discuss the reasons behind her ambivalence and reluctance since this is not an uncommon defensive orientation. She accepted what I call a transference interpretation, the wish to prove me right, but she also had to pose some objections because she was still afraid of total acceptance.

To reinforce her negative self-appraisal, she told me of two incidents. The first concerned an interaction with a mechanic. He had quoted her a price for some minor repair on her automobile. She had a little less money on her than what he quoted. The mechanic then asked her how much money she had on her and she told him. He accepted that amount, but the patient felt foolish and verbally chastised herself for having told him. She should have revealed only what she felt she could afford.

I surmised that she might have manipulated the mechanic into giving her a price that was lower than what he customarily charged. He felt guilty about taking advantage of her supposed vulnerability. Instead of being cheated, she had struck a good bargain. His price seemed low to me.

The patient had some difficulty in accepting my explanation, and in fact I was far from firm in my belief. I was interpreting manipulative behavior and what might be viewed as a transference resistance. In childhood she had maintained a depreciated view of herself. To reinforce her doubts about my speculation, she told me of a second incident.

She had been given a speeding ticket and had paid the officer $50 at a local police station. She was not particularly concerned about the money, but she did not want a mark on her driver's license because if she had two other offenses, she would lose it. The officer was sympathetic and conjectured that if she went to court and explained to the judge how concerned she was about the purity of her driving record, he would not penalize her. She followed his suggestion, but when she appeared in court the judge simply dismissed her and she was unable to speak to him. Again, she reviled herself for her passivity and ineffectiveness, because she felt she had not accomplished what she set out to do.

I made a bold speculation. I told her that I believed she had succeeded admirably. When the judge dismissed her he dismissed the case, and there would be no marks on her driver's license. She was incredulous about my sanguine outlook. I challenged her to get in touch with the courthouse to see whether I were correct. She called and learned that I was correct. Furthermore, several days later she received a check for $50 as a refund of the fine.

These clinical examples illustrate what I have repeatedly stated, that is, that interpretations are part of a complex communicative process. Simple distinctions between transference and nontransference interpretations cannot be made. Clinicians cannot prejudge what will be therapeutically effective.

Formulations and treatment approaches concerning psychoneurotic patients are simplistic, especially when compared with concepts about psychopathology of, and therapeutic interaction with, patients who belong in the borderline spectrum. The chief therapeutic tool of psychoanalytic treatment is interpretation, and, as has been emphasized in this chapter, interpretations have to take into account our increasingly expanding perspectives.

References

Abend, S. M., Porder, M. S., and Willick, M. S. (1983). *Borderline Patients: Psychoanalytic Perspectives*. New York: International Universities Press.

Adler, G. (1981). The borderline-narcissistic personality disorder continuum. *American Journal of Psychiatry* 138:46–50.

————— (1985) *Borderline Psychopathology and Its Treatment*. Northvale, NJ: Jason Aronson.

Adler, G., and Buie, D. H. (1979). Aloneness and borderline psychopathology. *International Journal of Psycho-Analysis* 60:83–96.

Alexander, F. (1961). *The Scope of Psychoanalysis.* New York: Basic Books.

Alexander F., and French, T. (1946). *Psychoanalytic Therapy.* New York: Norton.

Bateson, G. (1951). Conventions of communication. In *Communication: The Social Matrix of Psychiatry,* ed J. Ruesch and G. Bateson, pp. 212–218. New York: Norton.

Bleuler, E. (1911). *Dementia Praecox or the Group of Schizophrenias.* New York: International Universities Press.

Bollas, C. (1987). *The Shadow of the Object: Psychoanalysis of the Unthought Known.* London: Free Association.

———— (1989). *Forces of Destiny: Psychoanalysis and Human Idiom.* Northvale, NJ: Jason Aronson.

Boyer, L. B. (1978). Countertransference experiences with severely regressed patients. *Contemporary Psychoanalysis* 14:48–72.

———— (1983). *The Regressed Patient.* New York: Jason Aronson.

Boyer, L. B., and Giovacchini, P. L. (1967). *Psychoanalytic Treatment of Schizophrenic and Characterological Disorders.* New York: Jason Aronson.

———— (1980). *Psychoanalytic Treatment of Schizophrenic, Borderline and Characterological Disorders.* New York: Jason Aronson.

Breuer, J., and Freud, S. (1895). Studies on hysteria. *Standard Edition* 2:1–307.

Brunswick, R. M. (1928). A supplement to "Freud's History of an Infantile Neurosis". *International Journal of Psycho-Analysis* 9:439–476.

Deutsch, F. (1960). *The Mysterious Leap from the Mind to the Body.* New York: International Universities Press.

Deutsch, H. (1942). Some forms of emotional disturbances and their relationship to schizophrenia. *Psychoanalytic Quarterly* 11:301–321.

Eissler, K. (1953). The effect of the structuring of the ego on psychoanalytic technique. *Journal of the American Psychoanalytic Association* 1:104–143.

Ellenberger, H. (1970). *The Discovery of the Unconscious.* New York: Basic Books.

Emde, R., Goensbauer, T., and Harmon R. J., (1976). *Emotional Expression in Infancy.* New York: International Universities Press.

Erikson, E. H. (1959). *Identity and the Life Cycle.* New York: International Universities Press.

Fairbairn, R. (1954). *On Object Relations Theory of the Personality.* New York: Basic Books.

Federn, P. (1952). *Ego Psychology and the Psychoses.* New York: Basic Books.

Feinsilver, D. (1980). Transitional relatedness and containment in the treatment of a chronic schizophrenic patient. *International Review of Psycho-Analysis* 7:309–318.

Fenichel, O. (1945). *The Psychoanalytic Theory of Neurosis.* New York: Norton.

———— (1953). *The Collected Papers of Otto Fenichel.* New York: Norton.

Fraiberg, S. (1969). Libidinal object constancy and mental representation. *Psychoanalytic Study of the Child* 24:48–70. New York: International Universities Press.

Freud, S. (1896). Further remarks on the neuro-psychoses of defences. *Standard Edition* 3:157–187.

_____ (1900). The interpretation of dreams. *Standard Edition* 4, 5.

_____ (1904). Fragments of an analysis of a case of hysteria. *Standard Edition* 7:1–123.

_____ (1905a). My views on the part played by sexuality in the aetiology of the neuroses. *Standard Edition* 7:269–281.

_____ (1905b). Three essays on the theory of sexuality. *Standard Edition* 7:123–244.

_____ (1908). Character and anal erotism. *Standard Edition* 9:167–177.

_____ (1909a). Analysis of a phobia in a five-year-old boy. *Standard Edition* 10:1–48.

_____ (1909b). Notes upon a case of obsessional neurosis. *Standard Edition* 10:151–319.

_____ (1910). The future prospects of psychoanalytic therapy. *Standard Edition* 11:139–153.

_____ (1911). Psycho-analytic notes on an autobiographical account of a case of paranoia (dementia paranoides). *Standard Edition* 12:10–85.

_____ (1911–1914). Papers on technique. *Standard Edition* 12:85–172.

_____ (1912). Recommendations to physicians practicing psycho-analysis. *Standard Edition* 12:109–121.

_____ (1913). On beginning the treatment (further recommendations on the technique of psycho-analysis). *Standard Edition* 12:121–145.

_____ (1914a). On narcissism: an introduction. *Standard Edition* 14:67–105.

_____ (1914b). Remembering, repeating and working through. *Standard Edition* 14:145–157.

_____ (1915a). On the history of the psychoanalytic movement. *Standard Edition* 14:1–67.

_____ (1915b). Instincts and their vicissitudes. *Standard Edition* 14:109–141.

_____ (1916). Introductory lectures on psycho-analysis. *Standard Edition* 16:241–478.

_____ (1917). Mourning and melancholia. *Standard Edition* 14:237–259.

_____ (1918). From the history of an infantile neurosis. *Standard Edition* 17:1–123.

_____ (1919). Lines of advance in psycho-analytic therapy. *Standard Edition* 17:157–169.

_____ (1920). Beyond the pleasure principle. *Standard Edition* 18:3–66.

_____ (1923). The ego and the id. *Standard Edition* 19:1–60.

_____ (1924a). The loss of reality in neurosis and psychosis. *Standard Edition* 19:183–191.

_____ (1924b). Neurosis and psychosis. *Standard Edition* 19:149–155.

_____ (1925). A note upon the "Mystic Writing Pad." *Standard Edition* 19:227–235.

_____ (1926). The problem of anxiety. *Standard Edition* 20:75–177.

_____ (1931). Female sexuality. *Standard Edition* 21:221–247.

_____ (1938). Splitting of the ego in the process of defence. *Standard Edition* 23:271–279.

Gill, M. (1979). The analysis of transference. *Journal of the American Psychoanalytic Association* 27:263–288.

Giovacchini, P. (1990). Absolute and not quite absolute dependence. In *Tactics and Techniques in Psychoanalytic Therapy: The Implications of Winnicott's Contributions*, vol. 3, ed. P. L. Giovacchini, pp. 142–160. Northvale, NJ: Jason Aronson.

Giovacchini, P. L. (1956). Defensive meaning of a specific anxiety syndrome. *The Psychoanalytic Review* 43:373–380.

_____ (1958). Mutual adaptation in various object relationships. *International Journal of Psycho-Analysis* 39:1–8.

_____ (1961). Resistance and external object relations. *International Journal of Psycho-Analysis* 42:246–254.

_____ (1965a). Transference, incorporation and synthesis. *International Journal of Psycho-Analysis* 46:287–296.

_____ (1965b). The ego-ideal of a creative scientist. *Psychoanalytic Quarterly* 34:79–101.

_____ (1967). The frozen introject. *International Journal of Psycho-Analysis* 48:61–67.

_____ (1972). *Tactics and Techniques in Psychoanalytic Therapy.* Vol. I. New York: Jason Aronson.

_____ (1975a). *Psychoanalysis of Character Disorders.* New York: Jason Aronson.

_____ (1975b). Self-projections in the narcissistic transference. *International Journal of Psychoanalytic Psychotherapy* 4:142–167.

_____ (1977). A critique of Kohut's theory of narcissism *Annals of Adolescent Psychiatry* 5:213–235.

_____ (1979a). *Psychoanalysis of Primitive Mental States.* New York: Jason Aronson.

_____ (1979b). The sins of the parents: the borderline adolescent and primal confusion. In *Annals of Adolescent Psychiatry*, ed. S. Feinstein, and P. L. Giovacchini, pp. 213–234. Chicago: University of Chicago Press.

_____ (1981). Creativity, adolescence and inevitable failure. *Annals of Adolescent Psychiatry* 9:35–60.

_____ (1984). *Character Disorders and Adaptive Mechanisms.* New York: Jason Aronson.

_____ (1986). *Developmental Disorders: The Transitional Object in Mental Breakdown and Creative Integration.* Northvale, NJ: Jason Aronson.

_____ (1989). *Countertransference Triumphs and Catastrophes.* Northvale, NJ: Jason Aronson.

_____ (1990). Erotism and chaos. *Journal of the Academy of Psychoanalysis* 18:186–204.

Grotstein, J. (1981). *Splitting and Projective Identification.* New York: Jason Aronson.

Haesler, L. (1991). Extratransference and transference interpretations. *International Journal of Psycho-Analysis* 72:463–479.

Hartmann, H. (1939). *Ego Psychology and the Process of Adaptation.* New York: International Universities Press.

_____ (1950). Comments on the psychoanalytic theory of the ego. *Psychoanalytic Study of the Child* 5:74–96. New York: International Universities Press.

Hawthorne, N. (1950). Rappaccini's daughter. In *Great Short Stories,* ed. E. Schramm, pp. 60–93. Chicago: Harcourt, Brace and World.

Horner, A. (1991). *The Primacy of Structure: Psychotherapy of Underlying Character Pathology.* Northvale, NJ: Jason Aronson.

Janet, P. (1929). *The Major Symptoms of Hysteria.* New York: Macmillan.

Kardiner, A. (1977). *My Analysis with Freud.* New York: Norton.

Kernberg, O. F. (1975). *Borderline Conditions and Pathological Narcissism.* New York: Jason Aronson.

_____ (1984). *Severe Personality Disorders: Psychotherapeutic Strategies.* New Haven, CT: Yale University Press.

Kernberg, O. F., Selzer, M. A., Koenigsberg, H. W., et al. (1987). *Psychodynamic Psychotherapy of Borderline Patients.* New York: Basic Books.

Klaus, M., and Kennell, J. (1982). *Parent–Infant Bonding.* St. Louis, MO: Mosby.

Klein, M. (1935). A contribution to the psychogenesis of manic-depressive states. *International Journal of Psycho-Analysis* 27:145–174.

_____ (1946). Notes on some schizoid mechanisms. *International Journal of Psycho-Analysis* 27:99–110.

_____ (1952). *Developments in Psycho-Analysis.* Ed. J. Riviere. London: Hogarth.

Knight, R. P. (1953). Borderline states. *Bulletin of the Menninger Clinic* 19:1–12.

_____ (1954). Borderline states. In *Psychoanalytic Psychiatry and Psychology,* pp. 97–109. New York: International Universities Press.

Kohut, H. (1966). Forms and transformations of narcissism. In *The Search for the Self: Selected Writings of Heinz Kohut*, ed. P. H. Ornstein, pp. 427–460. New York: International Universities Press, 1978.

———— (1971). *The Analysis of the Self*. New York: International Universities Press.

———— (1977). *The Restoration of the Self*. New York: International Universities Press.

———— (1978). *The Search for the Self: Selected Writings of Heinz Kohut*. Ed. P. H. Ornstein. New York: International Universities Press.

———— (1979). The two analyses of Mr. Z. *International Journal of Psycho-Analysis* 60:3–27.

Kraepelin, E. (1883). *Dementia Praecox and Paraphrenia*. Edinburgh: Livingston.

———— (1903). *Lehrbuch der Psychiatrie*. 7th ed. Leipzig: Barth.

Kuhn, T. S. (1962). *The Structure of Scientific Revolutions*. Chicago: University of Chicago Press.

Langer, S. (1948). *Philosophy in a New Key*. New York: New American Library.

Little, M. (1990). *Psychotic Anxieties and Containment*. Northvale, NJ: Jason Aronson.

Mahler, M. (1968). *On Human Symbiosis and the Vicissitudes of Individuation*. New York: International Universities Press.

Masterson, J. F. (1976). *Psychotherapy of the Borderline Adult*. New York: Brunner/Mazel.

———— (1978). *New Perspectives on Psychotherapy of the Borderline*. New York: Brunner/Mazel.

McDougall, J. (1985). *Theaters of the Mind*. New York: Basic Books.

———— (1989). *Theaters of the Body*. New York: Basic Books.

Meissner, W. W. (1988). *Treatment of Patients in the Borderline Spectrum*. Northvale, NJ: Jason Aronson.

Modell, A. H. (1963). Primitive object relationships and the predisposition to schizophrenia. *International Journal of Psycho-Analysis* 44:282–292.

Ogden, T. (1982). *Projective Identification: Psychotherapeutic Technique*. New York: Jason Aronson.

Ornstein, P. H. (1979). The bipolar self in the psychoanalytic treatment process: clinical-theoretical considerations. *Journal of the American Psychoanalytic Association* 27:353–374.

Reichard, S. (1956). A re-examination of "Studies in Hysteria." *Psychoanalytic Quarterly* 25:155–179.

Rinsley, D. (1982). Object relations theory and psychotherapy with particular reference to the self-disordered patient. In *Treatment of the Severely Disturbed Patient*, ed. P. Giovacchini and L. B. Boyer, pp. 187–217. New York: Jason Aronson.

Roth, S. (1987). *Psychotherapy: The Art of Wooing Nature*. Northvale, NJ: Jason Aronson.

Schafer, R. (1968). *Aspects of Internalization*. New York: International Universities Press.

Searles, H. F. (1975). The patient as therapist to his analyst. In *Tactics and Techniques in Psychoanalytic Therapy, vol. 2, Countertransference*, ed. P. L. Giovacchini, pp. 95–151. New York: Jason Aronson.

_____ (1976). Transitional phenomena and therapeutic symbiosis. *International Journal of Psychoanalytic Psychotherapy* 5:145–204.

_____ (1984). Transference responses in borderline patients. *Psychiatry* 47:37–49.

_____ (1986). *My Work with Borderline Patients*. Northvale: NJ: Jason Aronson.

Spence, D. P. (1982). *Narrative Truth and Historical Truth*. New York: Norton.

Spitz, R. (1945). Hospitalism. *Psychoanalytic Study of the Child* 1:53–74. New York: International Universities Press.

_____ (1946). Hospitalism: a follow-up report. *Psychoanalytic Study of the Child* 2:113–117. New York: International Universities Press.

_____ (1959). *A Genetic Field Theory of the Ego*. New York: International Universities Press.

_____ (1965). *The First Year of Life*. New York: International Universities Press.

Sterba, R. (1934). The fate of the ego in analytic therapy. *International Journal of Psycho-Analysis* 15:117–126.

Stern, R. (1985). *The Interpersonal World of the Infant*. New York: Basic Books.

Stone, L. (1954). The widening scope of indications for psychoanalysis. *Journal of the American Psychoanalytic Association* 2:567–594.

Strachey, J. (1934). The nature of the therapeutic action of psycho-analysis. *International Journal of Psycho-Analysis* 15:127–160.

Szurek, S., and Johnson, A. (1954). Etiology of anti-social behavior in delinquents and psychopaths. *Journal of the American Medical Association* 54:814–817.

Volkan, V. (1976). *Primitive Internalized Object Relationships*. New York: International Universities Press.

Winnicott, D. W. (1953). Transitional objects and transitional phenomena. In *Playing and Reality*, pp. 1–26. London: Tavistock, 1971.

_____ (1955). Metapsychological and clinical aspects of regression within the psycho-analytic set-up. *International Journal of Psycho-analysis* 36:16–26.

_____ (1956). Primary maternal preoccupation. In *Collected Papers*, pp. 300–306. New York: Basic Books, 1958.

_____ (1958a). *Collected Papers*. New York: Basic Books.

———— (1958b). The capacity to be alone. *International Journal of Psycho-Analysis* 39:416–440.

———— (1960). Ego distortions in terms of true and false self. In *The Maturational Processes and the Facilitating Environment*, pp. 140–153. New York: International Universities Press.

———— (1963a). The development of the capacity for concern. In *The Maturational Processes and the Facilitating Environment*, pp. 73–83. New York: International Universities Press.

———— (1963b). The mentally ill in your case load. In *The Maturational Processes and the Facilitating Environment*, pp. 217–230. New York: International Universities Press.

———— (1969). The use of an object. *International Journal of Psycho-Analysis* 50:711–716.

———— (1972). Fragment of an analysis. In *Tactics and Techniques in Psychoanalytic Treatment*, vol. 1, ed. P. L. Giovacchini, pp. 455–697. New York: Jason Aronson.

Index